Saveur Cooks Authentic French

SAVEUR COOKS AUTHENTIC FRENCH

BY THE EDITORS OF SAVEUR MAGAZINE

CHRONICLE BOOKS
SAN FRANCISCO

First Chronicle Books LLC paperback edition,
published in 2005.

ISBN 0-8118-5069-2
The Library of Congress has cataloged the previous
edition as follows:
Saveur cooks authentic French: rediscovering the recipes,
traditions, and flavors of the world's greatest cuisine /
by the editors of Saveur magazine.
p. cm.
ISBN 0-8118-2564-7 (hardcover)
1. Cookery, French. I. Saveur.
TX719.S346 1999
641.5944—DC21 99-40932

Manufactured in China.

Designed by
Jill Armus, Michael Grossman, and Amy Henderson
Typeset in Bernhard Gothic, Della Robbia, and Garamond 3

10 9 8 7 6 5 4 3 2 1

Chronicle Books LLC
85 Second Street
San Francisco, California 94105

www.chroniclebooks.com

Acknowledgments

FRANCE HAS BEEN the source of so many of our most memorable stories, of so many of our most memorable meals. What if—we wondered—we were to assemble in one volume all the French classics we love to cook? Not only would this save us from frantically rifling through five years of issues for a favorite recipe, it would also affirm our reverence for this venerable (and lately overlooked) cuisine. Et voilà! *Saveur Cooks Authentic French* appears just a year after our first book, *Saveur Cooks Authentic American*, and is brought to you by the same merry band—the people who turn out every issue of SAVEUR magazine: Colman Andrews, Editor (and award-winning writer); Christopher Hirsheimer, Executive Editor (and acclaimed photographer); our crack conceptual design team: Michael Grossman, Creative Director; Jill Armus, Art Director; María Millán, Photography Editor; and to keep us all in line, the wonderful Ann McCarthy, Assistant Managing Editor. We're grateful for the help of Meg Matyia and Victoria Rich, Assistant Photography Editors; Amy Henderson, Designer; Christiane Angeli, Copy Editor; Gabrielle Hamilton, recipe tester; Melissa Moss and Zoë Pellegrino, who demand the highest production quality; and, above all, our superb project editor in France, Megan Wetherall. Others in our group were drafted into service: Catherine Whalen, Melissa Hamilton, Shoshana Goldberg, Mindy Fox, Sophie Cramer, Marina Ganter, Toby Fox, Julie Pryma, Chad Tomlinson, Jenny Chung, Robin Malik, Johanna Guevara, and Samantha Smith. Our team's high spirits and commitment to excellence is evidenced on every page. I am profoundly grateful for their generosity.

Most of the recipes in this book have been researched in the kitchens of the French cooks who prepared them. We cover the country (see map, page 20) from populous (and popular) cities to tiny hamlets, from three-star kitchens to humble home stoves, always looking for the memorable story that connects each recipe to its origins. To tell these stories, we have drawn on the work of the great photographers and writers who regularly appear in our magazine. Photography credits are listed on page 310. The writers are: R.W. Apple Jr., Michael Balter, Michael Bateman, Claudia M. Caruana, David Case, David Downie, Judy Fayard, Jacqueline Friedrich, Eric Goodman, Richard Goodman, Mireille Johnston, Marie-Pascale Lescot, Connie McCabe, Kevin McDermott, Thomas McNamee, Colette Rossant, Sally Schneider, Warren Schultz, George Semler, William Sertl, Elaine Sterling, Corinne Trang, Lucian K. Truscott IV, John Willoughby, and Clifford A.Wright.

More thank-yous are due to Cullen Stanley, our agent at Janklow & Nesbit, for her loyalty and smarts; to Bill LeBlond, our trusty editor at Chronicle Books, and to Chronicle's Laura Lovett and Shona Bayley as well. To our leaders, Chairman Chris Meigher and President Doug Peabody; to SAVEUR Publisher John McCarus and Marketing Director Stephanie Sandberg; and to all our colleagues at Meigher Communications: We're delighted to present you with another Christmas gift.—DOROTHY KALINS, *Editor-in-Chief*, SAVEUR

Table of Contents

15
BY

INTRODUCTION

THREE OF US sat down to lunch one day, not long ago, at a pretty little restaurant in the pretty little French wine town of Chablis. We'd just arrived in France that morning, two of us from New York and

In a Parisian bistro, left, where hearty food is served family style, the proprietors enjoy ample portions of their own cuisine. The year is 1953.

Some French Essentials

Picking wine grapes in front of a windmill in Bussac, in the Dordogne, in the early 1940s, top. Above, an array of cheeses on an early-20th-century poster advertising Fromageries Ch. Dayot, a chain of cheese shops. Right, outside an artisanal bakery in rural France in the early 1920s. The French, it is said, consume more bread than the citizens of any other country in the world; this photograph purports to show the quantity of bread eaten by the average peasant family every three or four days.

one from Moscow, and we were hungry, both physically and emotionally, for the succor that a good French meal can provide. We expected to be well fed...but when we took our first bites of our appetizers—snails in a buttery, garlic-accented parsley sauce (see page 130), chicken liver terrine with chablis-based gelée, and sautéed medallions of foie gras with apples and red currants—something extraordinary happened: In an instant, we rediscovered French food. All of us had traveled and eaten extensively in France for decades, and would have claimed to know the country's cuisine very well. Yet those first flavors were somehow a revelation to us—an epiphany. Maybe it was jet lag; maybe it was too many months of silly "fusion" cooking in America—but for whatever reasons, we were dazzled. What we had on our plates, we realized, wasn't just ingredients arranged; it was *cooking*—and it reminded us (though these may be fighting words in today's culinary climate) that good French food can be the best food in the world. It sent us this message so strongly, so immediately, in fact, that we pretty much decided then and there that our next SAVEUR book had to celebrate the cuisine of France.

French cuisine is far more than just a collection of recipes. It's a philosophy, an aesthetic, an attitude towards life. It is a way of preparing food—which is to say, a way of approaching (and assimilating) the natural world—

The Art of Food Shopping

A fashionably dressed and coiffed Parisian picks out non-French fruit at a stand in Montparnasse, probably in the 1950s, top. Above, the open-air market called the Marché des Innocents, on the rue St-Denis in Paris, around 1840, as depicted in a lithograph by one W. Parrott. Facing page, a covered food market somewhere in France, filled with shoppers on the first day of January 1950.

based on an immensely complex and sophisticated system of complementary, interlocking bases, part chemical, part mathematical, part artistic. French cooking can certainly involve trickery (marinating lamb to resemble venison, for instance), but at its best, it acknowledges and respects an old and surprisingly coherent canon, even when it sometimes deviates from it in pursuit of creativity. (French chefs are trained draftsmen even when they're painting abstract canvases, and it shows.) It is also a remarkably accommodating cuisine, capable of borrowing from other kitchens without compromising its own identity. Why is French cuisine ultimately greater than that of, say, China? Because it can adopt ingredients and techniques from the Chinese and remain true to itself, while the converse is not true.

For so many of us Americans, French food started it all. It was our introduction to the whole idea of cooking as an art, and to eating as an ennobling experience. Whether we learned to make it ourselves at home from Julia Child or Richard Olney or first experienced it in France itself, French was our first Cuisine with a capital C. But it is a cuisine that has been very much out of fashion in America in recent years. It is heavy and unhealthy, we are told. Italian food (it is said) is better—celebrating the integrity and purity of impeccable raw materials, while French food is culinary obfuscation,

based on sauces probably invented to cover up the stink of rotten meat. Oh, and by the way, the Italians taught the French to cook in the first place....

These are mindless libels. French food is rich, its flavors concentrated, but it can satisfy in small amounts. No one eats cassoulet every day, and none but the most voracious have a second helping. But that one serving, once in a while, is a treasure house of flavors, resonant of good living; it feeds the soul as well as the body. And it implies no disrespect to the gastronomic glories of Italy to say that, apart from introducing some ingredients to their Gallic neighbors, the Italians have taught the French little about cooking (historians have long since disproven the myth about Catherine de Médicis bringing haute cuisine to France). As for culinary ingredients, the French are absolutely fanatical about them, at least as much so as their peninsular neighbors—but while Italian food tends to be intentionally simple and accessible, the French seem more concerned with the extension of possibilities. They approach their foodstuffs with an almost Augustinian conceit, as if they are saying to each succulent guinea fowl or earthy truffle or juicy pear: "God made you, thus imbuing you with a certain natural perfection. Now, what can you become?"

France is a vast hexagon at the heart of western Europe—a nation of about 54 million inhabitants (those

The French at Table

An engraving from the late 18th century, top, suggests that food, drink, music, and love were all on the menu at a French country auberge. Above, Parisians gather at a café in the Quartier Latin in 1986. Facing page, vineyard workers moisten the remains of their soup with red wine (see page 74) at a harvesttime lunch in 1993—though this scene could have taken place a century or two ago.

Good Food in the Open Air

The French don't need a restaurant to share a meal—but they usually find a way to eat around a table. A family of cycling enthusiasts sets up their lunch table in a field to watch the 1997 Tour de France, top. Above, a young couple shares a cheese platter at a sidewalk table at La Bohème, a café in Paris, in 1972. Facing page, a couple enjoys a holiday lunch next to their Citroën 4-Cheveaux, in the Camargue, in 1956.

famous "50 million Frenchmen [who] can't be wrong"), covering some 212,918 square miles and encompassing an immense variety of geography, from Alpine fastnesses to farmlands rippling with grain, from craggy Atlantic coastlines to Mediterranean hillsides covered with vines and olive trees. Despite the legendary chauvinism (in the original sense) of the French, France is a country, too, of many accents—German in Alsace, Flemish in Nord-Pas-de-Calais, Celtic in Brittany, Italian on the Côte d'Azur, Spanish in parts of Provence, Catalan in the Pyrenees. France's larder is thus abundant and diverse, and its cuisine is polyglot—even when it doesn't look to China.

But at the core of French cuisine are two parallel traditions: One is that of a rigorous classical culinary culture, descended from the kitchens of royalty and the nobility by way of men like Taillevent (who wrote the first French cookbook, back in the 1370s), Beauvilliers (who opened what was probably the world's first real restaurant, in 18th-century Paris), Carême (who once famously remarked that pastry making was a branch of architecture; see page 308), and Escoffier (the first "modern" chef, and the great encyclopedist of French recipes). The other tradition is that of home cooking, the food of ordinary Frenchmen and, even more so, Frenchwomen (like the famous *mères* of Lyon), who follow no rules but those of making-do and of nourishing a family as best

MASTERING THE ART OF French Cooking
alibel
ENDIVES

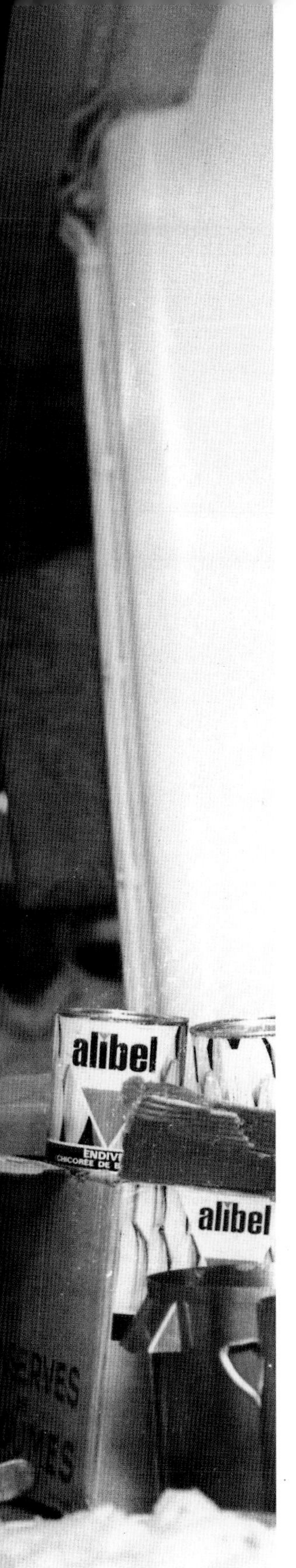

they can, but who seem to have an unerring sense of flavor and of culinary harmony, and who ultimately inspire formal cuisine much more than they are influenced by it.

From the first issue of our magazine, SAVEUR—whose name is French for "flavor" or "savor"—in the summer of 1994, we've made the food and wine of France a specialty. We've introduced readers to the gloriously simple cooking of "hidden" Provence; revealed the culinary secrets of modest bistros in Lyon and three-star restaurants in Paris; celebrated the wonderful food of Nice, Alsace, Burgundy, Brittany, and more. We've gone to the source to learn the truth about black truffles, foie gras, dijon mustard, and walnut oil. And we've deconstructed and then reproduced such definitive French dishes as bouillabaisse, boeuf à la bourguignonne, ratatouille, cassoulet, and soufflé au chocolat (all of which appear in this book), among many others. Along the way, as we tested recipes for this book—as aromas from simmering pots filled our offices and samples of French cooking made grown editors swoon—we became ever more enamored of this exquisite cuisine, and ever more convinced of its continuing importance, its eternal viability. There's a lot of talk these days about getting back to the culinary basics. These, in the Western world at least, are indisputably, and authentically, French. —COLMAN ANDREWS, *Editor*, SAVEUR

Gastronomy and Gourmandise

The staff of Mère Poulard, the famous omelette restaurant in Mont-St-Michel, in northwestern France, top. Above, an undated lithograph captures the moment of the toast at a formal dinner party. Facing page, Julia Child, who introduced so many Americans to real French food, on a visit to a Parisian kitchen in 1967.

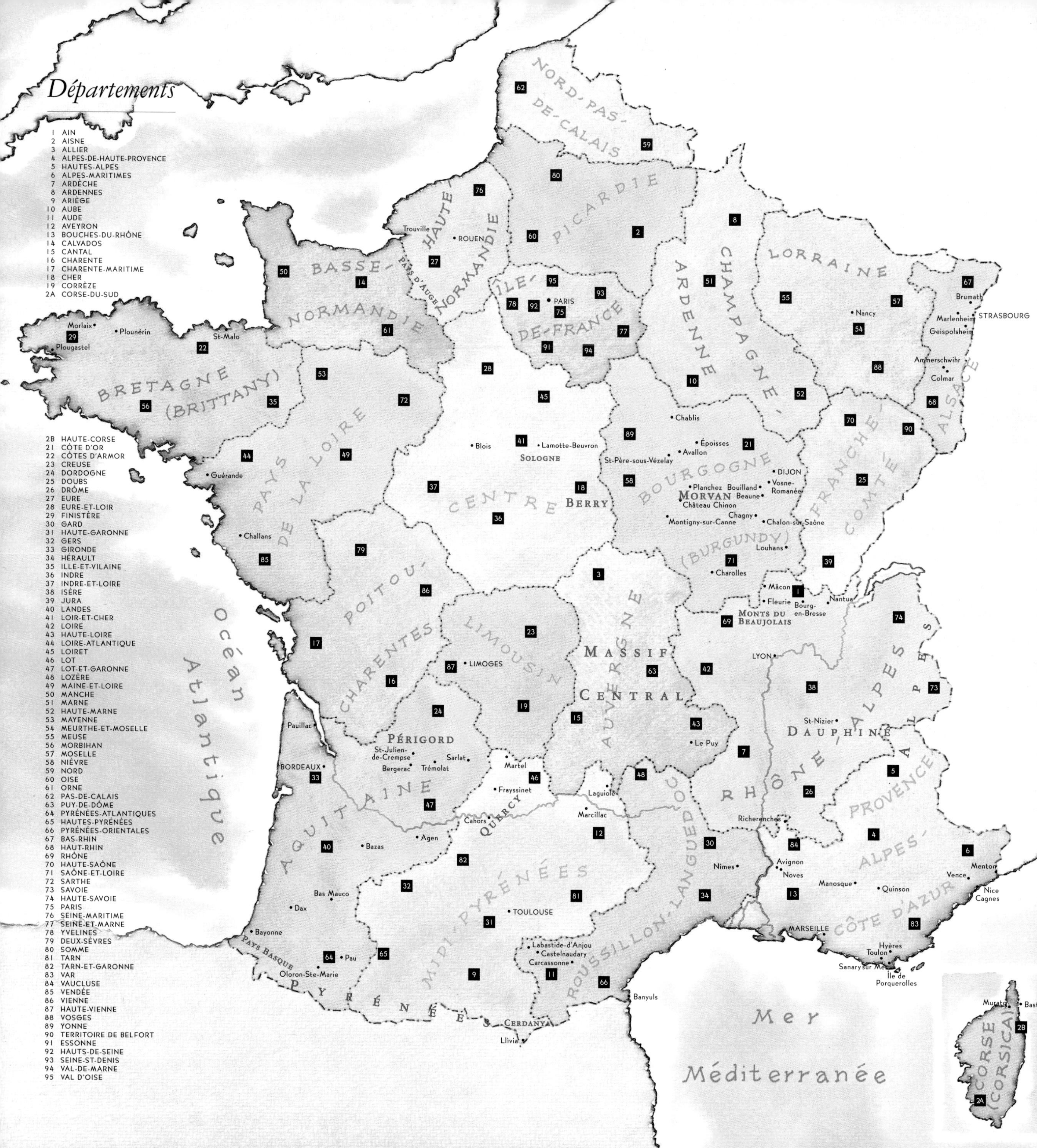

Départements
1 AIN
2 AISNE
3 ALLIER
4 ALPES-DE-HAUTE-PROVENCE
5 HAUTES-ALPES
6 ALPES-MARITIMES
7 ARDÈCHE
8 ARDENNES
9 ARIÈGE
10 AUBE
11 AUDE
12 AVEYRON
13 BOUCHES-DU-RHÔNE
14 CALVADOS
15 CANTAL
16 CHARENTE
17 CHARENTE-MARITIME
18 CHER
19 CORRÈZE
2A CORSE-DU-SUD
2B HAUTE-CORSE
21 CÔTE D'OR
22 CÔTES D'ARMOR
23 CREUSE
24 DORDOGNE
25 DOUBS
26 DRÔME
27 EURE
28 EURE-ET-LOIR
29 FINISTÈRE
30 GARD
31 HAUTE-GARONNE
32 GERS
33 GIRONDE
34 HÉRAULT
35 ILLE-ET-VILAINE
36 INDRE
37 INDRE-ET-LOIRE
38 ISÈRE
39 JURA
40 LANDES
41 LOIR-ET-CHER
42 LOIRE
43 HAUTE-LOIRE
44 LOIRE-ATLANTIQUE
45 LOIRET
46 LOT
47 LOT-ET-GARONNE
48 LOZÈRE
49 MAINE-ET-LOIRE
50 MANCHE
51 MARNE
52 HAUTE-MARNE
53 MAYENNE
54 MEURTHE-ET-MOSELLE
55 MEUSE
56 MORBIHAN
57 MOSELLE
58 NIÈVRE
59 NORD
60 OISE
61 ORNE
62 PAS-DE-CALAIS
63 PUY-DE-DÔME
64 PYRÉNÉES-ATLANTIQUES
65 HAUTES-PYRÉNÉES
66 PYRÉNÉES-ORIENTALES
67 BAS-RHIN
68 HAUT-RHIN
69 RHÔNE
70 HAUTE-SAÔNE
71 SAÔNE-ET-LOIRE
72 SARTHE
73 SAVOIE
74 HAUTE-SAVOIE
75 PARIS
76 SEINE-MARITIME
77 SEINE-ET-MARNE
78 YVELINES
79 DEUX-SÈVRES
80 SOMME
81 TARN
82 TARN-ET-GARONNE
83 VAR
84 VAUCLUSE
85 VENDÉE
86 VIENNE
87 HAUTE-VIENNE
88 VOSGES
89 YONNE
90 TERRITOIRE DE BELFORT
91 ESSONNE
92 HAUTS-DE-SEINE
93 SEINE-ST-DENIS
94 VAL-DE-MARNE
95 VAL D'OISE
NORD-PAS-DE-CALAIS
PICARDIE
HAUTE-NORMANDIE
BASSE-NORMANDIE
PAYS D'AUGE
ÎLE-DE-FRANCE
CHAMPAGNE-ARDENNE
LORRAINE
ALSACE
BRETAGNE (BRITTANY)
PAYS DE LA LOIRE
CENTRE
SOLOGNE
BERRY
BOURGOGNE (BURGUNDY)
MORVAN
FRANCHE-COMTÉ
POITOU-CHARENTES
LIMOUSIN
MASSIF CENTRAL
AUVERGNE
MONTS DU BEAUJOLAIS
RHÔNE-ALPES
DAUPHINÉ
ALPES
PÉRIGORD
AQUITAINE
QUERCY
MIDI-PYRÉNÉES
LANGUEDOC-ROUSSILLON
PROVENCE-ALPES-CÔTE D'AZUR
PAYS BASQUE
PYRÉNÉES
CERDANYA
CORSE (CORSICA)
Océan Atlantique
Mer Méditerranée
Trouville
ROUEN
PARIS
Morlaix
Plounérin
Plougastel
St-Malo
Guérande
Challans
Blois
Lamotte-Beuvron
Chablis
Époisses
Avallon
St-Père-sous-Vézelay
DIJON
Vosne-Romanée
Planchez
Bouilland
Beaune
Château Chinon
Chagny
Montigny-sur-Canne
Chalon-sur-Saône
Louhans
Charolles
Mâcon
Fleurie
Bourg-en-Bresse
Nantua
Nancy
Brumath
Marlenheim
STRASBOURG
Geispolsheim
Ammerschwihr
Colmar
LYON
LIMOGES
St-Nizier
Le Puy
Pauillac
BORDEAUX
St-Julien-de-Crempse
Bergerac
Trémolat
Sarlat
Martel
Frayssinet
Laguiole
Marcillac
Cahors
Agen
Bazas
Richerenches
Avignon
Noves
Nîmes
Manosque
Quinson
Vence
Menton
Nice
Cagnes
Bas Mauco
Dax
TOULOUSE
Bayonne
Pau
Oloron-Ste-Marie
Labastide-d'Anjou
Castelnaudary
Carcassonne
MARSEILLE
Hyères
Toulon
Sanary-sur-Mer
Île de Porquerolles
Banyuls
Llivia
Murato
Bast

Our France

THERE ARE good things to eat in every part of France, but we find ourselves returning time and again to the food of certain regions—Burgundy, Alsace, the Southwest, Provence, and few others—and in so doing, we find ourselves drawing our own map of France, defined by flavor and aroma more than geography. These are its essential compass points.

■ GOLD: Region
■ GREEN: Département
■ BLUE: Town or village

CHAPTER

I

HORS D'OEUVRES

"CURVING sinuously around the Baie des Anges, about 20 miles west of the Italian border, the ancient city of Nice, capital of

Radis
4F

the Côte d'Azur, has a palpable Italianate flavor—especially in the city's southeastern quarter, between the Vieux Port and the Promenade des Anglais. Here, the architecture is baroque, the language (Nissart, a dialect of Provençal) has a peninsular accent, and family names tend to end in vowels. Indeed, the old quarter, Vieux Nice, resembles an Italian hill town more than a French village. Streets are overhung with narrow balconies, open shutters, flower boxes, laundry fluttering in the breeze; building colors are earthy but memorable—clay yellow, desert beige, the pink of a Mediterranean dawn; little shops sell cheese, pasta, coffee, bread, wine. Along one flank of Vieux Nice runs the Cours Saleya—a handsome tile-paved promenade lined with cafés, restaurants, and shops—and here, six mornings a week, one of the most famous flower and produce markets in France sets up. The particulars change with the seasons, of course, but the display is fragrant and colorful and evocative of the bounty of the Mediterranean and beyond. Wild mushrooms leach their damp perfume into the air in autumn; the first precocious fava beans and baby purple artichokes shine luminously in early spring; and all year long there are heaps of pungent olives, mounds of fresh-ground spices, rows of farm-made oils and cheeses, a panoply of breads. And always there is market fare: the famous chickpea flour crêpes called socca and the onion-topped tart known as pissaladière (see page 26)—which I've always thought of as the market itself arranged on a crust." —COLMAN ANDREWS

RECIPES

Pissaladière

(Niçois Onion Tart)

SERVES 6

THE TRADITIONAL formula for this classic Niçois specialty, most often eaten as street (and market) fare, calls for the layer of onions to be fully half as thick as the crust.

FOR DOUGH:
1 7-gram packet active dry yeast
Extra-virgin olive oil
3 cups flour
1 tbsp. salt
Cornmeal

FOR TOPPING:
¼ cup extra-virgin olive oil
2½–3 lbs. yellow onions, peeled and very thinly sliced
Salt and freshly ground black pepper
Bouquet garni (see sidebar, page 59) with 2 sprigs marjoram and 1 sprig rosemary added
Anchovy paste
⅓ cup niçoise olives
12 anchovy filets (optional)

1. For dough, dissolve yeast in 1 cup warm water in a small bowl, let stand for 5 minutes, then add ¼ cup oil. Combine flour and salt in a medium bowl, add yeast mixture, and stir with a wooden spoon, adding a bit more water if necessary, until ingredients are well mixed. Turn out dough on a lightly floured surface, dust hands with flour, and knead until dough is smooth, firm, and elastic, about 3 minutes. Form dough into a ball, then place in a lightly oiled medium bowl and cover with a damp cloth. Allow dough to rise in a warm spot for about 1 hour.

2. For topping, heat oil in a large pan over medium-low heat. Add onions and season generously with salt and pepper. Add bouquet garni and cover pan to let onions slowly simmer for 45 minutes, stirring occasionally. Uncover and continue cooking until the moisture has evaporated and the onions have cooked down to a very tender marmalade-like consistency, 30–40 minutes. Remove and discard bouquet garni, then set onions aside.

3. Place a pizza stone in oven and preheat to 450°. Roll dough out on a floured surface into a thin, flat rectangle. Transfer dough to a baker's peel, a cookie sheet or inverted baking sheet, dusted with cornmeal. Cover dough with a damp cloth and allow to rest for 30 minutes.

4. Remove cloth from dough and spread a thin layer of anchovy paste over top. Spread onion mixture evenly over anchovy paste. Arrange olives and anchovy filets (if using) over the onions, season lightly with pepper, then slide pissaladière onto hot pizza stone. Bake until crust has browned, 15–20 minutes. Serve warm or at room temperature, cut into squares.

Anchovies and Onions

Because pissaladière is sometimes described as the Niçois pizza, it is tempting to think that the names of the two dishes are related. Not so. The term *pizza* is apparently Germanic in origin and has something to do with a word for piece or bit; *pissaladière*, on the other hand, derives from the Nissart words *pèi salat*, salted fish—and is named for the pissala, or fermented anchovy sauce, with which it was traditionally anointed. This ancient product, a relative of the garum of the Romans, is rarely found today, and a good-quality anchovy paste (like the superlative one from Jean-Gui, below) is a fine substitute. Anchovies aside, it is onions that define pissaladière, with the help of olives. The Niçois poet Victor Rocca, in fact, hailed pissaladière, in 1930, as "a sweet and proud synthesis / Which joins, beneath a triumphantly dry sky, / The white onion of the Berber and the olive of the Greek."

Chez Clovis

Crudités

(Raw Vegetable Salads)

Serves 6

An assortment of raw vegetables tossed in simple dressing—usually vinaigrette—is a staple of the old-style French bistro menu. Celery root and carrots are de rigueur.

CAROTTES RAPÉES
5–6 young carrots, peeled and julienned
2–3 tbsp. fresh lemon juice
Salt and freshly ground black pepper
2 tbsp. minced fresh parsley

CÉLERI RÉMOULADE
1 tbsp. dijon mustard
2 tbsp. fresh lemon juice
2 tbsp. peanut oil
Salt and freshly ground black pepper
1 bulb celery root, peeled and julienned

SALADE DE TOMATES
2 tsp. dijon mustard
2 tbsp. red wine vinegar
4 tbsp. peanut oil
Salt and freshly ground black pepper
6 small ripe tomatoes, sliced
1 clove garlic, peeled and minced
1 small red onion, peeled and finely chopped

SALADE DE CONCOMBRES
2 tsp. dijon mustard
2 tbsp. red wine vinegar
4 tbsp. peanut oil
Salt and freshly ground black pepper
2 cucumbers, peeled and thinly sliced

Carottes Rapées (Grated Carrot Salad): Put carrots and lemon juice in a small bowl and toss to mix well. Season to taste with salt and pepper. Arrange on a platter or divide evenly between 6 small plates, and garnish with parsley.

Céleri Rémoulade (Celery Root in Mustard Dressing): Whisk together mustard and lemon juice in a large mixing bowl. Drizzle in oil, continuing to whisk until dressing is smooth and emulsified. Season to taste with salt and pepper. Add celery root, toss to mix well, and adjust seasoning. Arrange on a platter or divide evenly between 6 small plates.

Salade de Tomates (Tomato Salad): Whisk together mustard and vinegar in a small mixing bowl. Drizzle in oil, continuing to whisk until dressing is smooth and emulsified. Season to taste with salt and pepper. Fan out tomato slices on a platter or divide evenly between 6 small plates. Drizzle with vinaigrette, then scatter garlic and onion over tomatoes and season to taste with salt and pepper.

Salade de Concombres (Cucumber Salad): Whisk together mustard and vinegar in a small mixing bowl. Drizzle in oil, continuing to whisk until dressing is smooth and emulsified. Season to taste with salt and pepper. Arrange cucumbers on a platter or divide evenly between 6 small plates. Drizzle with vinaigrette and season to taste with salt and pepper.

A Grand-Mère's Trick

Bière d'Avallon, the beer of Avallon, was first made in the town of the same name, in northwestern Burgundy, in 1780. It was still being produced, and appreciated, in the early years of this century—until, in fact, World War II. "When the Germans came through," recalls Marcelle Gueneau (above), who then owned the brewery with her husband, Fernand, "they took all the copper. You can't make beer without copper, so after the war, we made lemonade instead." Today, she is retired and her husband is deceased—but she still cooks good old-fashioned meals in her roadside house, next door to where the brewery used to be. When she invited us to lunch not long ago, for instance, she offered us little pastries filled with cheese and blood sausage, hearts of palm in a luxuriant vinaigrette, and a definitive coq au vin. "I stir a little potato starch into my vinaigrette so that it doesn't separate," she told us proudly. "That's not a chef's trick. It's a grandmother's trick!"

Island Cooking

The Île de Porquerolles is a tiny, verdant piece of land just off the Provençal coast near Hyères, about a dozen miles east of Toulon and 50 southeast of Marseille. The island is an unexpected Eden of dirt roads and rock beaches, thick with stands of Aleppo pines, eucalyptus, live oak, plane trees, and palms, accented everywhere by purple pelargoniums, fuchsia-hued bougainvillea, fragrant bushes of mock orange. There are even vineyards (below). On one end of the island is Le Mas du Langoustier, a low-key but polished hotel-restaurant owned by Marie Caroline Le Ber and her husband, Georges Richard, and put on the culinary map by the talent of their young chef, Joël Guillet (facing page, upper right). Guillet draws enthusiastically from the vocabulary of Provençal cooking—using garlic, olive oil, basil, rosemary, sage, licorice, saffron, tomatoes, eggplant, artichokes, fennel, and olives with calculated abandon. He also fills his menu with adaptations of such regional specialties as escabèche, panisses, mesclun, soupe de poisson, and tapenade. He surrounds classic brandade (see page 163) with sweet tiny clams in their own juices; he mixes flavors and textures with high-wire bravura by combining tender island octopus with puréed artichoke hearts, raw baby spinach leaves, and deep-fried periwinkles; he redefines steak au poivre by skewering pieces of filet on rosemary branches, grilling them, then serving them in black pepper sauce with crushed (not silkily puréed) potatoes. And his gâteau d'ail confit, which uses one of the world's most vivid flavors not for shock value but as an accent and an illumination, is as good a definition as any we can think of for contemporary Provençal cuisine.

Gâteau d'Ail Confit

(Garlic Custard with Chanterelles and Parsley Sauce)

SERVES 4

NO FLAVOR is more definitive of Provence than that of garlic, and chef Joël Guillet of Le Mas du Langoustier uses it freely. This recipe is for serious garlic lovers only.

4 large heads garlic
6 tbsp. olive oil
1 tsp. sugar
Salt and freshly ground black pepper
¾ cup half-and-half
⅓ cup heavy cream
2 eggs, lightly beaten
2 plum tomatoes, peeled, seeded, and coarsely chopped
4 cups coarsely chopped fresh parsley leaves and stems, plus additional sprigs for garnish
1 tbsp. butter
½ lb. chanterelles or other wild mushrooms, trimmed and sliced

1. Preheat oven to 350°. Halve 3 heads garlic crosswise, place on a large sheet of aluminum foil, drizzle with 1 tbsp. of the oil, sprinkle with sugar, season to taste with salt and pepper, and tightly wrap garlic in foil. Bake until soft, about 1½ hours. Remove from oven, unwrap, allow to cool, then squeeze garlic pulp from cloves into a small bowl; discard peels.

2. Separate remaining head of garlic into cloves, and peel and slice each clove lengthwise as thinly as possible. Heat 2 tbsp. of the oil in a small nonstick skillet over medium-low heat. Add garlic slices and cook, stirring, until soft, about 5 minutes. Drain on paper towels.

3. Reduce oven to 300°. Combine roasted garlic pulp, half-and-half, cream, and eggs in a food processor and purée until smooth. Lightly brush 4 ramekins, 3" wide and about 1½" high, with 1 tbsp. of the oil, then line the bottom of each with garlic slices. Spoon about 2 tbsp. garlic custard into each ramekin, evenly divide tomatoes between ramekins, then cover with about 3 more tbsp. custard.

4. Transfer ramekins to a roasting pan, place pan in oven, then add enough water to come 1" up the side of the pan. Bake custards until set, about 30 minutes, remove from pan, and allow to cool for about 20 minutes.

5. Meanwhile, blanch chopped parsley in a large pot of boiling salted water until bright green, 20–30 seconds. Drain, and transfer to a food processor. Add ¼ cup water and purée until smooth. Transfer pulp to the center of a clean thin kitchen towel and squeeze out juice into a small saucepan. Discard parsley. Warm over low heat, then whisk in butter.

6. Heat remaining 2 tbsp. oil in a medium skillet over medium-high heat. Add mushrooms and cook, stirring, until tender, 2–5 minutes. Adjust seasoning to taste with salt and pepper. To serve, turn each custard out onto a medium plate and garnish with parsley sauce, mushrooms, and parsley sprigs.

Terrine de Canard

(Duck Terrine)

SERVES 10–12

THIS LUXURIOUS terrine was inspired by a recipe from cookbook author Richard Olney, an American living in France, who regularly inspires the creation of good food.

2 1½-lb. muscovy ducks
Salt and freshly ground black pepper
¼ tsp. saltpeter (optional; see sidebar, page 38)
1 tbsp. olive oil
¼ cup cognac
4 sprigs fresh thyme
4 sprigs fresh parsley
1 medium yellow onion, peeled and halved
1 carrot, peeled and halved
1 clove garlic, peeled and minced
½ cup fresh bread crumbs
1 lb. fatback (ask butcher to slice into thin sheets to line a terrine)
¼ lb. ground veal
¼ lb. ground pork
1 egg
¼ tsp. ground nutmeg
1 tsp. juniper berries, coarsley ground
¾ cup shelled pistachios
¼ lb. foie gras, cut into 3" pieces

1. Rinse ducks and pat dry. Remove skin, then remove meat, setting leg meat and bones aside. Cut breast meat into ½" strips, season to taste with salt and pepper, and sprinkle with saltpeter (if using). Put in a bowl with oil, cognac, and 2 sprigs each of thyme and parsley. Cover and marinate in refrigerator for 2 hours.

2. Put duck bones, onions, carrots, remaining 2 sprigs each of thyme and parsley, ½ tsp. salt, and 4 cups water in a saucepan. Bring to boil over high heat, then reduce heat to medium and simmer until broth is reduced to ½ cup, about 1¼ hours. Strain.

3. Preheat oven to 350°. Mix broth, garlic, and bread crumbs in a small bowl to make a paste. Finely chop reserved leg meat and place in a medium bowl. Chop enough fatback to make ⅓ cup, then add to leg meat with bread paste, veal, pork, egg, nutmeg, juniper berries, pistachios, and 1 tbsp. salt. Mix well with a wooden spoon.

4. Cut 1 sheet of fatback into 3 pieces, then use each to individually wrap foie gras pieces. Line a 1½-quart terrine with remaining fatback, allowing a 2" overhang. Spoon half the meat mixture into terrine. Lay half the strips of marinated breast meat (lengthwise) on top, then place wrapped foie gras down the center. Top with remaining breast meat, then with remaining meat mixture. Fold over fatback to enclose. Cover, place in a pan, and add enough hot water to come halfway up the side. Cook in oven until juices run clear, about 1¼ hours. Cool, then pour off juices.

5. Cut a piece of cardboard to fit into terrine. Wrap cardboard in aluminum foil, place in terrine, and weigh down with a few cans. Refrigerate for at least 2 hours. Remove cardboard lid, run a thin knife under warm water, slide around edge of terrine, and invert onto a platter. Serve chilled. The terrine may be stored in the refrigerator for up to 1 week.

Ducks Deluxe

Foie gras, confit de canard, free-range organic chickens and turkeys, capons and poussins, wild and farmed game birds and venison, buffalo, rabbit, nitrite-free bacon, demi-glace, and at least four kinds of ducks, just for starters. At SAVEUR, we'd be lost without D'Artagnan—our favorite one-stop source for countless culinary riches, most of them with a southwestern French accent. D'Artagnan, named for the celebrated fictional Gascon musketeer, was founded in 1985 by George Faison, a Texan with an MBA from Columbia University, and Ariane Daguin (the two are below), daughter of André Daguin, one of the preeminent chefs of southwestern France. Today, the company is the largest wholesaler of fresh foie gras and game meats in the country, and about the only place to get scores of other products on a consistent, dependable basis. We find ourselves calling 800/DARTAGN (or signing on to www.dartagnan.com) about as often as we phone home.

La Nouvelle Escoffier

Fabienne Parra was born in Australia to French parents, and brought up outside Lyon. Her father is a chef/restaurateur, and she apprenticed in his kitchens. He still runs a restaurant, called Hermitage Corton, in the Burgundian wine capital of Beaune (home of the world-famous annual wine auction at the Hospices de Beaune, facing page)—and it was while working for her father as sommelier that she met and fell in love with another apprentice, Pierre Escoffier. The two were married in 1983, opened a wine shop in Beaune called Cave Ste-Hélène in 1989, and in 1996 turned the space next to the shop into a highly personal, absolutely wonderful little restaurant called Ma Cuisine. Fabienne wants her cooking to be simple and true, she says, and to have "heart"—and to make the wines she and Pierre have chosen shine. She succeeds on all counts.

Terrine de Foies de Volaille

(Chicken Liver Terrine)

Serves 10–12

THE TINY Ma Cuisine in Beaune, a great favorite among local vintners, is literally a two-person show: Pierre Escoffier serves as maître d'hôtel, waiter, busboy, and sommelier; his wife is the entire kitchen staff—which is why she likes to serve dishes that can be made up in advance, like this one.

1 tbsp. butter
1 medium yellow onion, peeled and minced
12 oz. chicken livers (about 8)
1½ lbs. ground lean pork
2 cloves garlic, peeled and minced
1 tsp. minced fresh thyme
¼ tsp. ground cloves
¼ tsp. ground nutmeg
¼ cup cognac
2 eggs, lightly beaten
Salt and freshly ground black pepper
¼ tsp. saltpeter (optional; see sidebar, page 38)
1 lb. fatback (ask butcher to slice into thin sheets for a terrine)
2 bay leaves

1. Melt butter in a skillet over medium heat, and sauté onions until soft, about 15 minutes. Meanwhile, coarsely chop about ⅓ of the chicken livers, then combine with whole livers, pork, garlic, thyme, cloves, nutmeg, cognac, and eggs in a large mixing bowl. Add sautéed onions and use your hands to mix well, taking care to leave livers whole. Season to taste with salt and pepper. Sprinkle with saltpeter (if using), mix well, cover and refrigerate for about 2 hours.

2. Preheat oven to 325°. Line a 1½-quart terrine with sheets of fatback. Fill with pâté mixture, packing mixture well to release any air pockets. Place bay leaves on top, then cover with a single layer of fatback. Cover terrine with lid or several layers of foil and put it in a large baking pan filled with enough boiling water to come halfway up the sides of the terrine. Bake to an internal temperature of 180°, about 1½ hours.

3. Allow to cool, then cut a piece of cardboard to fit into terrine. Wrap cardboard in aluminum foil, place in terrine, and weigh down with a few cans. Refrigerate for at least 24 hours before serving, then remove cardboard lid, run a thin knife under warm water, slide around edge of terrine, and invert onto a platter. Serve chilled. The terrine may be stored in the refrigerator for up to 1 week.

Gâteau de Foies Blonds de Volaille

(Chicken Liver Mousse)

SERVES 4

AT THE POPULAR Café des Fédérations in Lyon (below), this mousse is served with a hearty tomato sauce. We like their recipe, but prefer a more traditional crayfish sauce.

10 oz. chicken livers (about 6)
2 tbsp. flour
2 whole eggs
2 egg yolks
½ cup milk
½ cup cream
Pinch ground nutmeg
Salt and freshly ground black pepper
1 tbsp. butter
4 sprigs fresh flat-leaf parsley
1 cup crayfish sauce (see page 190)

1. Preheat oven to 325°. Combine chicken livers, flour, whole eggs, egg yolks, milk, cream, and a pinch nutmeg in a food processor. Season to taste with salt and freshly ground black pepper and purée.

2. Divide liver mixture between 4 buttered 3" ramekins. Place ramekins in a baking pan, place pan in oven, then add enough hot water to come three-quarters of the way up sides of ramekins. Bake until mixture is firm, 25 minutes. Loosen sides with a paring knife, unmold, garnish with parsley, and serve with warm crayfish sauce.

Pâté? Cake?

The French love to eat rich appetizers of ground, shredded, or puréed meat, fish, or fowl, and they distinguish between several varieties: **MOUSSE** Light, soft preparations, sweet or savory, in which ingredients are blended and then folded together; mousses are often set in a mold (in this form they are also sometimes called gâteaux, literally cakes). **PÂTÉ** According to *Larousse Gastronomique*, the word meant a filled pastry shell baked in the oven and served hot—a kind of pie. In today's usage, *pâté* more commonly means a terrine (see below)—though pâté en croûte (see page 38) conforms to the original definition. **RILLETTES** Pork, rabbit, goose, poultry, or oily fish cooked in lard or its own fat with herbs, then pounded to a coarse paste in a mortar, potted, and served as a cold hors d'oeuvre. **TERRINE** Technically, any food cooked or served in a terrine dish (see page 256). Terrines are commonly of meat, but can also be made with fish, seafood, or vegetables. Meat terrines are usually served cold or at room temperature; their ingredients may be marinated in alcohol, and terrines are typically lined with caul fat or other pork fat, and covered with a layer of fat or gelée.

Pink Salt

Besides the obvious ingredients—pork, salt, spices—most French charcuterie contains a substance not exactly common in the average American home kitchen: potassium nitrate, or saltpeter. A trace mineral that used to be present in all salt (but is now usually refined out), saltpeter helps inhibit spoilage and lends an attractive pinkish-red color to meat even after it has been cooked. Already used to cure sausages as long ago as the 16th century, saltpeter—available in drugstores—is still employed by many charcutiers today. Some chefs, however, prefer a derivative called sel rose, or pink salt—a blend of saltpeter, salt, cochineal (a natural red dye) and other natural colorings, and various spices. Home cooks, who are less likely to mind if their terrines or sausages turn grayish during cooking, don't need either one—but those who wish to try it the professional way should follow this rule of thumb: When mixing the ingredients for a 1½-quart terrine, add about a ½ teaspoon of saltpeter to every 5 lbs. of meat in addition to the salt called for in the recipe. If you find sel rose, usually only available from restaurant-supply firms, follow the manufacturer's directions.

Pâté en Croûte

(Pâté in a Pastry Crust)

Serves 6–8

A SPECIALTY of the region of Berry in central France (lower left), this complexly flavored pâté is one of the glories of traditional French cooking. Serve the pâté either warm or cold, accompanied by a green salad. And unless you're a professional, don't make your own puff pastry; Dufour and other store-bought brands are excellent.

8 oz. smoked bacon
1 12-oz. duck breast, skin removed
2 6-oz. chicken breasts, skin removed
3 tbsp. olive oil
1 cup sancerre or other dry white wine
¼ tsp. saltpeter (optional; see sidebar, left)
1 tsp. crushed coriander seeds
½ tsp. ground nutmeg
2 tsp. fresh thyme leaves
¼ cup chopped fresh chervil
¼ cup chopped fresh chives
3 eggs
2 tbsp. crème fraîche
Salt and freshly ground black pepper
½ cup flour
1 lb. frozen puff pastry, defrosted but cold
3 hard-cooked eggs, peeled

1. Cut bacon, duck breast, and chicken into medium pieces. Put in a medium bowl, add olive oil, wine, and saltpeter (if using), mixing to coat pieces well. Cover and marinate for 1 hour in the refrigerator.

2. Preheat oven to 400°. Drain meat, discarding marinade. Put meat, coriander, nutmeg, herbs, 2 of the eggs, crème fraîche, and salt and pepper to taste in a food processor fitted with a metal blade. Pulse until finely chopped.

3. On a floured work surface, unfold cold puff pastry and cut into two rectangles. Roll both sheets of pastry into 8" x 11" shapes. Place one pastry rectangle on a nonstick baking sheet. Divide meat mixture in half and spread half down the center of pastry. Put hard-cooked eggs in a line down middle of meat. Pat remaining meat over eggs. Pull up the pastry on the sides, then completely cover with second rectangle of pastry. Cut off and reserve excess pastry, wet edges with water, and press together. Cut a small hole in center of pâté and place a small piece of rolled parchment in it to allow steam to escape during baking. Beat remaining egg with a little water and brush egg wash over pâté. Cut decorative shapes out of excess pastry and press onto pâté. Brush again with egg wash.

4. Bake for 20 minutes, then lower heat to 350° and bake for another 20 minutes. The pâté should rest for 30 minutes before serving so that it is firm enough to slice.

Ham in France

The French do love their ham. Annual per capita consumption of cooked ham (jambon cuit, also known as jambon blanc, or white ham) in France is over ten pounds. Some of it is eaten in dishes like the jambon persillé at right—but much more is consumed in the form of "jambon beurre" (ham and butter) sandwiches on split baguettes. The best-known French cooked ham is jambon de Paris, easily identified by its oblong shape. France also produces jambon sec, or cured ham, rubbed with salt and aged in the manner of Italy's prosciutto crudo or Spain's jamón serrano. Excellent jambon sec is made in the Savoie, the Vendée, the Massif Central, and the Ardennes, but most connoisseurs consider that of Bayonne, in the French Basque country, to be the best.

Jambon Persillé Maison

(Parsleyed Ham in Aspic)

SERVES 20

WE HAVE ALWAYS loved this Burgundian specialty and have eaten it all over France—but we have never found a better version than this one, made by Fabienne Escoffier at Ma Cuisine, her little jewel of a restaurant in Beaune.

1 6–7 lb. cured ham, bone in
2 2½–3 lb. calfs' feet, split
3 carrots, trimmed
1 large yellow onion, peeled
1 clove
1 leek, trimmed and washed
Bouquet garni (see sidebar, page 59)
1 bottle dry white wine
Salt and freshly ground black pepper
4 egg whites
2 cloves garlic, peeled and minced
2 shallots, peeled and minced
2 cups minced fresh parsley
¼ cup red wine vinegar
2 tbsp. vegetable oil

1. Put ham, calfs' feet, carrots, onion studded with the clove, leek, bouquet garni, and white wine in a stockpot, add water to cover, and bring to a simmer over high heat. Reduce heat to low, cover, and simmer until ham is fork tender, about 5 hours.

2. Remove ham and allow to cool. Strain stock through a cheesecloth-lined sieve, discarding all solids, then return to pot. Bring stock to a gentle boil over medium-high heat and cook until reduced to about 8 cups. Skim fat and season to taste with salt and pepper.

3. Beat 4 egg whites with a whisk in a clean metal bowl until they form stiff peaks. Spread egg whites onto surface of stock and simmer for 15 minutes, until solids get caught in the egg-white "raft" that forms and stock is clarified. Strain stock, pouring carefully to avoid disturbing raft, then discard raft.

4. Shred ham into long pieces, then coarsely chop. Combine ham, garlic, shallots, parsley, and vinegar in a bowl and use your hands to mix well. Season to taste with salt and pepper.

5. Pour about ½ cup stock into each of 2 oiled 1½-quart terrines, then divide and layer about ⅓ of the ham mixture into the terrines, pressing the mixture down to compact it. Pour about ¾ cup of stock over each layer of ham mixture. Repeat process twice more, ending with stock. Refrigerate for 24 hours. Unmold terrines and serve with cornichons and dijon mustard on the side, if you like.

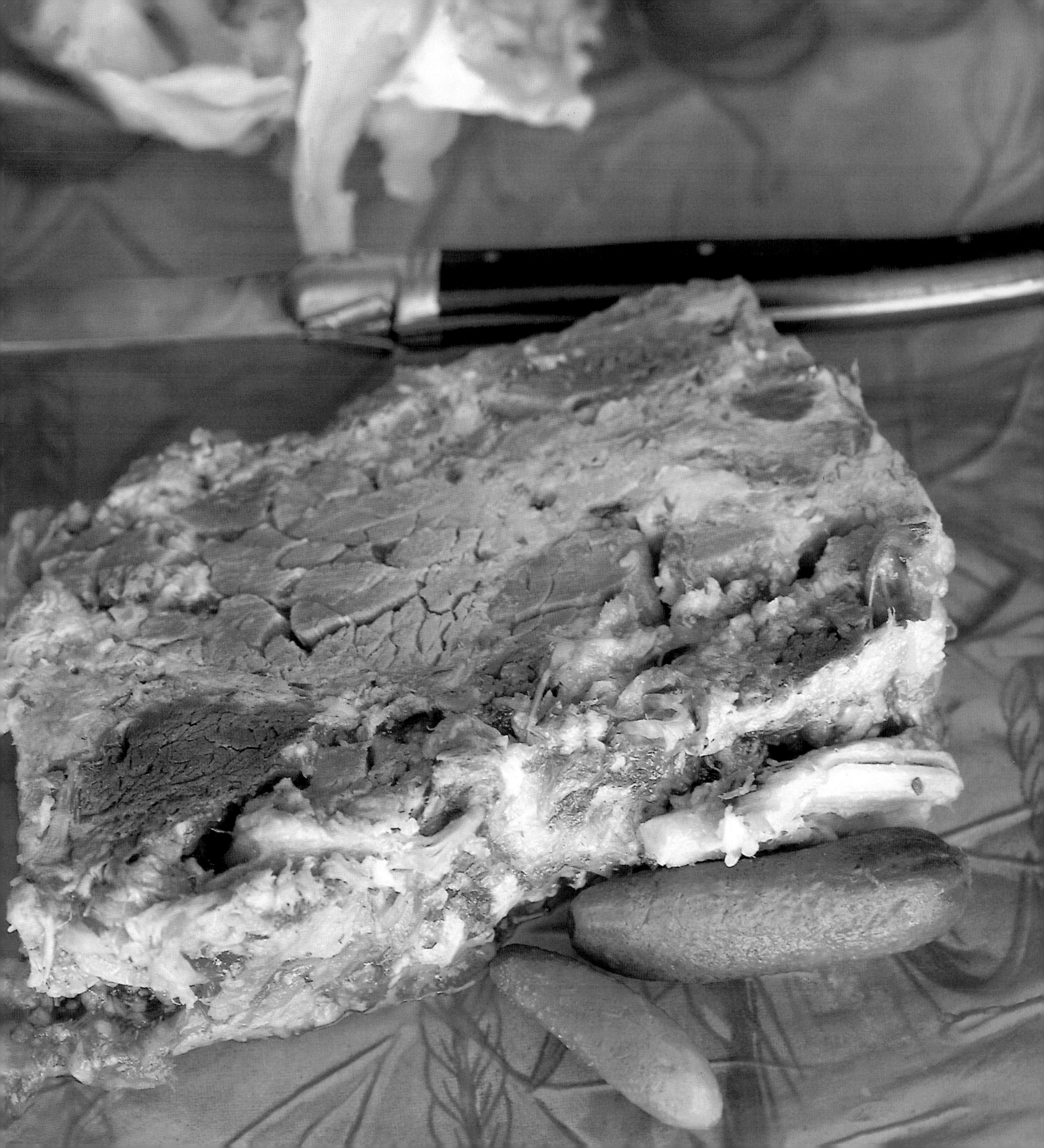

Home Cooking

Jacques Maximin is one of the most celebrated and notorious chefs in France—celebrated for his prodigious talents, notorious for his moods. Born in rainy northern France, he came of age professionally in the sunny south. As chef at Chantecler in Nice's Hôtel Negresco, and then in his own grand place, set in a 39,000-square-foot former theater in the center of Nice (where he installed the kitchen on the stage, behind a red velvet curtain that rose solemnly after dinner), he gained critical acclaim for his inventive, pure-flavored cooking. Alas, the theater closed—but in 1996, he opened a more modest restaurant, on the ground floor of his house in Vence, about a dozen miles from Nice. Sampling dishes here like a salad of crisp haricots verts tossed in a tomato-spiked cream dressing with fresh hazelnuts (see page 111), white beans with miniature squid in ink sauce, tiny scallops stuffed with dried mushrooms (above), and broiled baby pigeon with lentils—all simple, confident, and very good—it was clear to us that Maximin is at home in more ways than one.

Pétoncles Farcis à la Provençale

(Stuffed Scallops Provençal-Style)

SERVES 6

WHEN HE MAKES this simple appetizer at his restaurant in Vence, Jacques Maximin (right) uses the small Mediterranean scallops known as pétoncles provençals and serves them in their own shells. It can also be made with shelled bay scallops and presented in separately purchased shells.

- *2 oz. dried porcini mushrooms*
- *8 tbsp. butter, slightly softened*
- *2 shallots, peeled and minced*
- *3 cloves garlic, peeled and minced*
- *2 tbsp. cognac*
- *¼ cup finely chopped fresh parsley*
- *Salt and freshly ground black pepper*
- *30 fresh bay scallops, in shell (or 30 shelled bay scallops and 30 scallop half-shells); ask your fishmonger*
- *2 tbsp. freshly grated parmigiano-reggiano*

1. Rinse mushrooms, then put in a medium bowl. Add very hot water to cover, top with a plate, and set aside to soften for about 20 minutes. Drain, rinse, then finely chop mushrooms.

2. Heat 2 tbsp. butter in a medium skillet over medium heat. Add shallots, garlic, and mushrooms and cook, stirring, until shallots are soft, about 5 minutes. Add cognac and simmer until almost completely evaporated, about 30 seconds. Remove from heat and set aside.

3. Place remaining 6 tbps. butter in a medium bowl. Add mushroom mixture and parsley. Season to taste with salt and pepper and mix thoroughly.

4. Preheat broiler. Gently pry open scallops by running a paring knife through scallop muscle to separate it from shell. Remove and discard dark stomach. Using your fingers, pull away and discard small muscle, which wraps partially around scallop. Set scallops aside. Thoroughly wash and dry half the shells. (Remaining shells can be cleaned and stored for future use.)

5. Place scallop shells in a single layer on a cookie sheet. Put a scallop in each shell and top with about 1 tbsp. of mushroom butter. Sprinkle with parmigiano-reggiano and broil until cheese is golden, 1–2 minutes. Serve warm. (Shells can be washed and reused.)

Huîtres Glacées en Sabayon

(Oysters in Champagne Sauce)

SERVES 4–6

RAW OYSTERS on the half shell are a tradition in France, of course, but the classical French repertoire includes cooked oyster dishes, too, like this one from À Sousceyrac in Paris.

¾ lb. fresh spinach, trimmed and washed
Salt
24 large oysters (about 3" in length) such as bluepoint
Rock salt
¾ cup French champagne
¾ cup fish stock (see page 62)
¾ cup heavy cream
3 egg yolks
Freshly ground white pepper

1. Plunge spinach in a pot of boiling salted water for about 30 seconds. Drain, squeeze dry, and set aside.

2. Shuck oysters, reserving liquor and half the shells and discarding the rest. Put oysters in a medium saucepan with oyster liquor, cover, and simmer over medium-low heat until oysters are opaque and slightly firm, 1–3 minutes (**A**). Remove oysters with a slotted spoon. Strain liquor through a fine sieve, return to pan, and set aside. Wash and dry oyster shells. Make a ½" bed of rock salt on 4 or 6 ovenproof plates and divide shells between plates, arranging them in a circle in the salt.

3. Bring champagne to a boil in a small saucepan over medium-high heat. Cook until reduced by half, about 5 minutes, then set aside to cool.

4. Add fish stock to reserved oyster liquor. Bring to a boil over medium-high heat and cook until almost syrupy, 12–15 minutes, then add cream and cook, stirring, until reduced by two-thirds, 10–12 minutes.

5. Transfer reduced champagne to the top of a double boiler over simmering water on medium-low heat. Whisk in egg yolks and cook until thick and shiny, about 5 minutes. Remove from heat and slowly whisk in fish stock mixture. Season to taste with salt and pepper.

6. Preheat broiler. Spread a thin layer of spinach in each shell and top with 1 oyster (**B**). Spoon 1–2 tbsp. sauce over each (**C**) and broil for 3–5 minutes. Serve hot.

A

B

C

Oyster Culture

Two species of oyster are grown in France today: huîtres plates, or flat oysters (*Ostrea edulis*) and huîtres creuses, or concave oysters (*Crassostrea gigas*). The belon, named for the Belon River in Brittany (but also grown elsewhere, including Maine and the Pacific Northwest), is the most highly prized of the flats. Raised in a combination of fresh- and saltwater, the belon has what the French describe as "un petit goût de noisette" or slight hazelnut flavor, and an iodine character. The most prominent creuses are fines de claires and spéciales de claires from the Marennes basin in the Charente-Maritime. Another well-regarded creuse is the bouzigue, a Mediterranean oyster from the Thau basin in the Hérault. The French classify oysters according to weight. Flats are numbered from 000 (the largest) down to n°6 (the smallest). Confusingly, fines, spéciales, and all other creuses are rated according to a different system, with n°1 being the largest and n°6 the smallest (n°2 and n°3 are the most common). Very small but meaty oysters are called huîtres papillons, or butterfly oysters.

Cidre

Crêpes de Sarrasin

(Savory Buckwheat Crêpes)

Makes 8 crêpes

Buckwheat, called *sarrasin* or *blé noir* in French, is eaten in parts of France where wheat doesn't grow readily, and is often associated with the cuisine of poverty. In Breton tradition, the first crêpe in every batch, often considered to be substandard, was torn up and tossed into soup.

3 eggs
1 cup white buckwheat flour
¼ cup whole buckwheat flour
Salt and freshly ground black pepper
½ lb. gruyère, freshly grated
4 tbsp. butter

1. Whisk eggs and 1½ cups water together in a large mixing bowl. Sift together white buckwheat flour, whole buckwheat flour, salt and pepper to taste, then stir into egg mixture. Cover with plastic wrap and refrigerate overnight.

2. To cook, heat a large nonstick pan over medium-high heat. When pan is very hot, remove from heat and pour ¼ cup batter into the center. Tilt pan to distribute batter and return to heat. Cook crêpe until lightly browned, about 2 minutes, then flip with a spatula and cook for 1 more minute. Transfer to a plate and keep warm in a low oven while making remaining crêpes.

3. Return cooked crêpes to pan one at a time, sprinkle ¼ cup of the cheese in the middle, and fold to make a square. Cook until cheese melts, about 30 seconds. Serve immediately, seam side down, with a pat of butter.

Pancake Ceremony

"The crêpe symbolizes all that is Brittany," says chef Patrick Jeffroy (below), from the Breton town of Plounérin. More basic to the region's gastronomy than bread, crêpes come in two main varieties: sweet ones made with plain wheat flour mixed with eggs and milk and generally folded over a sweet filling of some kind, and salted ones, also called galettes, made with buckwheat flour, eggs, and water, and usually filled with savory ingredients. Crêperies, which dot almost every street in Brittany, serve extensive all-crêpe menus, offering fillings ranging from a sprinkling of sugar or a bit of jam to layers of ham, vegetables, and cheese. Crêpes are eaten at any time of day, as a snack or as a full meal—and are almost always accompanied by a cup or bowl of locally pressed cold hard cider. "There is a whole ceremony based around making crêpes at home," says Jeffroy. "The entire house smells good and the whole family comes together."

Queen of Crêpes

Millette Coquillon is famous for her coq au vin and her boeuf à la bourguignonne (see page 204), but she is known in the Morvan region— where she has run her La Petite Auberge (Chez Millette) for the last 36 years—most of all as "la reine de la grapiau", the queen of the Burgundian crêpe. Coquillon first worked in restaurants as a waitress, and claims to have learned to cook simply by watching what the chefs were doing. The daughter of Morvandelle *paysans,* she calls her cooking, which is based on fresh produce and on the region's excellent meats and charcuterie, *cuisine familiale.* Most of her clientele during the week, she says, is local— workers, generally. (We also saw a coterie of gendarmes enjoying a long lunch there one day.) On weekends, adds Coquillon, a few tourists are likely to be added to the mix. "But don't say too much about me," she cautions. "There isn't much to say anyway. What I really like is just simplicity."

Grapiaux

(Burgundian Crêpes)

Makes 16 crêpes

THIS SAVORY appetizer pancake, which is heartier than its Breton cousins, was once eaten in some form all over Burgundy—but today it is found mostly only in the Morvan (see page 205), a region famous for its pork products, and for its simple cooking. Millette Coquillon of La Petite Auberge in Planchez, considered by local connoisseurs to be the master of the grapiau, shared her recipe with us.

2 cups flour
2 ½ cups milk
4 eggs
Salt and freshly ground black pepper
8 oz. salt pork, diced

1. Sift flour into a mixing bowl, then gradually add milk, whisking constantly until batter is smooth. Add eggs, one at a time, and continue whisking until they are incorporated into the batter. Season to taste with salt and pepper, cover, and set aside for 1 hour.

2. Scatter 5–6 cubes salt pork into an 8" seasoned crêpe pan or nonstick skillet and fry over medium-high heat until just crisp. Pour about ¼ cup batter into the pan and cook until the crêpe is crispy and richly browned on 1 side, about 1 minute. Flip crêpe over and fry for an additional 30 seconds. Repeat process to make 16 crêpes.

CHAMOUX (89)
sur D 951 à 7 km
33 28 33

ROUGE
FRAGILE

and as the clock struck midnight, they'd turn from soup to champagne, and cries of 'Bonne Année!' would ring out across the room.... Until 1969, when the immense Parisian wholesale market complex called Les Halles began closing, this was the typical New Year's Eve scene at Chez Clovis, one of the many market bistros. 'On New Year's Eve,' recalls Claude Cornut, second-generation proprietor of Chez Clovis (with his wife, Françoise, facing page, lower right), 'everybody had soupe à l'oignon. It was the tradition. People would come by after their parties, and between 2 and 8 in the morning, we'd serve 1,600 bowls of it.' But consumption of this rich onion-filled, cheese-topped broth, at places like Chez Clovis and the celebrated Au Pied de Cochon (whose chef ladles it up still, facing page, top left), was hardly restricted to the year's end. Every night, Parisian swells on their way home from a night out would join workers from the market for bowls of this restorative tonic. 'Les Halles was a village unto itself in the very heart of Paris,' Cornut continues. 'We were so content and self-sufficient that we would forget that there was a world outside. Imagine the ambience of a place that is alive at least 20 hours of the day! It was extraordinary! There was never a void, never a dull moment. You'd see the pork butcher, spattered with blood, and the scale-covered fishmonger, laughing and drinking, right across from a party of elegant characters just arrived from an evening at the opera. There was this kind of colorful and hearty interaction at all hours of the night, any night of the year, with all the richness of the smells and sounds that accompanied it.'" —MEGAN WETHERALL

RECIPES

SOUPE À L'OIGNON GRATINÉE *(French Onion Soup)*, page 55; FOND BLANC DE VOLAILLE *(Clear Chicken Stock)*, page 56; FOND BRUN DE BOEUF *(Brown Beef Stock)*, page 59; FOND BRUN DE VEAU *(Brown Veal Stock)*, page 60; FUMET DE POISSON *(Fish Stock)*, page 62; SOUPE D'ÉCREVISSES *(Crayfish Soup)*, page 65; BISQUE DE HOMARD *(Lobster Bisque)*, page 66; CRÈME DE POTIRON *(Cream of Squash Soup)*, page 69; SOUPE DE FÈVES *(Fava Bean Soup)*, page 70; SOUPE CORSE *(Corsican Soup)*, page 73; SOUPE PAYSANNE À BOIRE ET À MANGER *(Peasant Soup to Drink and Eat)*, page 74.

CHAPTER

2

SOUPS

"THEY'D CROWD against the zinc bar, their heads bent over steaming bowls of soupe à l'oignon, their mouths connected to it by endless ribbons of golden cheese—

Soupe à l'Oignon Gratinée

(French Onion Soup)

SERVES 8

WE DEVELOPED this recipe based on the many early-morning onion soups we've enjoyed at Parisian bistros like Au Pied de Cochon (right) and Chez Clovis (pages 51-52).

6 tbsp. butter
1 tbsp. olive oil
3 lbs. medium yellow onions, peeled and thinly sliced
1 tsp. sugar
Salt
1 tbsp. flour
8 cups beef stock (see page 59)
2 cups dry white wine
Freshly ground black pepper
1 baguette
1 lb. gruyère, shredded

1. Melt 3 tbsp. of the butter and the oil in a large heavy pot over medium-low heat. Add onions, cover and cook, stirring occasionally, until soft and translucent, about 20 minutes. Increase heat to medium-high, uncover, and add the sugar and season to taste with salt. Sauté, stirring often until onions are very soft and a deep golden brown.

2. Reduce heat to medium, sprinkle in flour and cook, stirring constantly, for 2–3 minutes. Add about 2 cups of stock and stir to blend, then add remaining 6 cups of stock and the wine. Season to taste with salt and pepper and simmer for about 30 minutes. Adjust seasoning to taste.

3. Preheat oven to 425°. Meanwhile, slice the bread into at least 8 thick slices. Butter both sides of the bread with the remaining 3 tbsp. of butter, then toast until golden brown on both sides in the oven.

4. Place a slice of toast in each of 8 ovenproof bowls, then fill bowls with the onion soup. Spread a thick layer of cheese on top of soup. Set bowls in 2 baking pans, place in the oven and bake until cheese has browned.

A Sensible Soup

An oft-repeated culinary legend notwithstanding, it is extremely unlikely that soupe à l'oignon was invented by Louis XIV (who concocted it, according to one story, with champagne!). Nor did the soup necessarily originate in Lyon, despite the fact that the region is famous for its onions (and that dishes cooked à la lyonnaise inevitably contain them). According to Dr. Paul Henry, a respected Lyonnais historian, the origins of the soup are probably quite pedestrian. Until relatively recently in rural France, soup was a staple of every household, kept simmering on the stove and eaten daily, often for breakfast. It was made of anything that was cheap, or grew plentifully in the garden—and the onion certainly qualified. It also had the virtue of being available most of the year—and was one of the more flavorful of vegetables. "The addition of cheese to the soup and its evolution to a 'gratinée'," adds Henry, "would probably have come from the Savoie, where cheese is often used in cooking."

Fond Blanc de Volaille

(Clear Chicken Stock)

MAKES ABOUT 2 QUARTS

FAR FROM LOSING its flavor, the chicken used to make stock by this method soaks up lots of flavor from the vegetables, and is delicious in salads, soups, and sandwiches.

1 3-lb. chicken
3 leeks, trimmed, washed, and chopped
2 carrots, peeled and chopped
2 stalks celery, chopped
Bouquet garni (see sidebar, page 59)
Black peppercorns
Salt

1. Put chicken, leeks, carrots, celery, bouquet garni, and a few peppercorns in a large heavy stockpot. Add 3 quarts water and 2 tsp. salt, then bring to a boil over high heat.

2. Reduce heat to low and gently simmer stock, partially covered, for 1 hour. (At this point, if you like, you may remove chicken from pot, pick the meat from the bones to reserve for another use, and return carcass to pot.) Uncover, and continue to simmer for another hour, occasionally skimming off any foam that rises to the surface.

3. Pour stock through a strainer lined with cheesecloth, discarding chicken carcass and vegetables. Transfer stock to a bowl, cover with plastic wrap, and refrigerate for at least 4 hours, or overnight. Remove and discard fat that has formed on surface. Stock may be stored in the refrigerator for up to 3 days, or in the freezer for up to 6 months.

Stock Options

Stocks are the "fonds de cuisine" in a French kitchen—literally the very foundations of cooking. Butter and cream and wine may be vital to many classical French dishes, but it is stock that gives them texture, richness, and real depth of flavor. Making stock involves the slow cooking of meat, poultry, or fish—including their bones—in water, with vegetables and seasonings added. (Stock can also be made from vegetables alone.) If meat and bones are browned first with the vegetables, the result will be a fond brun, or brown stock—darker in color and even richer in flavor than a fond blanc, or white stock, made without browning. (Below, from left: demi-glace, made by reducing brown veal stock [see sidebar, page 61]; fish stock; chicken stock; brown veal stock.) Making stock is a great activity for a rainy day: It requires virtually no labor, but does benefit from occasional attention (skimming impurities off the surface)—and a simmering stockpot will both warm and perfume your house. There is no point making just a little stock, incidentally. Make plenty, use what you need, and freeze the rest. Every kitchen needs solid foundations.

Fond Brun de Boeuf

(Brown Beef Stock)

MAKES ABOUT 2 QUARTS

HEARTY beef stock, like this one, is a classic building block for many traditional French dishes. Besides the foodstuffs called for in the recipe below, the most important ingredient here is patience: Long, slow cooking is essential.

- *6 lbs. beef bones (shin, oxtail, and neck)*
- *2 tbsp. vegetable oil*
- *Salt and freshly ground black pepper*
- *2 tbsp. tomato paste*
- *2 carrots, scrubbed and coarsely chopped*
- *4 stalks celery, coarsely chopped*
- *2 medium yellow onions, halved*
- *2 leeks, trimmed, washed, and coarsely chopped*
- *2 cloves*
- *8 cloves garlic, peeled and lightly crushed*
- *1 cup red wine*
- *Bouquet garni (see sidebar, right)*

1. Preheat oven to 375°. Brush beef bones with 1 tbsp. oil, season generously with salt and pepper, put in a large roasting pan, and roast until just browned, about 30 minutes. Smear tomato paste over bones and roast for 20 minutes more. Toss carrots, celery, onions, leeks, cloves, and garlic with remaining oil, and add to pan with bones. Roast for 20 minutes more.

2. Transfer bones and vegetables to a large stockpot. Deglaze roasting pan on stovetop over medium heat with red wine, scraping up browned bits from bottom of pan, then pour juices into stockpot. Add bouquet garni and cover with 5 quarts water. Bring to a boil over high heat, then reduce heat to low and simmer, uncovered, until stock is reduced by two-thirds, about 4 hours, occasionally skimming off any foam that rises to the surface. Strain stock and discard solids. Transfer stock to a bowl, cover with plastic wrap, and refrigerate for at least 4 hours, or overnight. Remove and discard fat that has formed on surface. Stock may be stored in the refrigerator for up to 3 days, or in the freezer for up to 6 months.

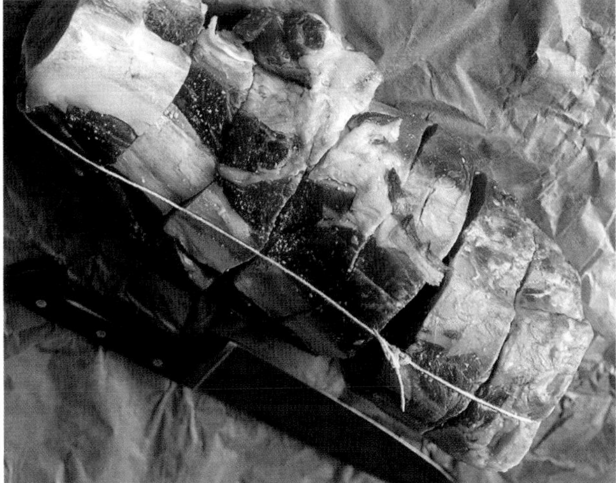

Bouquet Garni

For a classic bouquet garni, (above) the basic French bundle of herbs that flavors so many stocks, soups, and sauces, lay 3 sprigs of parsley, 2 sprigs of thyme, 1 bay leaf, and 3–5 peppercorns in the middle of a 6" square of washed cheesecloth, then gather up the edges and tie into a bundle with kitchen string. Or cut a 4" length of the light green part of a leek, split it in two lengthwise, and lay herbs and peppercorns inside one of the leaves, reassemble leek, and tie with kitchen string (see photos, page 57). Some cooks leave a little extra string on both kinds of bouquet garni to tie it to the pot handle, for easy retrieval.

Fond Brun de Veau

(Brown Veal Stock)

MAKES ABOUT 3 QUARTS

THIS INTENSELY flavorful stock is widely used in French cooking, both on its own and in twice-reduced form, as the chefs' "secret ingredient" known as demi-glace.

8 lbs. cracked veal bones
3 carrots, peeled and chopped
3 yellow onions, peeled and chopped
3 stalks celery, chopped
2 tbsp. tomato paste
2 cups dry white wine (optional)
2 plum tomatoes, chopped
2 cloves garlic, peeled
2 bay leaves
10 black peppercorns
3 sprigs fresh parsley

1. Preheat oven to 400°. Put veal bones in a large roasting pan and roast until browned, about 1 hour. Add carrots, onions, celery, and tomato paste, mix well, and continue roasting until vegetables and bones are well browned, 30–40 minutes.

2. Transfer bones and vegetables to a large stockpot. Deglaze roasting pan on stovetop over medium heat with white wine (if using) or 2 cups water, scraping up browned bits from bottom of pan. Simmer for 1 minute, then pour juices into stockpot.

3. Add tomatoes, garlic, bay leaves, peppercorns, parsley, and about 4 quarts water to stockpot. Bring to a boil over high heat, then reduce heat and simmer, uncovered, over medium heat until stock is reduced by about one-quarter, about 2 hours, occasionally skimming off any foam that rises to the surface. Strain stock and discard solids. Transfer stock to a bowl, cover with plastic wrap, and refrigerate for at least 4 hours, or overnight. Remove and discard fat that has formed on surface. Stock can be stored in the refrigerator in a sealed container for up to 3 days or frozen for up to 6 months.

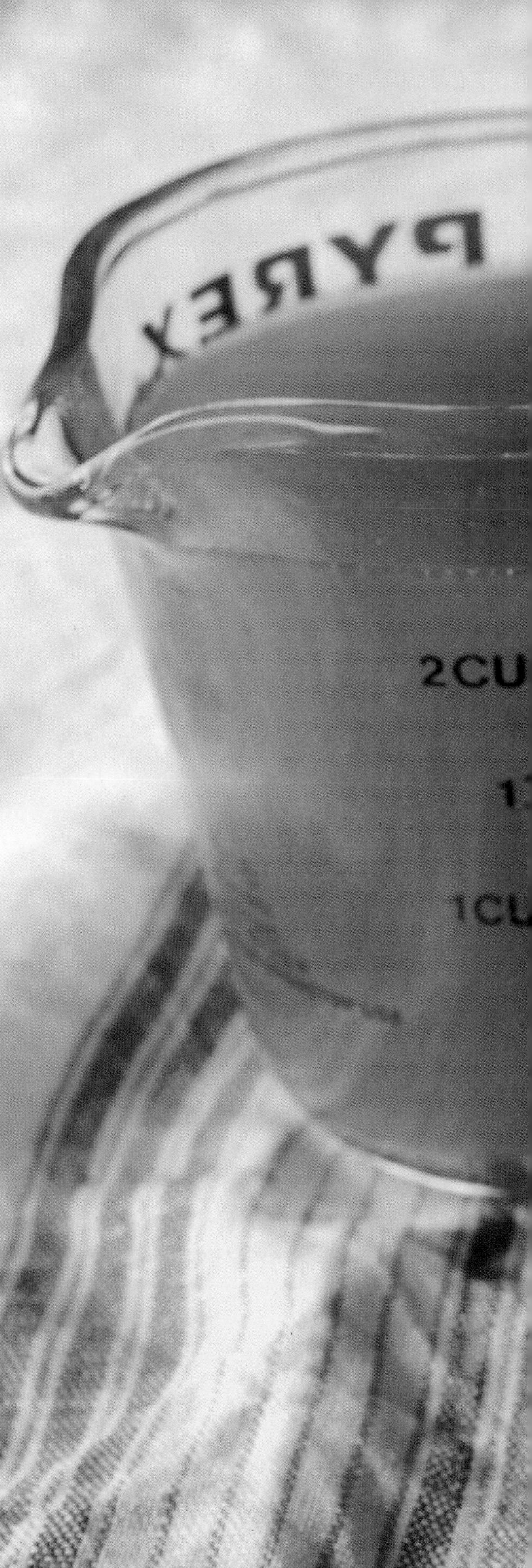

The Soul of Sauces

To make 2 cups of demi-glace, a rich, versatile brown "half-glaze", render fat from ¼ lb. finely chopped bacon in a large heavy pot over medium-low heat, cooking for about 15 minutes. Add 1 chopped, peeled yellow onion and 1 chopped, peeled carrot and cook, stirring occasionally, for 5 minutes. Sprinkle vegetables with ¼ cup flour and continue cooking, stirring occasionally, for 10 minutes. Add 2 tbsp. tomato paste, 10 sprigs fresh parsley, 2 bay leaves, 2 sprigs fresh thyme, and 2 quarts brown veal stock (see recipe, left). Simmer, skimming occasionally, over medium heat until sauce has reduced by three-quarters, about 2 hours. Strain sauce and return to pan. Add 2 more cups brown veal stock and simmer over medium-low heat until sauce has reduced by half, about 2½ hours, then strain. Store in refrigerator in a sealed container for up to 1 week or frozen for up to 6 months.

Fishmongers' Soup

Unsuspecting diners sometimes feel cheated in French restaurants when they order soupe de poisson and get something with no fish in it. That's because soup *with* fish is soupe aux poissons; soupe de poisson is an intense, orange-hued, long-reduced fish-flavored soup, traditionally served with croutons, spicy rouille (see recipe, page 146), and grated gruyère. Jars of this specialty (above) are sold in fish shops and markets all over France, and almost nobody bothers to make it at home. According to Dominique Pillet, a sixth-generation Trouville fishmonger, the soup must be made in large quantities in order to achieve the requisite concentration and intensity of flavor. He adds that in earlier times, fishmongers used to moonlight by cooking seafood specialties in for the Parisian vacationers who rented houses in the area. Soupe de poisson, perceived as a festive dish, ideal for serving at big family gatherings, was particularly popular among the holiday-makers. Not surprisingly, they took a taste for it back to Paris, and it soon became part of the standard French culinary repertoire.

Fumet de Poisson

(Fish Stock)

MAKES ABOUT 2½ QUARTS

IN BUYING fish carcasses for making fumet, avoid salmon and other freshwater varieties, and oily fish like mackerel and tuna. Monkfish and various kinds of rockfish are ideal.

3 tbsp. olive oil
3 small leeks, white part only, trimmed, washed, and diced
1 celery stalk, finely chopped
1 fennel bulb, finely chopped
2 medium carrots, peeled and finely chopped
Zest of ½ orange
3 cloves garlic, peeled
3 tomatoes, coarsely chopped
Bouquet garni (see sidebar, page 59)
6 lbs. fish carcasses (with heads)
1 bottle dry white wine

1. Heat oil in a large stockpot over medium-low heat. Add leeks, celery, fennel, carrots, and orange zest. Cook, stirring occasionally, until vegetables are soft, about 15 minutes. Add garlic, tomatoes, and bouqet garni. Continue to cook for 1–2 minutes.

2. Break fish carcasses into large pieces. Add to vegetables along with the wine and 4 quarts water. Increase heat to medium-high, bring stock to a boil, then reduce heat to medium and simmer, uncovered, for 1 hour, occasionally skimming off any foam that rises to the surface. Allow stock to cool slightly, then strain through a fine sieve, return to pot, and reduce by about half over medium-high heat for about 1 hour. Stock can be stored in the refrigerator in a sealed container for 3 days or frozen for up to 6 months.

Soupe d'Écrevisses

(Crayfish Soup)

Serves 4–8

Crayfish were once so plentiful in Alsace that soups like this one, served by father-and-son chefs Jean and Michel Orth (right) at their L'Écrevisse in Brumath, were common. Today, most "Alsatian" crayfish is imported from the U.S.

3 ¾ lbs. live crayfish, rinsed
2 tbsp. peanut oil
½ cup cognac
2 stalks celery, chopped
1 medium carrot, peeled and chopped
6 cloves garlic, peeled and finely chopped
2 tbsp. tomato paste
7 cups fish stock (see page 62)
5 sprigs fresh thyme
3 bay leaves
1 ½ tsp. arrowroot
1 cup crème fraîche
Salt and freshly ground black pepper
2 tbsp. finely chopped fresh chives

1. Bring a large pot of water to a boil over high heat. Add crayfish, cook for 5 minutes, then drain and run under cold water. Remove meat from tails, reserving shells. Devein crayfish as you would shrimp: run a paring knife along back of tail and lift out and discard intestine. (This is easiest under running water.) Set meat aside.

2. Heat oil in a large pot over medium-high heat. Add shells and cook, stirring, for 3 minutes. Add cognac, then carefully ignite cognac with a long-handled match. (Keep lid handy so flame can be extinguished if necessary.) Allow alcohol to burn off, about 1 minute. When flame has died down, reduce heat to medium and add celery, carrots, and garlic. Cook, stirring often, until vegetables are soft, 10–15 minutes.

3. Reduce heat to medium-low, stir in tomato paste, and cook, stirring constantly, for 2 minutes. Add stock, thyme, bay leaves, and 1 cup water. Simmer for 30 minutes.

4. Strain soup through a fine sieve, discarding shells, herbs, and vegetables. Return soup to pot and simmer over medium heat for 15–20 minutes. Ladle ½ cup of soup into a small bowl, stir in arrowroot, mix until dissolved, then whisk mixture back into soup. Simmer for 1–2 minutes, reduce heat to medium-low, then whisk in crème fraîche. Season with salt and pepper, stir in crayfish meat, and simmer until heated through, about 2 minutes. Serve warm, garnished with chives.

Crayfish Tales

Écrevisses, or crayfish, are freshwater crustaceans of the superfamily Astacoidea, looking a bit like small lobsters and a bit like shrimp. Generally just the tail is eaten (it's the only portion of the creature that has much meat), but the claws and shells ooze wonderful flavor and can be pounded to make bisques or stocks. These are the crustaceans commonly eaten in France:

ÉCREVISSE À PATTES ROUGES: Red-clawed crayfish, large and flavorful. Almost decimated by water pollution and overfishing, they are extremely rare, and usually found today only at France's top restaurants.

ÉCREVISSE À PATTES BLANCHES: White-clawed crayfish, the most common variety in France today, found wild in mountainous areas and also successfully farmed.

LANGOUSTINE: Related to the Dublin Bay prawn and to the scampi of the Adriatic; in effect, a kind of saltwater crayfish.

LANGOUSTE: Spiny or rock lobster, similar to homard (see below), but with very long antennae and no claws. There are many different varities fished in the Atlantic and the Mediterranean (and also the Pacific).

HOMARD: Lobster, the real thing, found in Europe off the coast of Brittany and in the cold waters off Britain and Norway. It is the largest of crustaceans as well as the meatiest (because of its large claws).

Bisque de Homard

(Lobster Bisque)

SERVES 8

A BISQUE IS a rich cream soup. For classic lobster bisque, female lobsters are preferred, because their roe lends flavor and color to the soup. (Ask your fishmonger to select females for you.) This recipe comes from Gabriel Biscay (lower right, foreground), chef at Prunier (see sidebar, page 157), the celebrated Parisian seafood restaurant.

3 1½ lbs. live female lobsters
¾ cup peanut oil
6 tbsp. butter
2 carrots, peeled and finely diced
4 shallots, peeled and finely diced
2 cloves garlic, peeled and minced
1 6-oz. can tomato paste
¾ cup dry white wine
2½ quarts fish stock (see page 62)
1 small stalk celery, chopped
Bouquet garni (see sidebar, page 59) with 2 sprigs fresh tarragon and 12 sprigs parsley added
Sea salt
Pinch cayenne
Freshly ground black pepper
4 tbsp. flour
1 tbsp. fresh tarragon, chopped, plus 8 sprigs reserved for garnish
4 tbsp. cognac
1 cup heavy cream

1. Set lobsters on a cutting board and, using a heavy knife, split lobsters in half through the heads lengthwise, taking care not to split the tail. Use the flat side of the knife to scoop up any juices from the lobster into a small bowl, and set aside. Discard the bitter, sandy interior of the head, but save tomalley and roe and add to bowl with reserved juices. Break or cut lobster into head, claws, and tail.

2. Heat oil in a large heavy pan over high heat. When the oil is hot, put lobster pieces in pan, flesh down, to sear. Use kitchen tongs to turn lobster pieces until shells are thoroughly red and almost blackened (add more oil if necessary), about 10 minutes. Transfer lobster to a large bowl and set aside.

3. Pour off leftover oil and return pan to stove. Melt 2 tbsp. of the butter in the pan over high heat then add carrots, shallots, and garlic and cook until soft and lightly browned. Add tomato paste and cook, stirring constantly, for 1–2 minutes. Add wine and cook for 3 minutes, then stir in fish stock. Return lobster to pan, add celery and bouquet garni, and bring to a boil. Skim off fat and any foam that rises to the surface with a large spoon. Reduce heat to medium-low, add 2 pinches of salt and the cayenne and season to taste with pepper. Gently simmer for 15 minutes, skimming regularly. Remove lobster from pan and set aside. Remove and discard bouquet garni and continue simmering stock for 15 minutes.

4. Meanwhile, melt remaining 4 tbsp. butter in a small saucepan over low heat. Whisk in flour, then add chopped tarragon and reserved tomalley, roe, and lobster juices and whisk until the mixture is smooth. Whisk in 1 tbsp. of the cognac and a little of the stock, then add butter mixture to bisque. Bring to a boil and continue whisking until smooth and thick. Reduce heat to medium, season to taste with salt and pepper, and simmer for another 15 minutes.

5. Remove meat from cooled lobster and discard shells. Cut meat into pieces and set aside, adding any juices to bisque. Pour bisque through a large, fine strainer into a large bowl, pressing solids with the back of a ladle, then return bisque to pan. Whisk in cream, adjust seasonings with salt and pepper, then add remaining 3 tbsps. of cognac.

6. Divide lobster between 8 bowls, then ladle bisque around it and serve garnished with tarragon sprigs.

Crème de la Crème

Almost any vegetable can be turned into a simple cream soup—turnips, cabbage, cauliflower, potatoes, whatever. To serve 6, peel and trim vegetables as needed to yield 1½–2 lbs. Melt 2 tbsp. butter with 1 tsp. vegetable oil in a large, heavy pot over medium heat. Add 1 chopped onion and cook until soft, about 15 minutes. Cut vegetables into small pieces, add to pot, and cook for 10 minutes. Add 2 quarts chicken stock (see page 56) and season to taste with salt and freshly ground white pepper. Bring to a boil, then reduce heat to low and simmer, uncovered, until vegetables are soft, about 40 minutes. Stir in ½ cup heavy cream and cool slightly. Purée in a blender or food processor, and adjust seasoning. Reheat before serving.

Crème de Potiron

(Cream of Squash Soup)

SERVES 8

"MANY'S the bride who has tried to duplicate her French mother-in-law's famous *potage au potiron*," note Julia Child and Simone Beck in their *Mastering the Art of French Cooking*, vol. 2, "and finds that the secret ingredient...was squash rather than pumpkin." This recipe came to us not from a mother-in-law but from chef Patrick Jeffroy (see page 242).

4 lbs. butternut squash, or princess or cheese pumpkin
½ small cauliflower
2 tbsp. butter
3 medium yellow onions, peeled and diced
6 cups chicken stock *(see page 56)*
6 tbsp. heavy cream
Salt and freshly ground white pepper
Freshly grated nutmeg
8 fresh chervil sprigs

1. Cut squash in half, remove seeds, and peel. Cut about an eighth of the squash into a fine dice and set aside. Cut remaining squash into pieces about 2" square and set aside.

2. Cut off about half of cauliflower florets, the smallest ones from the crown of the cauliflower, and set aside. Break remaining cauliflower into larger florets and set aside. Blanch diced squash and small cauliflower florets in a large pot of boiling water for 60 seconds then drain, refresh in a bowl of ice water, and set aside.

3. Melt the butter in a large heavy pot over medium heat. Add onions, 2" squares of squash, and large cauliflower florets, cover tightly and cook until slightly soft, about 15 minutes, lifting the lid occasionally to stir. Increase heat to high, add chicken stock, and bring to a simmer, then reduce heat to medium-low and simmer, partially covered, until vegetables are very soft, about 15 minutes more.

4. Transfer vegetables and broth to a blender or food processor and purée. Strain the puréed soup back into pot, set over low heat, stir in cream, and season to taste with salt, pepper, and nutmeg. Divide reserved vegetables between 8 bowls, then ladle hot soup over vegetables and garnish each bowl with a chervil sprig.

Harold l'Américain

The expression 'joie de vivre' was invented for my Dad, Harold Wright [in checked shirt, below and facing page, upper right and lower left],who now lives part of the year in France," writes author Clifford A. Wright. "Curiously and refreshingly, his love of the country has no similarity with any of the affected Francophilia popular among the cosmopolitan cognoscenti in America today. He doesn't care about the art, the literature, the wine; as far as he knows, a Michelin three-star is a kind of tire. But in 1984 he bought an old ramshackle barn in the village of Frayssinet [facing page, upper left] in the southwestern French département of the Lot. Dad is an outgoing and charming man, who kisses the ladies and bounces the children, and is now a fixture in the village—where he is known as Harold l'Américain. Once the mayor came by reminding everyone of a community meal being held in the village meeting hall. Dad remarked, 'But I only live here part of the year.' The mayor replied, 'Yes, but you're a part of our community.' After that, Dad really felt welcome, and his life in the village evolved into the idyllic retirement we all hope for. Dad doesn't cook much, but he eats well, thanks to his neighbors—enjoying such earthy local preparations as a fava bean soup that is memorably cooked in duck fat. 'They like to eat duck and lamb around here,' Dad once informed us, sounding genuinely surprised."

Soupe de Fèves

(Fava Bean Soup)

Serves 8

Odette Cocula sometimes cooks this rustic soup for her neighbor, Harold Wright, a well-liked part-time American resident of the village of Frayssinet in the Lot.

3 tbsp. duck fat
1 medium yellow onion, peeled and finely chopped
3 cloves garlic, peeled
2 leeks, white part only, split lengthwise, washed and sliced
1 tbsp. tomato paste or 1 ripe plum tomato, peeled and finely chopped
2 potatoes, peeled and diced
10 cups chicken stock (see page 56)
3 cups fresh fava beans, shelled, blanched, and peeled, or 3 cups frozen fava beans, blanched and peeled
Salt and freshly ground black pepper
8 slices country bread

1. Melt the duck fat in a large heavy pot over medium-high heat. Add onions, 2 cloves of the garlic, and the leeks and sauté until vegetables are soft, about 15 minutes.

2. Stir in tomato paste and cook for 1–2 minutes. Add potatoes and chicken stock and simmer for 1 hour. Use a potato masher to slightly crush vegetables. Add fava beans and cook for 5 minutes, then season to taste with salt and pepper.

3. Rub bread on both sides with remaining garlic clove, then toast the bread in a preheated broiler. Put a piece of toasted bread in each of 8 soup bowls, then ladle soup and vegetables over bread.

MOUSQUETAIRES
ici Paris
France Dimanche
JOHNNY
La fin d'un immense bonheur

Soupe Corse

(Corsican Soup)

Serves 8

When they make this hearty mountain soup, the Juillard sisters of Murato use the French beans called cocos roses. We found navy beans to be an excellent substitute.

½ lb. dried navy beans
3 tbsp. olive oil
3 large yellow onions, peeled and finely chopped
10 small potatoes, peeled and diced
2 medium leeks, trimmed, washed, and finely chopped
2 medium zucchini, trimmed and diced
½ small green cabbage, cored and finely chopped
½ lb. haricots verts, trimmed and finely chopped
1 medium carrot, peeled and diced
1 medium tomato, peeled, seeded, and chopped
4 sprigs fresh marjoram, chopped
1 ham bone with some meat attached (have butcher cut in half crosswise)
¼ lb. tagliatelle, broken in half
3 cloves garlic, peeled and minced
5 fresh basil leaves, minced
Salt and freshly ground black pepper

1. Put beans in a medium bowl, cover with cold water by 2", and set aside to soak for at least 4 hours or overnight. Drain and set aside.

2. Heat oil in a large stockpot over medium heat. Add onions, potatoes, leeks, zucchini, cabbage, haricots verts, carrots, tomatoes, marjoram, and soaked beans and cook, stirring often, until fresh vegetables are slightly soft, about 10 minutes. Add ham bones and 10 cups cold water, increase heat to medium-high, and bring to a boil. Reduce heat to medium and simmer, stirring often, until vegetables are very soft and soup is thick, about 2 hours.

3. About 20 minutes before soup is finished cooking, add tagliatelle, garlic, and basil and cook, stirring often, until pasta is tender. Remove ham bones and season soup to taste with salt and pepper. Soup will thicken as it sits, and may be thinned with a little water, if you like.

Universal Soup

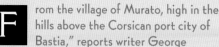

From the village of Murato, high in the hills above the Corsican port city of Bastia," reports writer George Semler, "I could just make out the French mainland to the northwest, hovering cloudlike in the distance. 'You're in luck,' said Henri Thiers. 'You can see the continent from here only two or three days a year.' Murato is justly famous for its extraordinary 12th-century polychrome church, San Michele de Murato—but there is another, almost equally compelling reason to visit the town: the 15-year-old restaurant Ferme Campo di Monte, which Thiers owns with sisters Pauline and Josiane Juillard. Corsicans seldom agree about anything, but they all seem to admire the place. When I arrived there that afternoon, the sisters were busy in the kitchen preparing the night's dinner: On the stove were goat stew, storzapreti—gratinéed cheese dumplings with mint and egg—and soupe corse. 'We took the soup off the menu once,' Pauline confides, 'but we had an uprising. Our patrons protested. It's the most universal Corsican dish.'"

Love and Garlic

Garbure is a hearty farmers' dish of cabbage, meat (usually salted pork and/or duck or goose confit), and seasonal vegetables, native to southwestern France. Rural households always had a pot of it on the stove, so it thickened and grew ever more intense in flavor; connoisseurs of garbure say that it should be so dense that a ladle will stand up in it. As with many traditional dishes, the recipe changes from season to season, from village to village, and even from house to house. The most famous of all garbures are those from Oloron-Ste-Marie, a town about 20 miles southwest of Pau, which styles itself La Capitale de la Garbure. Oloron hosts an annual Garburade, or garbure festival, which includes a competition for the best version of the dish. Basic ingredients include potatoes, leeks, and "corn beans", which are beans that grow around the cornstalk in the field—but vegetables as diverse as pumpkin, sugar-snap peas, dried chiles, nettles, and Chinese artichokes (crosnes) are also considered acceptable. Garbure, adds Fernand Pon, president of the Garburade, should be made with "a lot of love and a little bit of garlic"—though in the southwest of France, a little bit of garlic can turn out to be quite a lot.

Soupe Paysanne à Boire et à Manger

(Peasant Soup to Drink and Eat)

SERVES 12

IN BORDEAUX, when a few spoonfuls of soup are left in the bowl, locals pour in a few ounces of red wine, swirl it around, then drink the liquid directly from the bowl.

2 tbsp. duck fat
1 medium yellow onion, peeled and finely chopped
2 shallots, peeled and finely chopped
1 ham hock
1 head garlic, separated into cloves, then peeled and crushed
1 leek, trimmed, rinsed and thickly sliced
3 carrots, peeled and thickly sliced
2 large turnips, peeled and cut into large cubes
1 celery stalk, thickly sliced
1 small cabbage, cored and chopped into large pieces
1 ½ cups navy beans
Salt and freshly ground black pepper
1 large loaf rustic sourdough bread

1. Melt duck fat in a large heavy pot over medium heat. Add onions and shallots and cook until slightly softened, about 5 minutes. Add ham hock and brown, turning occasionally, for another 10 minutes.

2. Increase heat to high, add garlic, leeks, carrots, turnips, celery, cabbage, and beans, then add 5 quarts water and season to taste with salt and pepper. Once soup has come to a boil, reduce heat to low, partially cover, and simmer gently for 4 hours. Adjust seasoning, then serve with bread to soak up any leftover broth.

who traverse them, whether on foot, on skis, or by car, an enormous hunger—and, as a result, old-fashioned French mountain cooking is robust and satisfying. It thrives most vigorously today in the départements of Savoie and Haute-Savoie, in the heart of the French Alps. It is not sophisticated fare. Polenta and buckwheat pasta are common in traditional kitchens, as is the hearty one-pot meal called potée (see page 222). Though there are wild mushrooms and glorious apples, pears, plums, and cherries in summer and fall, and wild game well into the winter, many of the region's dishes are based on charcuterie, potatoes, and dairy products—above all cheese. One specialty combines all of these: reblochonnade (also called tartiflette), a dish of thinly sliced potatoes sautéed with bacon and onions, moistened with cream, baked, and finally topped with generous slices of creamy reblochon, the Haute-Savoie's most famous cheese—which is melted over it. Another variation of the cheese-and-potato theme is raclette (facing page, upper right), made by melting the cheese of that name over potatoes and cornichons. The region's most celebrated cheese dish, of course, is fondue savoyarde (see page 80)—gruyère-like beaufort (or French-made gruyère) melted with white wine and kirsch and scooped up with cubes of bread. Beaufort, like reblochon (and its larger relative, beaumont), is also much appreciated on its own. Another great cheese of the region is the medium-rich, slightly nutty-tasting tomme de Savoie, which cheese expert Steven Jenkins has called 'the most accessible cheese taste experience in the world.'" — GASTON PINARD

RECIPES

CHAPTER

3

CHEESE AND EGGS

"THE ALPS are an emblematic range, romantic, imposing, operatic—mountains as metaphor. They inspire us to poetry and to heroic deeds. They also inspire, in those

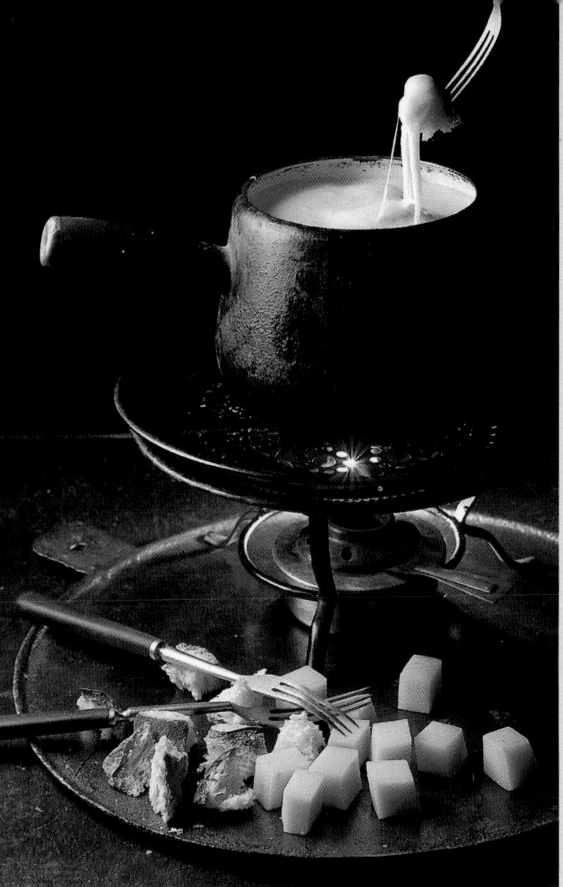

Fondue Savoyarde

Serves 4

Fondue pots, essential in any "gourmet" household of the 1960s, are back in the stores. The best ones, though, are the old models, which turn up sometimes at garage sales. According to fondue tradition, if your bread cube slips off your fork into the pot, you must buy the next round of drinks—or, some say, kiss the man or woman to your left.

1 clove garlic, peeled and crushed
1 ½ cups Savoyard white wine, such as chignin or crépy, or other light, dry white wine
1 lb. beaufort or gruyère cheese, grated or cubed
1 tsp. freshly grated nutmeg
Freshly ground black pepper
¼ cup kirsch
8 thick slices French country bread, cut into 1" cubes, each one with a piece of crust

1. Rub a medium-size heavy pot with garlic, then discard garlic. Add wine and bring to a boil over high heat. Reduce heat to medium and gradually add cheese, stirring constantly with a wooden spoon, until it has melted. Do not allow to boil. Continue to cook, stirring frequently, until mixture has thickened, about 20 minutes. Add nutmeg, pepper to taste, and kirsch. Transfer to a chafing dish or fondue pot.

2. To serve fondue, put the fondue pot in the middle of the table, with the bread cubes in a basket. Diners spear cubes with their fondue forks and dip them in the pot. Stir the pot frequently to prevent the cheese from coagulating. If fondue becomes too thick, stir in ¼ cup of dry white wine.

Cheese Fight

Is gruyère, that most popular of Alpine cheeses, Swiss or French? It's hard to say. In 1115, the first count of Gruyère, in what is now Switzerland, accepted taxes from the Priory of Rougemount in the form of a cheese whose description matches that of modern-day gruyère. (The town, in turn, was named after the *grue*, or crane, that appears on the count's coat of arms.) The French, though, maintain that during the time of Charlemagne (A.D. 742–814), forestry authorities known as *agents gruyers* (from the Old German word *grüejen*, to grow, as in greenery) roamed what is now France, collecting taxes on firewood—and that they, too, were paid in cheese, eventually lending it their name. The issue of gruyère's paternity was officially, but inconclusively, contested at the International Cheese Conference in Rome in 1930 and at the 1951 Convention of Stresa. Finally, the French-Swiss Treaty of 1974 settled the matter: The glory of gruyère was to be shared by France and Switzerland.

1 CUP
A
B
C

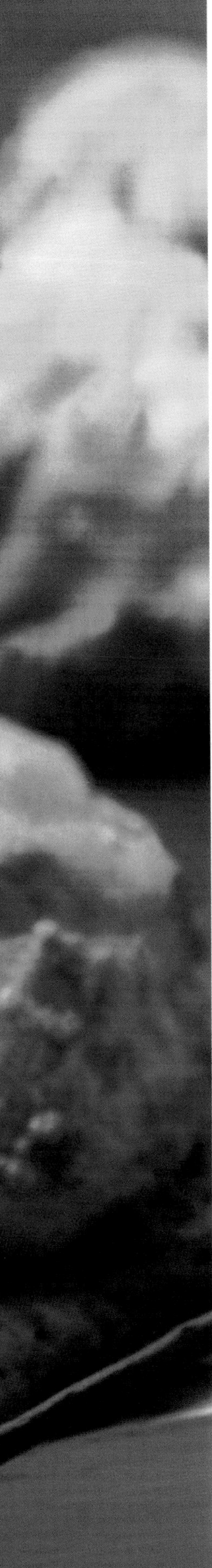

Gougères

(French Cheese Puffs)

MAKES 3 DOZEN

IN BURGUNDY, where they originated, gougères are considered the perfect hors d'oeuvre—complementary to wine and satisfying to the palate without being filling. According to Jean-Pierre Silva of Le Vieux Moulin in Bouilland, whose recipe this is, the secret of successful gougères is to add the flour all at once and the eggs one at a time.

8 tbsp. butter, cut into pieces
¾ cup milk
Salt and freshly ground white pepper
1 cup flour
4 large eggs, at room temperature
1 ½ cups grated comté or gruyère cheese

1. Preheat oven to 400°. Combine butter, ½ cup of the milk, and ½ cup water in a medium saucepan over high heat. Season generously with salt and pepper. Bring to a boil, and when butter has melted, remove pan from heat. Add flour all at once and stir vigorously with a wooden spoon until mixture forms a thick dough and pulls away from the sides of the pan, 1–2 minutes. Return pan to heat for 1 minute, stirring constantly. Remove from heat.

2. Let dough cool to room temperature, then beat in eggs, one at a time, making sure each egg is completely incorporated into mixture and dough is smooth after each addition. Dough should be thick, shiny, and smooth. Add 1 cup of the cheese and beat in until well combined.

3. Spoon tablespoon-size mounds of dough on nonstick baking sheets, leaving about 1" between each. Brush tops with remaining ¼ cup milk, then sprinkle with remaining ½ cup cheese. Bake one tray at a time in lower third of oven until gougères have doubled in size and are golden, 20–25 minutes. Serve warm or at room temperature.

Mastering the Puff

French grandmothers can make gougères in their sleep—but for the rest of us, despite the simplicity of the recipe, they can be a little tricky. These tips will help: Correct measurements are vital (**A**). For the flour, fill a dry measuring cup, then sweep it clean with the flat side of a knife. Always use a glass measuring cup for liquids so that you can see the level of the liquid. And be sure that the eggs are graded large, not extra-large or jumbo; this is one case where bigger is not better. Dump the flour into the hot milk and butter all at once, then begin beating mixture vigorously with a wooden spoon (**B**). The batter should almost seize up and pull away from the sides of the pan. Beat the eggs into the cooled batter one at a time (**C**). The batter will be slippery and a little hard to beat, but it will eventually absorb the eggs and become a smooth, shiny mass.

Plateau de Fromages

(Assorted Cheese Platter)

RESTAURANTS in France typically offer diners a choice of 20 or 30 cheeses (as at the three-star Arpège in Paris, left). At home, two or three of varying pungency (see below) is sufficient; half a dozen would be generous. The cheeses below are made in France, but available in the U.S.; feel free to make substitutions from America, Italy, Holland, Spain, Switzerland, or anywhere else that makes good cheese.

MILD CHEESES:
Brillat-savarin (cows' milk; triple cream)
Chaource (cows' milk)
Explorateur (cows' milk; triple cream)
Montrachet (goats' milk; usually wrapped in chestnut or grape leaves), fresh
Port-Salut (cows' milk; a brand name for cheese known generically as st-paulin)
Reblochon (cows' milk)
St-Marcellin (goats' or cows' milk), fresh
St-Nectaire (cows' milk; can grow stronger)
Vacherin (also called mont-d'or; cows' milk)

FULL-FLAVORED CHEESES:
Bleu de Bresse (cows' milk; blue)
Brie de Meaux (cows' milk)
Brindamour (sheeps' milk; coated with rosemary and savory)
Camembert (cows' milk)
Cantal (cows' milk; reminiscent of English farmhouse cheddar)
Montrachet (goats' milk; usually wrapped in chestnut or grape leaves), aged
Rocamadour (sheeps' or goats' milk; the latter is somewhat stronger)
St-Marcellin (goats' or cows' milk), aged
Tomme de Savoie (cows' milk)

PUNGENT CHEESES:
Beaufort (cows' milk; sometimes sold as French gruyère)
Comté (cows' milk; also sometimes sold as French gruyère)
Crottin de Chavignol (goats' milk)
Époisses (cows' milk)
Fourme d'Ambert (cows' milk; blue)
Livarot (cows' milk)
Munster (cows' milk; not to be confused with mild deli-counter muenster)
Pont-l'Évêque (cows' milk)
Roquefort (sheeps' milk; blue)
Valençay (goats' milk), aged

Cheese Platter Tips

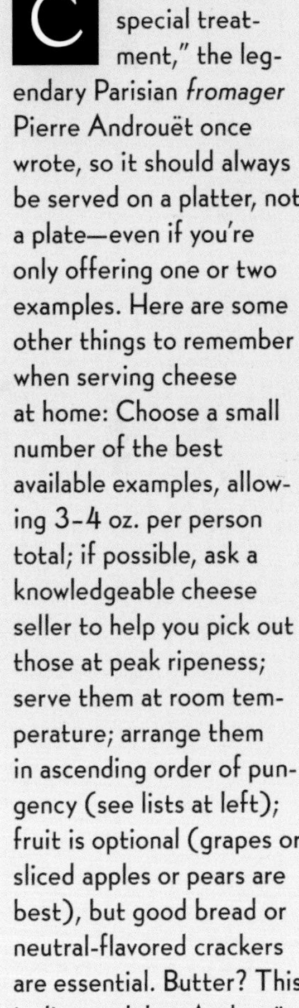

"Cheese deserves special treatment," the legendary Parisian *fromager* Pierre Androuët once wrote, so it should always be served on a platter, not a plate—even if you're only offering one or two examples. Here are some other things to remember when serving cheese at home: Choose a small number of the best available examples, allowing 3–4 oz. per person total; if possible, ask a knowledgeable cheese seller to help you pick out those at peak ripeness; serve them at room temperature; arrange them in ascending order of pungency (see lists at left); fruit is optional (grapes or sliced apples or pears are best), but good bread or neutral-flavored crackers are essential. Butter? This is disputed, but Androuët says yes—and we agree.

Unimposing Perfume

"In France," reports writer Claudia M. Caruana, "shallots are considered positively essential in the kitchen. The best thing about them is their flavor—onionlike, but without the onion's bite. The 19th-century French gourmet Charles Monselet observed that the shallot 'perfumes without imposing'. This is a distinction much appreciated by the French. Botanically speaking, the shallot is either *Allium cepa*, var. *Aggregatum* (a descendant of the wild onion native to Turkmenistan's Kopet-Dag mountains) or *Allium ascalonicum*, a name that is most likely a corruption of Ashkelon, an ancient port in Palestine. The Crusaders supposedly first introduced the 'Ascalonian onion' to Europe on their return from the Holy Land. There is quite a range in shallot flavor: The standard French red shallot, also known as the Brittany red, since the bulk of French production comes from that region, has a pronounced but muted flavor. The Dutch yellow (facing page), which has a higher sulfur content, is spicier. The gray shallot has the most complex and attractive flavor of all—but it's ugly and hard to peel, and not found very often in America anyway."

Crème d'Échalotes

(Shallot Custard)

Serves 4

THE PRICE of shallots has come down noticeably in recent years, due at least partially to an increase in domestic production. They are also easy to grow, and most seed catalogues offer several varieties—even the ugly but tasty gray.

FOR SHALLOTS:
4 large shallots, peeled
1 tbsp. butter
1 tsp. sugar
Freshly grated nutmeg
Salt and freshly ground white pepper
¼ cup dry sherry

FOR CUSTARD:
2 eggs
1 ½ cups cream
½ tsp. salt
Freshly ground white pepper
Freshly grated nutmeg

1. For shallots, trim each bulb by removing any fibers from root end, leaving base intact. Using a paring knife, "fan" each shallot by thinly slicing from the tip to—but not through—the base. (Shallots should retain their original shape, but will open slightly during cooking.)

2. Melt butter in a medium skillet over medium-high heat. Add shallots, sprinkle with sugar, and season to taste with nutmeg and with salt and pepper. Turn shallots to coat with butter mixture, then cook until golden, 2–3 minutes per side. Add sherry, stir gently, then reduce heat to low. Cover and cook until shallots are tender and well browned, about 25 minutes. (If skillet becomes too dry during cooking, add 1–2 tbsp. water.) Drain shallots and cool on paper towels.

3. For custard, preheat oven to 275°. Put eggs, cream, and salt in a medium bowl. Add a pinch of pepper and nutmeg and whisk until mixture is just smooth; do not overbeat.

4. Arrange shallots in 4 ramekins (1" high and 4¾" across), gently fanning and separating slices. Ladle ½ cup custard into each dish, cover tightly with plastic wrap, then place in a large baking pan.

5. Place baking pan in oven. Add enough hot water to come about halfway up sides of custard dishes, then cook until custards are set, about 20 minutes. To check for doneness, carefully lift plastic wrap from one custard and insert a toothpick in the center. Custards are done if toothpick comes out clean. Remove remaining custards from baking pan, lift off plastic wrap, then set custards aside to cool. Serve warm or at room temperature.

Soufflé aux Artichauts et aux Champignons

(Artichoke and Mushroom Soufflé)

SERVES 4

THE PARCHMENT technique described below yields soufflés with dramatic golden crowns (left). As always with soufflés, the egg whites must be beaten in a *very* clean bowl.

4 globe artichokes
Salt
4 tbsp. butter
2 tbsp. olive oil
3 white mushrooms, finely chopped
Freshly ground black pepper
3 tbsp. flour
1 cup hot milk
¼ cup hot heavy cream
Freshly grated nutmeg
5 eggs, separated

1. Trim artichokes, then cook in boiling salted water until tender, about 30 minutes. Drain and set aside until cool enough to handle. Break off leaves, scrape off meat with a spoon (this should yeild about 1½ cups), discard leaves and set meat aside. Remove and discard choke from artichoke heart, then trim stem so heart that it sits flat.

2. Put each trimmed heart into a buttered, individual (1½ cups) soufflé dish. Use 2 tbsp. of the butter to grease 4 strips of parchment paper or foil, 12" x 4". Wrap and tie buttered parchment collars around soufflé dishes with kitchen string. Put dishes on a baking sheet.

3.Heat oil in a sauté pan and add mushrooms and reserved artichoke meat. Sauté until mushrooms have released and reabsorbed their juice. Season to taste with salt and pepper. Divide mushroom mixture evenly between artichoke hearts.

4. Preheat oven to 400°. Melt remaining 2 tbsp. butter in a heavy-bottomed pan and stir in flour. Cook over medium heat for 2 minutes, then remove pan from heat and slowly whisk in milk and cream. Return saucepan to heat and cook, whisking constantly, until smooth and very thick, about 2 minutes. Remove pan from heat and season with salt, pepper, and a pinch of nutmeg. Beat in egg yolks one at a time. Set aside.

5. In a very clean metal bowl, beat egg whites with a pinch of salt until stiff peaks form. Add a third of the egg whites into thickened milk mixture and gently fold together, then fold mixture into remaining egg whites. Divide mixture evenly between soufflé dishes, spooning it over filled artichoke bottoms. Bake until puffed and golden, about 15 minutes. Remove collars and serve immediately.

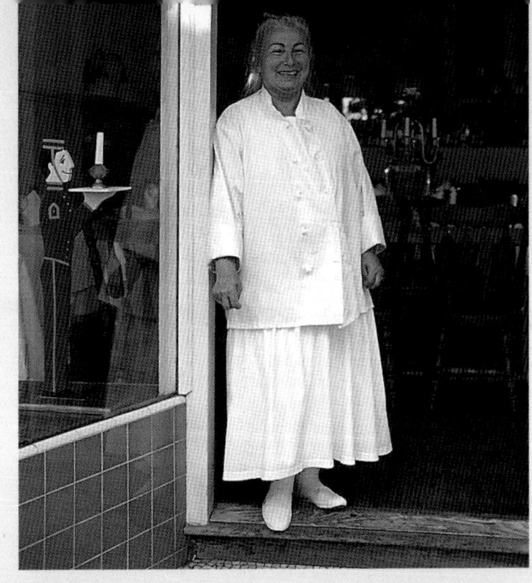

A Friend of Soufflé

Jacqueline Margulis (above) learned to cook soufflés at a convent in the countryside near Bordeaux—where, she recalls, "We were taught to smell, touch, and feel all sorts of food." In 1958, at 22, she emigrated to New York. Later she moved west, and in 1979 opened Café Jacqueline in San Francisco—where she offers diners nothing but soufflés. Does she ever get bored? "Never," she replies, "for every soufflé is different and I am forever inventing new ones." You must be among friends to enjoy a soufflé, she adds—"both to share it fairly and to enjoy the wait as the eggs are being cracked!" One of her favorite soufflés, says Margulis, is made with roquefort. To serve 2 or 3 (friends), preheat oven to 400°. Melt 2 tbsp. butter in a heavy-bottomed medium saucepan over medium heat. Add 3 tbsp. flour and cook, stirring constantly with a wooden spoon, for 1 ½ minutes (do not brown). Remove from heat and whisk in 1 cup hot milk. Return saucepan to heat and cook, whisking constantly, until smooth and very thick. Season with a pinch of salt and freshly ground white pepper to taste. Whisk in 4 extra-large egg yolks, one at a time. Set aside. Beat whites of 5 extra-large eggs until stiff peaks form. Add a third of the egg whites to milk mixture and gently fold together. While folding in remaining egg whites, sprinkle in 4 oz. shaved roquefort. Do not overmix. Spoon into a buttered medium (6 cup) soufflé dish. Bake until soufflé stands tall and is golden brown, 25–30 minutes. Serve immediately.

Real Quiche

If you think quiche lorraine is a frou-frou brunch dish, best accompanied by a healthy little green salad, you might be interested to learn that in this specialty's homeland—the Lorraine (above), next door to Alsace in northeastern France—it is traditionally served on May Day alongside roast suckling pig in aspic. In other words, it is serious food in these parts. Apparently invented in the 16th century in the city of Nancy, then capital of Lorraine, it derives its name from the German *Küchen*, or cake. Though quiche was originally made with bread dough, a short pastry crust has become standard, and the recipe rarely varies in Lorraine itself. About the only disagreements seem to be whether or not to add nutmeg (we do) and whether or not to blanch the bacon before sautéing it (we do this, too).

Quiche Lorraine

SERVES 4–6

ADAPTED from *Mastering the Art of French Cooking*, vol. 1, by Julia Child, Louisette Bertholle, and Simone Beck, this is the real thing, with no cheese, no onions, no vegetables.

FOR CRUST:
2 cups flour
½ tsp. salt
Pinch sugar
8 tbsp. cold butter, cut into small pieces
3 tbsp. cold vegetable shortening, cut into small pieces
1 egg, lightly beaten

FOR FILLING:
6 oz. slab bacon, diced
2 eggs, lightly beaten
1 ½ cups heavy cream
½ tsp. salt
Freshly grated nutmeg
Freshly ground black pepper

1. For crust, sift together flour, salt, and sugar into a mixing bowl. Use a pastry cutter or 2 knives to work butter and shortening into flour until it resembles coarse meal. Sprinkle in up to 6 tbsp. ice water, stirring the dough with a fork until it just begins to hold together. Using your hands, press the dough firmly into a rough ball, then transfer to a lightly floured surface. Give the dough several quick kneads with the heel of your hand to form a smooth dough, then shape into a ball, flatten slightly to make a disk, and dust with flour. Wrap disk in plastic and refrigerate for 2 hours.

2. Preheat oven to 400°. Allow dough to sit at room temperature to soften slightly before rolling out on a lightly floured surface into a 14" round. Fit dough, without stretching it, into a buttered 10" bottomless metal flan ring, 1½" deep, set on a parchment-lined cookie sheet with no rim. Press overhanging dough down slightly into sides of ring to make the sides of the crust a little thicker and sturdier. Run the rolling pin over the top of the ring to remove any overhanging dough. Using a fork, prick bottom lightly, then make a decorative edge around the rim. Line dough with buttered aluminum foil, then add pie weights or dried beans. Bake until crust is set and edge just begins to color, about 25 minutes. Remove foil and weights, brush bottom and sides with egg, and continue baking until crust is pale golden, another 2–5 minutes.

3. For filling, reduce heat to 375°. Put bacon in a medium pan, cover with cold water, and bring to a boil over medium-high heat. Boil for 5 minutes, then drain. Return bacon to pan, and cook over medium heat until lightly browned, about 3 minutes. Transfer bacon with a slotted spoon to a paper towel to drain, then arrange in bottom of crust.

4. Beat together eggs, cream, and salt in a medium bowl and season to taste with nutmeg and pepper; pour into crust. Bake until custard is puffed and golden and just set in the center, 30–35 minutes. Slide quiche off parchment paper onto a serving platter and remove ring. Serve quiche warm or at room temperature, sliced into wedges.

Oeufs Farcis à la Périgourdine

(Périgord-Style Stuffed Eggs)

SERVES 4

ONE OF THE dishes Lucian K. Truscott IV and his wife made in their kitchen in the Dordogne (the region historically known as the Périgord), these eggs may be served as an hors d'oeuvre or first course, or with a salad for lunch.

- *4 hard-cooked eggs, peeled and halved lengthwise*
- *2 tbsp. coarsely chopped smoked ham*
- *2 tbsp. walnut oil*
- *1 tsp. finely chopped fresh thyme*
- *1 tsp. finely chopped fresh rosemary*
- *1 tsp. finely chopped fresh parsley*
- *Salt and freshly ground black pepper*
- *2 tbsp. goose or duck fat or vegetable oil*
- *1 egg white, beaten until frothy*

1. Remove yolks from hard-cooked eggs, put them in a small bowl, and mash them with a fork. When they're mashed, stir in ham, walnut oil, thyme, rosemary, and parsley, and season to taste with salt and pepper. Spoon mixture into hard-cooked whites, rounding and smoothing it as you go.

2. Heat fat or oil in a large nonstick skillet over medium-high heat. Dip stuffed eggs into beaten egg white, then place in pan, stuffed side down first, and fry for about 30 seconds on each side, until lightly browned. Drain on paper towels, arrange on a platter, and garnish with thyme, if you like.

Being There

"Three years ago," reports writer Lucian K. Truscott IV, "my wife, Carolyn, our 2-year-old daughter Lilly [above], and I rented a house for a week in a little village called St-Julien-de-Crempse, just north of Bergerac in the Dordogne. The house was part of a 17th-century farm compound atop a hill, overlooking fields of hay and corn and sunflowers. From our bedroom window, we could see into a coop of chickens, with a rabbit hutch just beyond. The yard in front of the house had a walled garden planted with roses, fragrant lavender, and lilies, and the kitchen was a delightfully serious cooking space. Every day, we'd shop at one of the region's farmers' markets [facing page], then come back here to cook ourselves dishes like pasta with a sauce of fresh peas, white asparagus, and melted chèvre; eggs stuffed in the Périgord style with ham and herbs; grilled duck breast with fresh cherry and apple sauce; and guinea hen stuffed with green onions and Toulouse sausage and wrapped in smoked pork. One day we bought plump, tiny mussels from the coast near Bordeaux that were so good they left us wondering, Why don't we just move here?"

French Locomotive

A rich, old-fashioned bistro dish, oeufs en meurette—its name is thought to derive from *muire*, an Old French term for brine—is hard to find these days. One place that still serves it (and makes it the right way, poaching the eggs in good red wine instead of acidulated water as other establishments apparently do) is a sophisticated Parisian restaurant called Le Récamier (facing page). Opened in 1969 by a dedicated amateur named Martin Cantegrit, it specializes in the cooking of Burgundy, and has proven remarkably consistent in quality over the years. Cantegrit is a culinary chauvinist, who maintains that "The French are gastronomic because only in France do you find such a concentration of products in one small hexagon"— and that "France must teach the rest of the world about fine food; it must be the locomotive by which each country rediscovers its own culinary traditions." Sampling chef Robert Chassat's snail and wild mushroom fricassée, stuffed cabbage, truffled pork sausage with puréed split peas, or, well, oeufs en meurette, it is easy to agree with him.

Oeufs en Meurette

(Poached Eggs in Red Wine Sauce)

SERVES 4

USE EGGS that come straight from the refrigerator for this dish, counsels Robert Chassat, chef at Le Récamier in Paris, who gave us this recipe; cold eggs hold their shape better while poaching. At the restaurant, he allots two eggs per serving, but at home, you may find one to be sufficient.

4 tbsp. butter, softened
¼ lb. slab bacon, coarsely chopped
½ lb. small white mushrooms, sliced
1 large shallot, peeled and minced
1 medium carrot, peeled and coarsely chopped
1 sprig fresh thyme
1 bay leaf
5 ¼ cups French red burgundy or other dry red wine
1 cup demi-glace (see sidebar, page 61)
1 ¾ cups beef stock (see page 59)
2 tbsp. flour
4–8 eggs
Salt and freshly ground black pepper
4 slices bread, preferably pain brioche, lightly toasted, crusts removed
4 sprigs fresh chervil

1. Melt 1 tbsp. of the butter in a medium skillet over medium heat. Add bacon and cook until crisp, 7–10 minutes. Remove bacon with a slotted spoon, drain on a paper towel, and set aside. Add mushrooms to skillet and cook, stirring occasionally, until golden, about 10 minutes. Transfer to a bowl and set aside.

2. In the same skillet, melt 1 tbsp. of the butter, add shallots, and cook, stirring, until fragrant, about 1 minute. Stir in carrots, thyme, and bay leaf and cook until carrots begin to brown, about 7 minutes.

3. Increase heat to medium-high, add 2 cups wine, and cook until reduced by three-quarters, about 25 minutes. Add demi-glace and stock and cook, skimming frequently, for 10 minutes. Remove skillet from heat and strain sauce through a fine sieve into a small saucepan. Combine flour and remaining 2 tbsp. butter in a small bowl, forming a paste. Whisk paste into sauce a little at a time, then simmer over medium-low heat for 2 minutes. Reduce heat to low and keep sauce warm.

4. Place remaining 3¼ cups wine in a small saucepan and bring to a simmer over medium heat. Poach eggs two at a time by cracking each egg into a saucer, then carefully slipping into wine. Poach until whites are firm and yolks just set, 5–7 minutes. Using a slotted spoon, transfer eggs to a plate and cover with foil. Repeat process with remaining eggs.

5. Add reserved bacon and mushrooms to sauce and season to taste with salt and pepper. Divide bread between 4 plates, place one or two eggs on each piece, spoon sauce over them, and serve garnished with chervil.

L'heure
de gloire
Monsieur
et madame
Chaussette
Le
doigt de Dieu

RICARD

Oeufs en Bouillon

(Eggs in Broth)

SERVES 4

AT HER CHEZ MILLETTE in Planchez (below), in the Morvan, Millette Coquillon sometimes serves guests these hard-cooked eggs in a rich meat stock before the plat du jour.

8 eggs
4–6 cups beef stock (see page 59)
¼ cup fresh parsley, chopped
Salt and freshly ground black pepper

1. Put eggs in a medium saucepan, cover with cold water, and bring just to a boil over medium heat. Reduce heat to low and simmer very slowly for 10 minutes. Drain, then run cold water over eggs until they are cool. Peel eggs and return them to pan.

2. Add enough stock to completely cover eggs, then bring to a simmer over medium heat and cook for 2 minutes. Remove from heat, cover, and set aside to marinate for 1 hour before serving. Serve eggs in stock, at room temperature, garnished with fresh chopped parsley. Serve salt and pepper on the side.

Ubiquitous Herb

The French, it is said, used to be wary of parsley, believing that it had magical powers. In a way, as it turns out, it does: It is impossible to imagine French cuisine without parsley today. It is an essential ingredient of the bouquet garni, that bundle of herbs that flavors so many French soups and sauces (see sidebar, page 59); it clings to meats in marinades; it is a special friend to garlic, often fried alongside it. And of course it garnishes plates and platters in bistros and at banquets alike, adding decorative accents with equal flair to modest, homey dishes like oeufs en bouillon (facing page) and elegant preparations of whole fish or roast meat (among many other things). It even shows up in idioms: *Avoir du persil*, to have some parsley, means to be witty or piquant. (On the other hand, *avoir du persil dans les oreilles*, to have parsley in one's ears, means to be unwashed.) *Faire son persil*, to do one's parsley, is to strut or preen. And not surprisingly, considering parsley's culinary ubiquity, a person who keeps turning up is said to be *partout, comme le persil*—everywhere, like you know what frilly green herb.

2F50
sucrine
Salade
plein Champs
Provenance
24
Batavia
Grenobloise
Provenance
24F
3F.00
pièce
4 pour 10F
Provenance
24
Sucrine
3F00
pièce

Mushrooms under the Trees

The Germans call it Eierschwamm (egg mushroom) or Gelbhahnel (yellow chick); to the Italians, it's capo gallo (cock crest) or orecina (little ear). The French identify it as the girolle, from the Old French word *girer*, to twist (a reference to its shape), or the chanterelle—a word derived from the Greek *kantharos*, meaning a kind of drinking vessel. Under whatever name, *Cantharellus cibarius* and other chanterelle species have apparently been plentiful throughout Europe since the beginning of recorded time; the first illustration of one supposedly appeared in Holland in 1581. Chanterelles grow only in the presence of living trees, with which they form a symbiotic relationship. The fungi draw nourishing sugar from the trees' younger roots, in turn providing them with phosphorus and other minerals. Thus, despite the best efforts of mycologists, all available chanterelles are still hand-gathered in the woods.

Salade de Chanterelles

(Chanterelle Salad)

SERVES 4

BECAUSE THEIR appearance is so distinctive and because they grow in such profusion when conditions are right, chanterelles are among the safest and easiest wild mushrooms to gather—which is fortunate, because they're expensive. Writer Lucian K. Truscott IV improvised this salad at a house he and his family rented in the Dordogne (see page 93).

- *¼ cup shelled walnut halves*
- *5 tbsp. walnut oil*
- *2 large cloves garlic, peeled and minced*
- *½ lb. chanterelles, cleaned and trimmed*
- *Salt and freshly ground black pepper*
- *1 medium tomato, seeded and diced*
- *2 oz. thinly sliced smoked ham, diced*
- *1 tbsp. finely chopped fresh parsley*
- *¼ lb. mixed baby greens*

1. Place walnuts in a single layer in a large skillet. Toast over medium heat, turning once, for 10 minutes. Coarsely chop and set aside.

2. Heat 3 tbsp. of the oil in a large skillet over medium heat. Add garlic and cook, stirring until fragrant, for about 2 minutes. Increase heat to medium-high, add mushrooms, season to taste with salt and pepper, and cook, stirring, until mushrooms soften, about 5 minutes.

3. Reduce heat to low, add tomatoes, ham, and parsley, and cook, stirring, for 1 minute. Remove from heat and set aside.

4. Put greens in a small bowl and dress with remaining 2 tbsp. oil. Season to taste with salt and pepper, then divide between 4 small plates. Arrange mushroom mixture over lettuce, garnish with toasted walnuts, and serve.

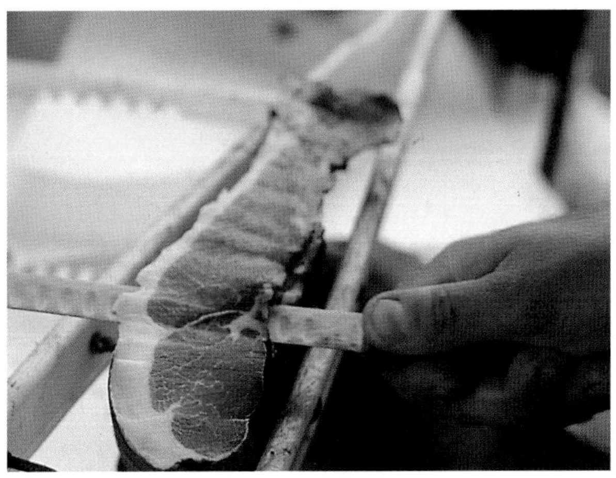

Huile de Noix

hamlets, and farms. The Lot is famous for foie gras, truffles, and other delicacies—among them exquisite handmade walnut oil, which has been produced in the region since the 11th century, and which many connoisseurs consider the ultimate condiment for salads. (Because it has a low smoke point, it is rarely used for cooking.) The only artisan still making the oil in the Lot is André Castagné (facing page, lower left), proprietor of Huilerie Familiale du Lac de Diane near the town of Martel. I was led to my first taste of his superlative product by a modest roadside sign—one of the many that fill the local landscape, advertising culinary specialties. When I arrived at Castagné's mill, I found the man himself feeding a fire with walnut shells. The rich aroma of roasting walnuts filled the air as he bounced back and forth between the three pieces of equipment that make up his entire operation: an ancient granite mill to grind the walnut meat to paste; a cast-iron basin in which the paste is roasted; and a hydraulic press layered with steel plates, to extract the rich, golden oil. Castagné bought his mill in 1985 and rebuilt it to its original form. Now he presses oil almost daily most of the year. He offered me a taste. The flavor of the roasted nuts was immediate, followed by a delicate hint of maple; it was a marvel. Before World War II, Castagné told me, virtually every village in the Lot had its own mill, but these died out. Today, walnut oil and other walnut products (including apéritifs, digestifs, and preserves) are becoming popular again, and it seems possible that more old mills might reopen in the future. 'Working at the mill,' Castagné added with a smile, 'is good for families. It keeps the children at home.'" —ELAINE STERLING

RECIPES

SALADE DE CHANTERELLES *(Chanterelle Salad)*, page 102; SALADE NIÇOISE, page 105; SALADE DES MOINES *(Green Salad with Cîteaux Cheese Croutons)*, page 106; SALADE DE LENTILLES DU PUY *(Lentil Salad with Roasted Carrots and Beets)*, page 109; SALADE DE HARICOTS VERTS AUX NOISETTES FRAÎCHES *(Salad of Haricots Verts and Green Hazelnuts)*, page 111; SALADE D'ARTICHAUTS À LA VENTRÈCHE *(Artichoke and Pork Belly Salad)*, page 112; SALADE TIÈDE DE ROUGETS AUX ARTICHAUTS *(Warm Red Mullet and Artichoke Salad)*, page 114.

CHAPTER

4

SALADS

"IN THE département of the Lot in south-western France, feudal castles and bastides loom high above strategic limestone cliffs, and rivers flow gently through fertile valleys connecting medieval market towns,

Salade Niçoise

SERVES 4

THE TRADITIONAL version of Nice's classic salad uses no lettuce, no cooked vegetables, no vinegar. And remember that the Niçois would never dream of making their salad with fresh tuna: This is a dish based on preserved fish.

4 ripe tomatoes, sliced
1 green bell pepper, stemmed, seeded, and finely chopped
8 radishes, thinly sliced
2 6⅛-oz. cans good-quality tuna packed in olive oil, well drained
4 hard-cooked eggs, peeled and quartered
8 oil-packed anchovies
4 fresh chives, chopped
Salt and freshly ground black pepper
½ cup niçoise olives
Extra-virgin olive oil, preferably French (see page 115)

1. Divide tomatoes, bell pepper, radishes, tuna, and eggs equally between 4 plates, arranging them attractively, working from the outside in.

2. Garnish each plate with 2 anchovy filets. Sprinkle with chives, and season to taste with salt and freshly ground black pepper. Scatter olives evenly over the salads, and drizzle with olive oil just before serving.

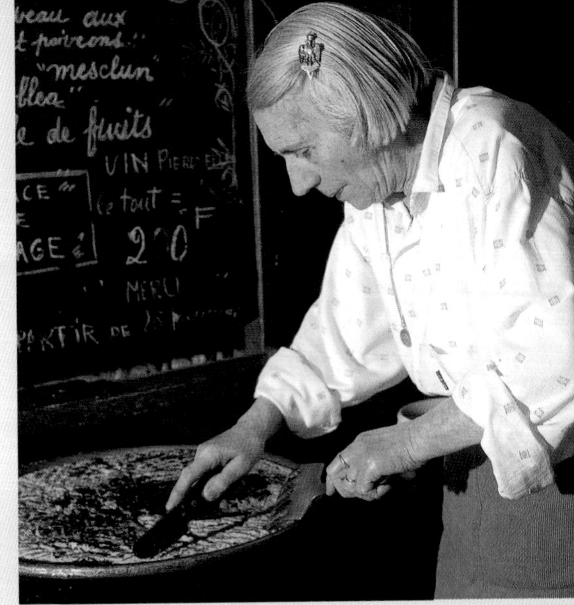

Nissa la Bella

At Barale, her restaurant near Nice's Vieux Port, Catherine-Hélène Barale (above) serves diners a nightly fixed-price encyclopedia of local cooking in an antiques-filled dining room. The procession begins with a wedge of crisp-crusted pissaladière (see page 26) and proceeds with a piece of socca (chickpea flour crêpe); a real salade niçoise; a healthy helping of ravioli, filled with swiss chard—the defining vegetable of Nice—and, moistened with meat juices; a main course of (usually) braised veal shoulder with mushrooms and sweet red peppers; and for dessert, a thick slab of tourte de blettes, a sweet swiss chard torte (see page 288). Then comes a big bowl of fruit, and finally a tiny glass of marc or cherry liquor. After dinner, Barale passes out little folders bearing the words to a patriotic Niçois anthem, "Nissa la Bella". Then she cranks up an old 78 on an ancient gramophone, and one and all—if they know what's good for them—bellow out "E toujou criderai / En la miéu ritournella, / Viva, viva Nissa la Bella" (And always I'll proclaim / Upon my return, / Viva, viva, Nice the Beautiful). After a meal like this—which is a revelation, a largesse, and a casually but shrewdly guided tour of the local gastronomic landscape, with all its simplicity and salt and savory intensity—it's hard to imagine anyone not wanting to join in.

Burgundy's Cheese

Burgundy's most famous cheese, and almost certainly its most distinctive, is époisses (above)—soft, politely pungent, pleasantly sharp on the palate, and a perfect foil for the region's famed red wines. Made from cows' milk in various parts of northwestern Burgundy—there is only one producer of the cheese in the pretty little town of Époisses itself, Fromagerie Berthaut—it is aged for three months by law, and traditionally has its rind rinsed two to three times a week for about a month with marc de bourgogne, the local version of grappa. (A law passed in early 1998 also awards recognition to a variation that is washed in chablis instead.) Époisses is one of only 40 French cheeses to have been granted an appellation d'origine contrôlée. The other famous cheese in this part of Burgundy is the not dissimilar, but milder, monastery-style cîteaux—named for the Cistercian monks who make it—which is aged two months and not marc-washed.

Salade des Moines

(Green Salad with Cîteaux Cheese Croutons)

Serves 4

At home at the family wine estate in Vosne-Romanée, Marielle Grivot mixes vinaigrette in the bottom of her salad bowl, puts greens on top of it, and tosses the salad at the table. To dress up a green salad, she adds croutons topped with melted cîteaux cheese (Canada's oka may be substituted). Her daughter Mathilde (right) often helps serve.

1 tbsp. sherry vinegar
2 tbsp. walnut oil
½ tsp. dijon mustard
Salt and freshly ground pepper
1 head butter lettuce, washed, dried, and torn into pieces
1 baguette
8 oz. cîteaux or oka

1. Place an oven rack in top third of oven and preheat broiler. Meanwhile, in a large salad bowl, whisk together the vinegar, oil, and mustard, and season to taste with salt and pepper. Add lettuce, toss with the vinaigrette, then divide between 4 plates.

2. Make croutons by cutting 12 thin round slices from the baguette, then place a slice of cîteaux cheese on top of each. Place slices on a baking sheet and broil until cheese is melted, 30–45 seconds. Garnish each salad with three croutons.

Salade de Lentilles du Puy

(Lentil Salad with Roasted Carrots and Beets)

SERVES 6

THIS RECIPE was developed for the esteemed lentils of Le Puy, but green lentils grown in America's best lentil country—an area, called the Palouse, stretching between Idaho, Oregon, and Washington—are similar, and work just as well.

3 small beets, peeled and diced
1 large carrot, peeled and diced
4 shallots, peeled and halved
½ cup extra-virgin olive oil, preferably French (see page 115)
2 sprigs fresh parsley
2 sprigs fresh thyme
Salt and freshly ground black pepper
¾ lb. lentilles du Puy, or other tiny French-style green lentils, picked over and rinsed
3 tbsp. sherry vinegar
¼ cup chopped fresh parsley

1. Preheat oven to 350°. Put beets, carrots, shallots, and ¼ cup oil in a medium roasting pan. Stir to coat vegetables evenly with oil. Add parsley and thyme, season to taste with salt and pepper, and cook, stirring once, until vegetables begin to brown, about 20 minutes. Add lentils and 3 cups of water, stir, then cover pan with foil. Continue roasting until lentils are tender and all water is absorbed, about 1 hour.

2. Remove pan from oven. Remove and discard herb sprigs. Whisk vinegar and remaining ¼ cup oil together in a small bowl, then pour over lentils. Allow lentils to cool slightly, then stir in chopped parsley. Adjust seasoning and serve.

Celebrated Legume

Lentilles du Puy, tiny gray-green earthy ones from Le Puy, a town in the mountainous French region of Haute-Loire, are arguably the best in the world. They even have their own appellation contrôlée. Agriculturalists credit the local climate—dewy mornings, temperate days, cool nights—and volcanic soil with producing the distinct flavor of this legume. At Le Puy's annual Fête de la Lentille, more than 800 farmers compare their lentils, and chefs create new dishes, like sweet lentil preserves and lentil-flour tuile cookies.

Salade de Haricots Verts aux Noisettes Fraîches

(Salad of Haricots Verts and Green Hazelnuts)

SERVES 4

JACQUES MAXIMIN makes this salad with haricots verts grown near his restaurant in Vence (left), in the hills above Nice, and with green hazelnuts gathered from a tree in his own backyard. In the absence of these ingredients, good, fresh green beans and mature hazelnuts will do nicely.

Salt
1 lb. haricots verts or green beans, trimmed
½ cup green hazelnuts, skins removed, or mature blanched hazelnuts
¾ cup crème fraîche
1 tbsp. red wine vinegar
Freshly ground black pepper
2 medium tomatoes, seeded and diced
4 cups mixed baby greens
4 sprigs fresh basil

1. Bring a medium pot of salted water to a boil over high heat. Add haricots verts and cook until tender, 5–8 minutes. Drain, refresh in ice water, then drain, wrap in a dish towel and set aside.

2. If using green hazelnuts, coarsely chop and set aside. If using mature hazelnuts, heat a medium skillet over medium-high heat. Add hazelnuts to the dry skillet, and toast, turning, until nuts are golden, 5–7 minutes. Remove, coarsely chop, and set aside.

3. Put crème fraîche in a medium bowl. Whisk in vinegar and season to taste with salt and pepper. Add tomatoes, stir gently, then set aside for 10 minutes, allowing tomatoes to flavor and color dressing.

4. To assemble, toss greens in a medium mixing bowl with about 2 tbsp. dressing, then evenly divide between 4 plates. Put haricots verts in the same bowl, add about ½ cup dressing, and toss to coat. Arrange haricots verts on top of greens. Spoon remaining dressing over salads, taking care that a few diced tomatoes are on top of each one. Sprinkle with hazelnuts and garnish with basil leaves.

Well-Regarded Nuts

Hazelnuts, also called filberts, are among the most aristocratic of nuts, with an inimitably sweet, mild flavor cherished in candies, cookies, tortes, and other confections (see page 307) all over Europe. They're grown commercially on a large scale in four countries: Turkey, Italy, Spain, and the United States. The majority of the world's crop comes from Turkey, where the nuts are picked by hand from unpruned bushes. A mere 3 percent of the annual production comes from America, all from the Pacific Northwest—but the hazelnuts from this region are generally larger than those from other countries, and are widely considered to be tastier as well. In France, small quantities are grown in Corsica, the département of Pyrénées-Orientales, and the southwest. Hazelnuts are also used in savory dishes like terrines, salads, and fish dishes—and in the Catalan regions of France and Spain, they are ground along with other ingredients and stirred into soups and sauces for thickening and flavor.

Delicious Thistle

The artichoke, which most likely originated in the Middle East or North Africa as the descendant of a wild thistle, is one of the many culinary treasures popularly thought to have been introduced to France by the 14-year-old Catherine de Médicis when she crossed the Alps to marry the future French king Henri II in 1533. Catherine was a native of Tuscany, where artichokes were popular, and she was very fond of the vegetable. It took the French a while to succumb to its thorny charms, however; at first it was eaten more for its supposed medicinal value than for its flavor. It was also reputed to be an aphrodisiac. In France nowadays, artichokes are mainly grown in Brittany and throughout the South (from Provence to the Pyrenees)—and the French, besides eating the thing abundantly, describe somebody with a fickle heart as having "un coeur d'artichaut"—implying that they fall in love with one person one day and another the next, with the ease and confidence of someone peeling off yet another artichoke leaf, knowing that the heart is still safely cushioned beneath many more layers.

Salade d'Artichauts à la Ventrèche

(Artichoke and Pork Belly Salad)

SERVES 4

VENTRÈCHE (pork belly), a specialty of southwestern France, is often cured for months in salt and pepper. A version of cured ventrèche is made in America—or pancetta may be substituted. This unusual salad is served by Jean-Pierre Xiradakis at La Tupiña in Bordeaux (see page 273).

4 large globe artichokes
1 lemon, halved
2 tbsp. duck fat
24 thin slices ventrèche or pancetta, cut into 2" strips
8 scallions, trimmed and finely chopped
8 red radishes, trimmed and halved lengthwise
½ cup fresh shelled and peeled fava beans (optional)
2 tbsp. balsamic vinegar
½ lb. mixed baby greens
2 tbsp. peanut oil
Salt and freshly ground black pepper
½ bunch fresh parsley
½ bunch fresh chervil
1 bunch fresh chives
2 tbsp. finely diced, peeled carrot

1. Bend back short lower leaves of artichokes until they snap, leaving the meaty bottom parts of the leaves. Then cut off the stems and slice off remaining cone of leaves, right above the heart. Scrape out and discard the hairy choke with a sharp spoon or melon baller. Cut artichokes into thick slices, transfer to a bowl, squeeze lemon juice over them to prevent discoloration. Melt duck fat in a large nonstick skillet over medium-low heat, add artichokes and sauté until soft and golden, 8–10 minutes. Transfer to a large bowl and set aside.

2. Arrange ventrèche in the same skillet and cook until brown and crisp, about 10 minutes. Remove ventrèche from skillet and drain on paper towels. Pour off all but 1 tbsp. of fat, then add scallions, radishes, and fava beans and sauté for about 2 minutes. Transfer to the bowl with the artichokes, add ventrèche and toss together. Drain fat from pan, then return pan to heat, add vinegar and deglaze, stirring with a wooden spoon for about 1 minute. Remove from heat and set aside.

3. Put greens in a large bowl, drizzle with oil, season to taste with salt and pepper, and toss together. Divide greens between 4 plates, then arrange artichoke mixture on top of greens. Drizzle vinegar over salads, then, with a pair of sharp scissors, snip parsley, chervil, and chives evenly over salads. Scatter carrots on top for color.

Salade Tiède de Rougets aux Artichauts

(Warm Red Mullet and Artichoke Salad)

SERVES 4

RED MULLET, one of the Mediterranean's tastiest fish, is occasionally sold in the U.S.; red snapper makes a more than adequate substitute in this salad from Jacques Maximin.

Salt
2 cups penne rigate (ribbed penne pasta)
1 tsp. balsamic vinegar
8 tbsp. extra-virgin olive oil, preferably French (see sidebar, facing page)
Freshly ground black pepper
6 baby artichokes, trimmed
8 cloves garlic, unpeeled
½ lb. cleaned squid, body sliced into rings, tentacles quartered
4 5-oz. red mullets, cleaned, deboned, head and tail left on (or 2 10-oz. boneless red snapper filets, halved crosswise)
½ cup flour
¼ lb. parmigiano-reggiano in 1 piece
12 fresh basil leaves
8 fresh chives
8 sprigs fresh chervil
¼ cup niçoise olives

1. Bring a pot of salted water to a boil over high heat. Add penne. Cook 7–10 minutes. Drain, then dress with vinegar and 1 tbsp. of the oil, season to taste with salt and pepper, and set aside.

2. Halve artichokes lengthwise, then heat 2 tbsp. of the oil in a skillet over medium heat. Add artichokes and garlic and brown on all sides, 5–7 minutes. Remove and set aside.

3. Add 1 tbsp. of the oil to the same skillet, add squid, and cook, stirring until squid is firm, about 1 minute. Season to taste with salt and pepper, then immediately remove from skillet and set aside.

4. Wipe out skillet. Dredge fish in flour. Shake off excess, then season to taste with salt and pepper. Heat remaining 4 tbsp. oil in skillet over medium heat. Add fish and fry, turning once, 2–4 minutes per side. Drain on paper towels.

5. To assemble, divide penne, artichokes, and squid evenly between 4 plates. Arrange fish on top and thinly shave parmigiano-reggiano over it. Garnish with basil, chives, chervil, and olives. Serve drizzled with additional olive oil if you like.

Huile d'Olive

French olive oil consumption has doubled in the past 20 years—to one whole liter per person per year. The Greeks, in comparison, manage 25 liters, and the Italians a respectable 13 (Americans barely manage half a liter). The French, in other words, don't live and breathe olive oil as much as their Mediterranean neighbors do. Peanut or colza (canola) oil is more likely to be used for cooking. Still, olives are grown and oil is made in some 13 *départements* throughout the south of France and in Corsica. From a recent tasting of French oils, we found the recurring notes to be buttery, nutty, and grassy—not peppery like Tuscan oils or strongly flavored like many of those from Greece or Spain. French olive oils found in the U.S. tend to be expensive, and frankly aren't always worth the price. (One that retails for about $70 per 750 ml bottle seemed heavy and disconcertingly tropical to us.) The European Union has approved a five-year plan to improve the quality of French olive oils. In the meantime, among the examples now sold here, we like the pale fresh Plagniol and the soft, opaque green Le Vieux Moulin, both from Provence, and the rich, complex, golden-hued Soulas from the Gard.

Terrine ovale à gibier,

CHAPTER

5

FOIE GRAS, FROGS' LEGS, SNAILS, AND TRUFFLES

"THE 19TH-CENTURY English cleric Sydney Smith once proposed that heaven was 'eating...foie gras to the sound of trumpets'. For me, you could hold the trumpets. Foie gras is the extravagance I crave most. It's my madeleine. Along with Romanesque cathedrals, foie gras was my first big discovery when I went to France as a kid. I never take a single silken bite without thinking back to the early 1950s, when I was so memorably disabused of my belief that all liver came from calves and all cathedrals were Gothic. Foie gras makes me feel young again, in other words. And it makes me feel, in the immortal words of Bob Strauss, the Texas politico, like 'a rich sumbitch'. People have been nuts about foie gras (it's pronounced 'fwah grah' and literally means 'fat liver') since antiquity. Egyptian paintings from 2500 B.C. show farmers holding geese by the neck and force-feeding them balls of grain. The Romans fed their geese figs, to obtain what they called *iecur ficatum*, or liver with figs; so closely was this fruit identified with this organ, in fact, that the modern Italian word for liver, *fegato*, derives from the Latin word for fig. Even the French don't argue that foie gras is the most easily digestible thing in the world. Don't eat too much of it, I'd advise, and certainly don't eat it too late at night. On the other hand, it is said that Bismarck used to drink a glass of milk and eat a slice of foie gras to cure his insomnia. No wonder they called him the Iron Chancellor." —R.W. APPLE JR.

RECIPES

TERRINE DE FOIE GRAS *(Foie Gras Terrine)*, page 120; **FOIE GRAS DE CANARD POÊLÉ AUX RAISINS BLANCS** *(Seared Foie Gras with Green Grapes)*, page 122; **BAECKEOFFE DE FOIE GRAS** *(Potted Foie Gras and Vegetables)*, page 125; **CUISSES DE GRENOUILLES AU BEURRE PERSILLADE** *(Frogs' Legs in Parsley Butter)*, page 126; **MILLE-FEUILLES DE GRENOUILLES** *(Frogs' Leg "Napoleons" with White Bean Sauce)*, page 129; **ESCARGOTS À LA BOURGUIGNONNE** *(Snails in Parsley Butter)*, page 130; **FRICASSÉE D'ESCARGOTS AU COULIS DE PERSIL** *(Fricassée of Snails with Parsley and Roasted Garlic Cream)*, page 133; **FRICASSÉE DE CÈPES AUX TRUFFES** *(Cèpe Fricassée with Truffles)*, page 134; **POMMES À LA SARLADAISE AUX TRUFFES** *(Sarladais-Style Potatoes with Truffles)*, page 137; **OEUFS BROUILLÉS AUX TRUFFES** *(Scrambled Eggs with Truffles)*, page 138; **POULET DEMI-DEUIL** *(Truffled Chicken)*, page 141.

Ferme de la
Veyrie
NOIX
FOIE GRAS

Terrine de Foie Gras

(Foie Gras Terrine)

SERVES 10

THIS OPULENT terrine, whose secrets we learned from chef Christian Guillut of Le Cordon Bleu in Paris, is one of the simplest but most memorable classics of French cuisine.

1 fresh duck foie gras (about 1 ½ lbs.), room temperature
⅓ cup good-quality sauternes
Salt and freshly ground black pepper
1 fresh black truffle, wiped clean and finely chopped (optional)

1. Starting with whole lobes of foie gras (**A**), pull any bits of translucent membrane from the surface of the foie gras and separate the two lobes, using a knife to sever any connecting veins (**B**). Probe for the main vein and its branches with your fingers, pulling it out as you follow its length. Inspect the folds for patches of bitter green bile and, if found, extract them with a knife. Slice off any bruises. Put foie gras in a nonreactive bowl with water to cover and plenty of ice cubes (**C**). Soak overnight in the refrigerator.

2. Drain foie gras and pat dry with paper towels, then break into even pieces. Put into a medium bowl or baking dish and drizzle sauternes over top. Season with salt and pepper and allow to marinate for 2 hours.

3. Preheat oven to 200°. Remove foie gras from marinade and press into a 2½-cup terrine, leaving a bit of space at top. Place terrine on 3 folded-over paper towels in the bottom of a deep ovenproof skillet (to steady terrine), and fill pan with hot water to reach halfway up sides of terrine. Place in the oven and cook until internal temperature of foie gras reaches 115° on a meat thermometer, about 30 minutes. Pour off and reserve fat. Set terrine aside to cool.

4. Cut a piece of cardboard to fit inside top of terrine and wrap it in plastic. Gently press cardboard onto foie gras and weight with a small can for 1 hour. Remove can and cardboard, return reserved fat to terrine, cover, and refrigerate 1–2 days.

5. To unmold, dip terrine in a bowl of warm water for 30 seconds, run a knife along edges, and invert onto a plate. (Reserve fat in terrine.) Serve sliced, garnished with truffle, if you like. If covered in reserved fat, foie gras will keep, refrigerated, for 1 week.

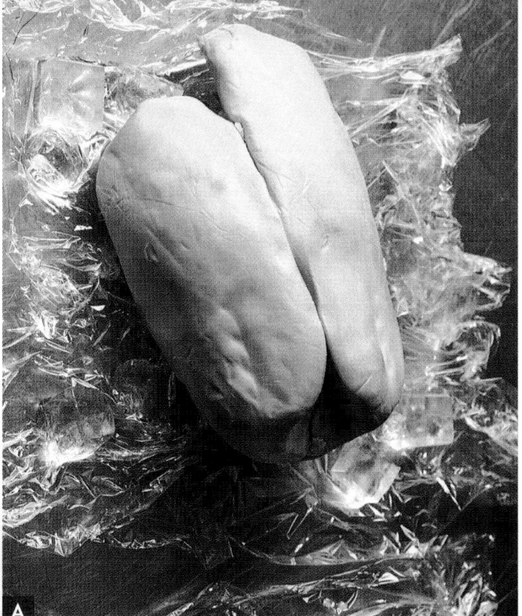

Liver Lore

The French grade and classify foie gras, whether of duck or goose, with a manic fervor that defies comprehension by foreign infidels. Here are brief definitions of a few of the more important terms for the foie-gras buyer to understand:

FOIE GRAS FRAIS: Fresh raw liver. You buy it, take it home, and cook it right away. This is what the chefs of the great restaurants start with, and what you will need for the terrine recipe on the facing page.

FOIE GRAS ENTIER: This is the same as a terrine made with an entire lobe. At home, serve this as an appetizer with toasted brioche (for a little sweetness) or rustic sourdough and a glass of sauternes or port or other sweet wine.

BLOC OR MOUSSE DE FOIE GRAS: Reconstituted from smaller pieces or trimmings of foie gras (or lower-grade foie gras) and puréed. Serve on toasted bread to accompany an apéritif of sweet wine.

PÂTÉ DE FOIE GRAS: Often includes pork or chicken livers, pork fat, and/or puréed pork or ham, as well as scraps of duck or goose livers. Great in a baguette sandwich with a glass of red wine, but it's more pâté than foie gras.

Foie Gras as Talisman

"I admit it," dancer and writer Marie-Pascale Lescot told us not long ago, "I smuggled a small, round, golden can of foie gras—my mother's homemade duck foie gras—into the United States. I couldn't help it. In the early 1970s, my parents settled into a sturdy 13th-century house in the middle of a cornfield in Bas Mauco, a 242-soul village in southwestern France. Before long, the local farmers had taught my mother an important local art: how to make duck foie gras. She became very good at it, and every November, she'd be flooded with orders from neighbors, friends, and relatives alike. But this was more than a small, homespun, under-the-table business. It became to us an autumn paean, a celebration of the richness, the generosity, the savor of the southwestern terroir. That's why I had to bring one of these cans with me to America when I left my French hometown—not as a gastronomic delicacy, but as an edible bond with a family, a region, a way of life. Passing through the airport in Boston, it did occur to me that I'd have no idea how to explain this rather Proustian concept to a U.S. customs official. Fortunately, I didn't have to—and when I finally got it to my new lodgings, I felt more than relief. I felt safe."

Foie Gras de Canard Poêlé aux Raisins Blancs

(Seared Foie Gras with Green Grapes)

Serves 8

The freshness of green grapes offsets the richness of the foie gras in this dish from Alain Dutournier's Au Trou Gascon in Paris—perhaps the most consistently satisfying outpost of southwestern French cooking in the capital.

1 fresh duck foie gras (about 1½ lbs.), room temperature
Salt and freshly ground black pepper
¼ tsp. ground nutmeg
2 cups good-quality sauternes
1 clove garlic, crushed and peeled
1 tbsp. ruby port
¼ cup chicken stock (see page 56)
1½ tsp. sugar
1 tbsp. fine bread crumbs
2 cups large green grapes, halved and seeded

1. Starting with whole lobes of foie gras, pull any bits of translucent membrane from the surface of the foie gras and separate the two lobes, using a knife to sever any connecting veins. Probe for the main vein and its branches with your fingers, pulling it out as you follow its length. Inspect the folds for patches of bitter green bile and, if found, extract them with a knife. Slice off any bruises. Rinse foie gras under cold water, then pat dry with paper towels. Season to taste with salt, pepper, and nutmeg.

2. Reduce sauternes in a medium saucepan over medium heat for about 20 minutes, to about ½ cup, then set aside.

3. Preheat oven to 400°. Rub a large cast-iron skillet with garlic clove, then sear foie gras over high heat until nicely browned and crisp on the outside, about 2 minutes on each side. Remove foie gras and set aside. Pour off fat and reserve for another use.

4. Deglaze skillet with port, stock, and reduced sauternes. Add sugar, bread crumbs, grapes, and salt and pepper to taste. Cook over high heat 3 minutes. Return foie gras to skillet and place in oven 10–12 minutes, until interior is pinkish beige or reaches 120° on a meat thermometer. Serve thinly sliced, with sauce and grapes.

Baeckeoffe de Foie Gras

(Potted Foie Gras and Vegetables)

Serves 4

ALSATIAN HOUSEWIVES used to fill crocks with meats and vegetables and take them to local bakers to be cooked; the resulting dish was called a baeckeoffe, literally a baker's oven. In Strasbourg (lower right), chef Émile Jung of the three-star Au Crocodile still seals his luxurious update of baeckeoffe with dough, lest we forget its humble origins.

- *3 large red bliss potatoes, peeled and sliced*
- *1 leek, white part only, washed and sliced*
- *1 small yellow onion, peeled and sliced*
- *5 small carrots, peeled and sliced*
- *3 small turnips, peeled and sliced*
- *1 ⅓ cups Alsatian riesling or other dry but fruity white wine*
- *4 cups chicken stock (see page 56)*
- *3 bay leaves*
- *3 sprigs fresh thyme*
- *1 tbsp. duck or goose fat*
- *Salt and freshly ground black pepper*
- *1 lobe of fresh duck foie gras (about ¾ lbs.), room temperature*
- *½ cup flour*
- *1 fresh black truffle, wiped clean and finely chopped (optional)*
- *½ small head savoy cabbage, julienned*

1. Put potatoes, leeks, onions, carrots, turnips, wine, stock, bay leaves, thyme, and fat in a large pot. Season to taste with salt and pepper. Bring to a boil over high heat. Reduce heat to medium, cover, and simmer until vegetables are tender, about 25 minutes. Drain, reserving broth, and set vegetables aside.

2. Pull any bits of translucent membrane from surface of foie gras and use a knife to remove any of the connecting veins. Probe for the main vein and its branches with your fingers, pulling it out as you follow its length. Inspect the folds for patches of bitter green bile and, if found, extract them with a knife. Slice off any bruises. Season generously with salt and pepper.

3. Preheat oven to 400°. Mix flour with 5 tbsp. water in a bowl. Roll dough on a floured surface into the shape of a rope, about 24" long. Spoon half of the vegetables into a 2-quart terrine (with lid). Add foie gras, then truffles (if using) and remaining vegetables. Top with cabbage and reserved broth. Cover terrine, and wrap dough around rim to seal. Bake for 30 minutes. Remove baeckeoffe from oven, break seal, and remove lid. Transfer vegetables to a platter. Slice foie gras, then arrange over vegetables. Ladle broth from terrine over foie gras and vegetables before serving.

From Home to Haute

Alsace can boast 28 Michelin-starred establishments, including three that bear three stars, making it indisputably one of the gastronomic strongholds of France. The cuisine in the region, like the rest of local culture, shows vivid influences from both sides of the Rhine Valley—German and French—and can be both hearty and refined. There is an old Alsatian saying that "Meat is the best vegetable", and this is borne out by the continued popularity of such traditional dishes as choucroute garnie (with its veritable anthology of pork products; see page 226), baeckeoffe (lamb, beef, and pork layered with potatoes and baked slowly in a casserole), and stewed tripe, as well as a wide range of charcuterie and foie gras in several forms. Other definitive Alsatian specialties include crayfish soup (see recipe, page 65), coq au riesling (chicken cooked in white wine), flammekueche (a pizzalike tart), and numerous preparations of frogs' legs and snails. It is one of the reassuring glories of regional cookery here that these specialties seem to be able to exist as happily in homey and sophisticated versions.

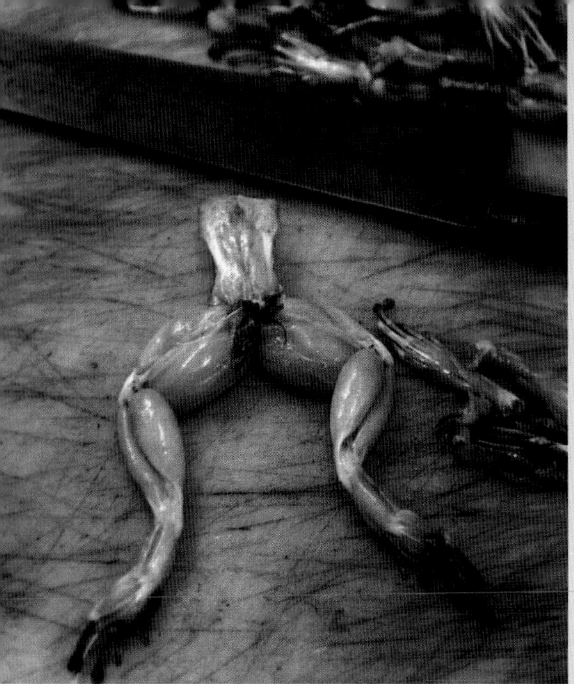

Frog Facts

Frogs apparently weren't eaten in Europe until the 16th century—before that time, they were associated with sorcery or thought to be poisonous (which in fact is true of some South American varieties)—and didn't become a gastronomic staple in France until the 1800s. Once the French nobility discovered the amphibians' culinary charms, however, they began devouring them at an alarming rate. By the end of World War II, the country's frog population was waning—helped towards oblivion by chemical pesticides polluting the ponds and marshes and by overfishing. In the 1960s, France began to import frogs from Yugoslavia and Albania, but those countries' stocks were quickly exhausted, too, and today the majority of the fresh frogs' legs imported by the French—some 600–700 tons of live creatures a year—come from Turkey and Egypt. France also imports, we are sorry to have to report, some 3,000–4,000 tons of frozen frogs' legs annually from Indonesia and China. Why is it only the legs of the frog that are consumed? Because the French prefer tiny frogs, whose muscular legs provide their only appreciable meat. However, many varieties of Asian frogs are bigger, and have bodies big enough to, well, suck on if not exactly chew.

Cuisses de Grenouilles au Beurre Persillade

(Frogs' Legs in Parsley Butter)

SERVES 4

SAUTÉING frogs' legs in butter with garlic and parsley is a classic Burgundian method of preparing this emblematic delicacy. We learned this simple procedure from chef Jean-Pierre Silva, whose Le Vieux Moulin in Bouilland, near Beaune (see sidebar, page 186), is one of Burgundy's best restaurants.

1 ½ lb. frogs' legs (about 8 large pairs), separated
½ cup flour
6 tbsp. butter
2 tsp. vegetable oil
Salt and freshly ground black pepper
4 cloves garlic, peeled and minced
½ cup minced fresh parsley

1. Rinse frogs' legs, drain, and thoroughly pat dry with paper towels. Dredge in flour and shake off excess.

2. Melt 4 tbsp. of the butter with the oil in a large nonstick skillet over medium-high heat. Add frogs' legs, season to taste with salt and pepper, and sauté until golden on all sides, about 4 minutes. Add garlic, parsley, and remaining 2 tbsp. butter and sauté 1 minute more. Divide frogs' legs between 4 warm plates, then drizzle with garlic parsley butter.

Mille-Feuilles de Grenouilles

(Frogs' Leg "Napoleons" with White Bean Sauce)

SERVES 4

THIS IMPROVISATION on a Burgundian theme was created by chef Jacques Lameloise at his three-star restaurant in Chagny. Look for fresh frogs' legs at Asian markets.

½ cup great northern beans
4 cloves garlic, peeled, 1 whole and 3 minced
1 small yellow onion, peeled and finely chopped
1 oz. salt pork, finely chopped
1 bay leaf
5 sprigs fresh parsley
2 sprigs fresh thyme
2 medium carrots, peeled and finely chopped
1 cup strong chicken stock (see page 56)
2 cups heavy cream
Salt and freshly ground black pepper
6 tomatoes, peeled, quartered, and seeded
1 small stalk celery, minced
1 small zucchini, minced
3 tbsp. butter
2 lbs. frogs' legs (about 12 pairs), separated
2 tsp. vegetable oil
4–8 sprigs chervil

1. Put beans, whole clove of garlic, half the onions, salt pork, bay leaf, parsley, thyme, and all but ⅓ cup of the carrots in a heavy pot. Add chicken stock and heavy cream. Bring to a boil over high heat, reduce heat to low, cover, and simmer until beans are very tender, about 2 hours. Season to taste with salt and pepper and cook 30 minutes more. Remove and discard bay leaf. Transfer beans and cooking liquid to a food processor and purée until smooth. Strain through a fine sieve back into the same pot. Cover to keep warm. Gently flatten tomato quarters, then season with salt and pepper and set aside.

2. Put remaining ⅓ cup carrots and 1 cup salted water in a saucepan, bring to a boil over high heat, reduce heat to medium, cover, and simmer for 3 minutes. Add celery and remaining onions and simmer, covered, for 3 minutes more. Add zucchini and simmer, covered, for another 4 minutes. Drain vegetables and return to pan. Add 1 tbsp. butter, and season to taste with salt and pepper. Cover and set aside.

3. Cut 8–12 of the frogs' legs into drumsticks and thighs. Melt remaining 2 tbsp. butter with oil in a nonstick skillet over medium heat, add minced garlic, and stir for 1 minute. Add all frogs' legs and sauté until golden on each side, about 3 minutes total, depending on size. Remove from heat and set aside 8–12 drumsticks. Remove and reserve meat from remaining frogs' legs, discarding bones.

4. Put a tart ring, 3" in diameter and 1½" deep, in the center of each of 4 plates. Arrange 2 tomato quarters, slightly overlapping, at bottom of each ring, then spread each evenly with ¼ cup reserved frogs' leg meat, then 2 tbsp. vegetables. Repeat layers, ending with tomatoes. Repeat process to make four "napoleons". Press down to help mold each one, then carefully slide off rings. Drizzle bean sauce around napoleons and garnish each plate with drumsticks and chervil.

Taste and Flavor

Lameloise in Chagny is one of the surprisingly few French three-star restaurants that looks the part: Its marble floors are warmed with Persian carpets, its vaulted ceilings crossed with massive dark wooden beams, its white-washed stone walls hung with much better paintings than most elevated French restaurateurs seem to buy.

It is a comfortable monument to good taste. Under the direction of third-generation chef-proprietor Jacques Lameloise (above), it is also a monument to good flavors—both delicately contemporary and, best of all, heartily Burgundian; the great chefs of Burgundy are rarely better than when they stay close to home.

Slow Food

Snails have been a part of the human diet since prehistoric times, according to the evidence of heaps of shells found in archaeological digs. Today, the French are the world's leading consumers of the little gastropod by far, managing about 30,000 tons of them each year. The best French snails—and in fact the only ones that the official French snail-growers organization, Maîtres Escargotiers de France, recognize as escargots—are of the genus *Helix*. These include the celebrated and now endangered

escargots de Bourgogne (which come from the Franche-Comté, Savoie, and Champagne regions as well as Burgundy itself) and the petits-gris (little grays) of Provence and the Languedoc—as well as plain old escargots from other parts of the country. French snail lovers differentiate between *coureurs*, or runners, available in spring and fall; the *voilés*, or veiled ones, of summer (so called because the snails seal their apertures with a thin veil of mucus so that they don't dry out in the heat); and *operculés*, the operculated or covered ones, which seal themselves with a less permeable calcareous veil before hibernating for the winter. Connoisseurs collecting snails in the wild prefer voilés and operculés to coureurs; the latter have a higher moisture content.

Escargots à la Bourguignonne

(Snails in Parsley Butter)

Serves 4

THE PLUMP, succulent snails of Burgundy (left), traditionally plucked from the vineyards, where they feed on vine leaves, were once among the region's gastronomic treasures—but like so many delicacies, they are disappearing. Fortunately, good-quality canned snails are fine in this dish.

½ lb. unsalted butter, softened
3 cloves garlic, peeled and minced
¼ cup minced fresh parsley
1 small shallot, peeled and minced
2 tsp. salt
½ tsp. freshly ground black pepper
Pinch freshly grated nutmeg
1 tbsp. dry white wine
1 tsp. cognac
2 dozen snail shells, cleaned
2 dozen canned giant snails (Burgundian if possible)
Rock salt

1. Beat together butter, garlic, parsley, shallots, salt, pepper, nutmeg, wine, and cognac in a medium mixing bowl. Cover and refrigerate for at least 4 hours, or overnight.

2. Preheat oven to 400°. Using a butter knife, fill each snail shell with about ½ tsp. butter mixture. Push a snail into each shell, then use remaining parsley butter to fill shells to the rim. Cover the bottom of a baking pan with rock salt and arrange escargots with butter side up. Bake until butter sizzles, about 10 minutes. Serve with good country bread, if you like, to soak up the butter.

Fricassée d'Escargots au Coulis de Persil

(Fricassée of Snails with Parsley and Roasted Garlic Cream)

SERVES 8

LIVE SNAILS (left) are preferred by most Burgundian chefs in preparing escargots. This elegant variation on the traditional local recipe (see page 130) is served at the Hostellerie des Clos in Chablis—an excellent restaurant noted both for its food and its encyclopedic local wine list.

3 small heads garlic
¼ cup olive oil
1 bunch flat-leaf parsley, trimmed
Salt
½ cup heavy cream
1 cup French chablis
Freshly ground black pepper
½ cup escargot brine (juice from canned snails, below)
6 tbsp. butter
4 dozen canned giant snails (Burgundian if possible)

1. Preheat oven to 250°. Slice off the top of each head of garlic, exposing cloves, and slightly spread cloves apart. Place garlic in a small baking dish, drizzle with oil, then cover dish with aluminum foil. Bake until cloves have softened, about 2 hours.

2. Reserve 8 parsley sprigs for garnish, and blanch the rest in a pot of boiling salted water over high heat for about 30 seconds. Drain and dry on paper towels, then finely chop and set aside.

3. Reserve 8 cloves roasted garlic in their skins for garnish, peel remaining cloves, and transfer to a blender or food processor. Add cream and 2 tbsp. of the chablis and purée until smooth. Season to taste with salt and pepper, transfer to a small saucepan, cover, and warm gently over low heat.

4. Combine escargot brine and remaining chablis in a small saucepan and bring to a simmer over medium heat. Season to taste with salt and pepper and cook for 5 minutes. Add 2 tbsp. of the butter, stirring until melted, then remove from heat. Stir in chopped parsley, and cover pan to keep warm.

5. Melt remaining 4 tbsp. butter in a large nonstick skillet over medium heat and sauté snails until hot, 3–5 minutes. Divide parsley sauce between 8 plates, then swirl garlic cream into each serving. Spoon snails in center of each plate and garnish with parsley sprigs and garlic cloves.

Chablis vs. Chablis

To Americans, chablis—much of it produced in California's hot, dry central valley—is cheap generic white jug wine; to the French, chablis—made only in and around the pretty little town of Chablis in the northwestern corner of Burgundy—is one of the world's great white wines. It all depends, of course, on whose "chablis" you're drinking; but under no circumstances confuse the two. The real thing, the original, is made entirely from chardonnay, and is sometimes said to embody that grape's flavor and aroma more purely and truly than any other wine. Some producers in the region have phased out the oak barrels traditionally employed for fermentation and/or aging in favor of stainless steel vats—on the theory that chablis is a wine whose unique character (it is famous for its mineraly *goût de pierre à fusil* or gunflint flavor) is best left uncomplicated by the vanilla-scented richness of oak. Other makers of the wine—including some of the best, like René and Vincent Dauvissat and François and Jean-Marie Raveneau—maintain that judicious use of oak fills out the chablis, complementing its acidity and flint. Chablis is usually consumed young, but the best examples—especially those from the grands crus vineyards of Les Clos, Blanchots, Bougros, Vaudésir, Valmur, Les Preuses, and Grenouilles—can grow positively stunning with 10 or 20 years of age.

Buried Treasure

The "black" wine of Cahors, in the Quercy region, has been famous for centuries. Another black treasure drawn from local earth, even more sought after, has earned its celebrity a bit more recently—only in the past 150 years or so: This is the black truffle, *Tuber melanosporum*, one of the greatest of all gastronomic delicacies. Though the truffles of the Périgord region, immediately northwest of Quercy, are better known, the precious tubers have been harvested on Quercy's *causses*, or arid plains, since at least the late 19th century, and are an integral part of the local cuisine. Ironically, it was the destruction of the region's vineyards by phylloxera around 1880 that gave impetus to the truffle industry here: Recognizing that the thin soil and porous limestone earth of the causses offered ideal growing conditions for truffles, many local farmers replaced their ravaged vines with truffle oaks—whose root systems provide nutrients for the soil, encouraging the tubers to form (even as the truffles feed the trees). Though no one has yet cultivated truffles consistently, these farmers were largely successful in their efforts. In the winter months today, many Quercy towns have truffle markets offering the black jewels to wholesale and retail customers alike.

Fricassée de Cèpes aux Truffes

(Cèpe Fricassée with Truffles)

SERVES 6

CÈPES (*Boletus edulis*)—the wild mushrooms known in Italy as funghi porcini—"little pig mushrooms", for their size and succulence—are greatly appreciated in southwestern France, where they are sometimes combined with that other noble fungus, the truffle, as in this recipe from Cahors.

2 lbs. fresh cèpes
4 tbsp. olive oil
7 cloves garlic, peeled
1 ½ cups chicken stock (see page 56)
10 sprigs fresh thyme
Salt and freshly ground black pepper
3 oz. fresh black truffles, wiped clean
4 tbsp. butter, cut into small pieces

1. Separate cèpe stems from caps with a paring knife and remove and discard spongy underpart of caps if soft. Peel stems and cut into ¼"-thick slices. Cut caps into quarters or sixths depending upon size.

2. Heat 2 tbsp. oil in a large skillet over medium heat. Add 5 cloves of garlic and cook, stirring frequently, for 2 minutes. Add cèpe stems and cook until tender, about 5 minutes.

3. Transfer garlic and stems to a food processor, add stock, and purée until smooth. Strain through a fine sieve into a small saucepan. Simmer over medium-high heat until reduced by half, 7–10 minutes. Cover and keep warm over low heat.

4. Wipe out large skillet and heat remaining 2 tbsp. oil over medium-high heat. Add cèpe caps and remaining 2 cloves garlic and sauté for 3 minutes, then add 4 sprigs of the thyme, season to taste with salt and pepper, and cook, stirring occasionally, until caps are golden, about 3 minutes.

5. Using a truffle slicer or vegetable peeler, thinly shave truffles into skillet, toss with cèpes, and cook just until heated through, about 1 minute. Whisk butter into sauce, and season to taste with salt and pepper. Remove and discard sautéed garlic and thyme, evenly divide cèpe and truffles between 6 plates, surround with sauce, and garnish with remaining thyme.

Pommes à la Sarladaise aux Truffes

(Sarladais-Style Potatoes with Truffles)

SERVES 6

THIS RECIPE is from Pierre-Jean Duribreux, chef at Le Vieux Logis in Trémolat; *à la sarladaise* means in the style of nearby Sarlat—which now implies truffles and goose fat.

2 lbs. russet potatoes, peeled and chopped into ½" pieces
Salt
5 tbsp. goose fat
1 clove garlic, peeled and minced
2 tbsp. finely chopped fresh parsley
1 3–4 oz. fresh black truffle, wiped clean and cut into matchsticks
Freshly ground black pepper

1. Blanch potatoes in a large pot of boiling salted water for 3 minutes. Drain and pat dry with paper towels.

2. Heat a large cast-iron or heavy skillet over medium-high heat for 1–2 minutes. Add 2 tbsp. of the fat and all the potatoes; be careful of spattering fat. Cook, stirring occasionally, until a crisp golden crust forms, about 10 minutes. Add 1 tbsp. fat and continue to cook, scraping crust off the bottom of the skillet and turning the potatoes to brown on all sides, for another 10 minutes. Crush potatoes slightly with a large fork, taking care not to turn them into a purée. Reduce heat to medium, then add garlic, parsley, and remaining 2 tbsp. fat. Cook, stirring often, for 2 minutes. Add truffles, continue stirring, and cook for another 2 minutes. Season to taste with salt and pepper.

A Mass for Truffles

The event of the season each January in the portion of Provence called the Vaucluse—where 70 percent of France's annual truffle production originates—is the Messe de la Truffe, or truffle mass, held on the third Sunday of the month at the little church in the village of Richerenches, one of the local truffle capitals. The villagers, many of whom are truffle gatherers, and their families (facing page), come here to thank Saint Anthony, patron saint of the village, and to ask for a good truffle harvest. (Saint Anthony, remember, blesses the search for things lost.) In return, they contribute truffles instead of money when the alms basket is passed; the truffles are to be auctioned off later, for the greater good of the parish. The sermon intermingles religious considerations with the spirit of the hunt: Search for faith with as much passion as you search for truffles, the pastor might say; truffles are a gift from God's earth, so return a fair share for His glory; and remember that faith gives flavor to your life, as the truffle gives flavor to an omelette.

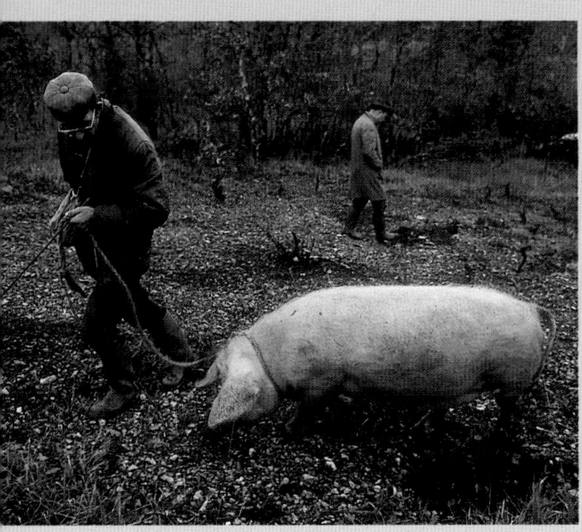

The Pig or the Dog?

Historically, France has been divided into regions that prefer the pig for truffle-hunting (the Dordogne, Quercy, and Provence) and those that swear by the dog (Burgundy, Champagne, and the Haut-Dauphiné). No one dog breed stands out for hunting truffles; spaniels, griffons, sheepdogs, and mongrels seem equally adept. Proponents of porcine truffle hunters point out that young female pigs have a very sharp, well-developed sense of smell—and that a well-trained sow will actually unearth the truffle with its snout, whereas dogs will only indicate its location. Why are dogs used more often than pigs today, then? The main reason, say experts, is the unfortunate extinction of most of France's indigenous porcine breeds. Dogs have more stamina and are more intelligent and obedient than the modern pig breeds, it is said, though the old breeds would have run them ragged. In the Dordogne and Quercy, truffle hunters who prefer the pig have high hopes for a newly imported breed, the Large White Yorkshire—said to be a natural.

Oeufs Brouillés aux Truffes

(Scrambled Eggs with Truffles)

SERVES 2

IN HER 1960 CLASSIC *French Provincial Cooking*, Elizabeth David shares a secret she learned from a French truffle hunter: Before cooking eggs with truffles, as in this recipe, mix the two ingredients together and let them sit for a while, so that the truffle flavor permeates the eggs.

6 eggs
½ oz. fresh black truffle, wiped clean and very thinly sliced
1 ½ tbsp. cold butter
2 tbsp. heavy cream
Salt and freshly ground black pepper

1. Beat eggs in a bowl, add truffle slices, cover, and refrigerate for 3–4 hours. Melt butter in a large heavy-bottomed skillet over medium heat just until it stops foaming, about 1 minute. Mix cream into eggs, then pour into skillet. Wait for 5 seconds, then using a wooden spoon pull eggs in towards center of skillet allowing uncooked eggs to flow into the empty part of pan. Do not stir. Cook until eggs are set but still moist, 2–3 minutes. Season to taste with salt and pepper.

Poulet Demi-Deuil

(Truffled Chicken)

Serves 4

THOUGH CHICKEN is the foodstuff most often prepared "demi-deuil" (in half-mourning), the term is also applied to truffled eggs, potato salad, and spiny lobster (langouste)—all "white" foods darkened with the black of la truffe. Chef and cookbook author James Peterson developed this simplification of the classic chicken version of the dish.

1 3½-lb. chicken, rinsed and dried
¾ oz. fresh black truffle, wiped clean and sliced into thin rounds
Salt and freshly ground black pepper
2 tbsp. butter, softened
1 clove garlic, peeled and halved lengthwise
1 tbsp. rainwater madeira
1 tsp. cognac

1. Working from the neck opening, use your fingers to gently pry chicken skin away from as much of the breast and legs as you can without tearing it. Slip truffle slices under skin in a single layer, covering as much flesh as possible. Truss chicken with kitchen string by tying legs together and binding the bird into a compact package. Wrap loosely in plastic, and refrigerate overnight.

2. Preheat oven to 400°. Rub chicken with salt and pepper and a little of the butter. Rub the inside of a small heavy casserole with garlic and remaining butter. (The casserole should have a tight-fitting lid and be just a little bigger than the chicken.) Pour madeira and cognac around chicken in casserole. Tightly cover and bake for 1 hour. Lift cover at the table to allow everyone to enjoy the fragrant steam. Serve with buttered egg noodles and good crusty bread, if you like.

Delicious Mourning

Mère Fillioux, one of the famous "mothers" of Lyonnais gastronomy, was famous for her poulet en demi-deuil, literally chicken in half-mourning—so called because of the black robe of truffles under its skin. Eugénie Brazier, another Lyonnais Mère, worked for Fillioux for three years at her restaurant, then went on to open her own place—where she became the first, and thus far only, female chef to earn the ultimate three-star rating in the Guide Michelin. In her honor, Paul Bocuse (who had worked in her kitchen as a young man) renamed the dish, which is traditionally made with the famous chickens of Bresse (see page 185), "poularde de Bresse truffée Mère Brazier". Today, Eugénie's granddaughter, Jacotte Brazier, runs the restaurant Eugénie founded, and still serves the classic chicken dish to which her ancestor's name has been attached.

CHAPTER

6

SEAFOOD

"IN THE FALL OF 1991, I moved to the pretty port town of Sanary-sur-Mer, just west of Toulon on the Mediterranean coast of France, to live for a time with a close-knit group of professional fishermen. For the better part of a year, I'd meet them at the dock in the predawn darkness, beneath a silvery moon, boarding one of their tiny fishing boats and heading out to sea. I learned a lot about these fishermen, and developed lasting friendships with them. Lucien Vitiello (facing page, lower left, in white shirt), the weathered leader of the group, spent the most time with me, and taught me about the passion that drives these men to devotedly pursue such a harsh existence. One beautiful spring afternoon, Vitiello invited me to his home in the hills above Sanary to share a bouillabaisse. I arrived to find him cleaning a large accumulation of fish, most of which he had netted the day before—a combination of soft-fleshed varieties like wrasse and forkbeard, which would disintegrate during cooking and enrich the soup, and firmer ones like john dory, conger eel, and of course rascasse, or scorpion fish [see page 147]. 'Of course,' he explained, 'you use what you're lucky enough to catch.' After cleaning the fish, Vitiello poured some fruity olive oil into an enormous pot, scattered onions and garlic into it, then added some fennel tops and herbs. Tomatoes and sliced potatoes went in next, then the fish, which were topped with a few more tomatoes. He doused everything with richly scented fish stock, tossed in a handful of tiny Mediterranean crabs and another of mussels, then gave the entire dish a spritz of pastis and a big pinch of saffron. His bouillabaisse was now ready for the fire. Less than an hour later, Vitiello's wife, Loulou, called out 'À table!'" —RICHARD GOODMAN

RECIPES

Bouillabaisse

SERVES 8

LUCIEN VITIELLO (facing page) makes bouillabaisse this way, using a wide variety of fish. Rouille is the traditional accompanying red-pepper mayonnaise (*rouille* means rust).

1 24" baguette, cut into ½"-thick slices
2 cloves garlic, peeled

FOR ROUILLE:
4 cloves garlic, peeled
2 tbsp. fish stock (see page 62)
½ tsp. saffron threads
1 cup mayonnaise
½ tsp. sweet paprika
Pinch cayenne
Salt

FOR BOUILLABAISSE:
½ cup olive oil
2 medium yellow onions, peeled and sliced
5 cloves garlic, peeled and crushed
3 sprigs fresh parsley
3 sprigs fresh thyme
1 bay leaf
¼ cup fennel tops
2 lbs. new potatoes, peeled and sliced
1 ½ lbs. tomatoes, peeled, seeded, and chopped
6 lbs. assorted cleaned fish (see sidebar, facing page)
16 mussels, scrubbed and debearded
2 ½ quarts warm fish stock (see page 62)
1 tsp. saffron threads
½ cup pastis
Salt and freshly ground black pepper

1. Preheat oven to 350°. Place bread on a cookie sheet and toast until golden, turning once, about 10 minutes per side. Rub toast on both sides with garlic, then discard them. Set bread aside.

2. For rouille, mince garlic and set aside. Put fish stock in a mortar, crumble in saffron, add minced garlic, and grind mixture with a pestle until smooth. Transfer to a bowl and stir in mayonnaise, paprika, and cayenne. Season to taste with salt and set aside. (Rouille should be made the day it is to be used; it does not keep well.)

3. For bouillabaisse, heat ¼ cup of the oil in a 10–12 quart pot over low heat. Add onions, garlic, parsley, thyme, bay leaf, and fennel tops. Add potatoes, then tomatoes. Add large, whole, firm fish first, then smaller, more delicate fish, and finally mussels.

4. Pour in stock and remaining ¼ cup of oil. Crumble in saffron and add pastis. Season to taste with salt and pepper and raise heat to high. Ingredients will cook as bouillabaisse comes to a boil; start checking after about 5 minutes and carefully transfer seafood to a platter as it cooks. (Discard any mussels that do not open.) When potatoes have cooked (this can take up to 25 minutes, depending on age of potatoes), transfer them to same platter, then strain broth and set aside.

5. To serve, for the first course, spread rouille on toast, put 3 or more pieces in each of 8 warmed soup bowls, and add broth. For the second course, serve a platter of fish and potatoes at room temperature. Moisten with additional broth and add a dollop of rouille, if you like.

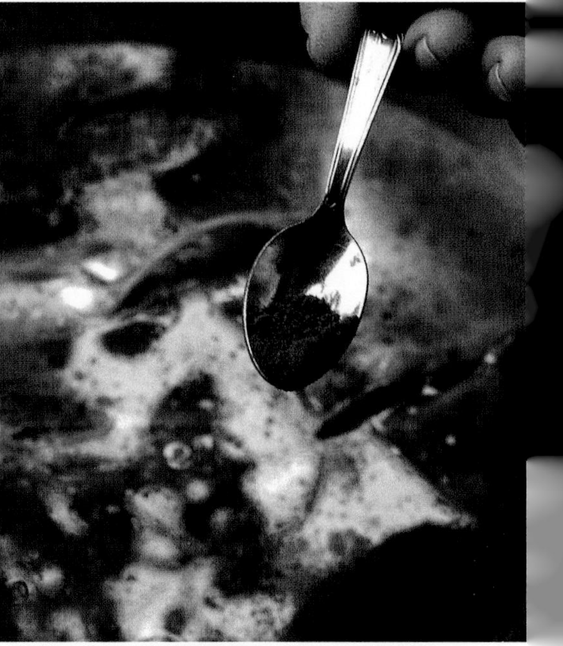

Without Rascasse

"Bouillabaisse without rascasse," asserts Lucien Vitiello, "is like paella without rice." Unfortunately for Americans, this common flavorful Mediterranean poisson, called scorpion fish in English, is rarely available here. The good news is that an excellent bouillabaisse can indeed be made without it. The important thing, French and American chefs alike agree, is to use the freshest, tastiest seafood available. Red snapper, sea bass, tilefish, grouper, striped bass, monkfish, halibut, john dory, even squid or cuttlefish are among the possibilities. Paul Bertolli, chef and part-owner of Oliveto in Oakland, California, recommends a selection of the small, inexpensive rockfish found in Asian markets. Most experts agree, though, that the American bouillabaisse-maker would do well to avoid freshwater fish like trout and catfish; mild fish, like swordfish or salmon; flaky fish, like cod; and strong, oily fish, like mackerel.

Cotriade

(Breton Seafood in Broth)

Serves 6

THE FLAVOR of this Breton fisherman's dish is subtler than that of bouillabaisse. At his restaurant in Plounérin, Patrick Jeffroy sometimes dresses up cotriade with saffron and shellfish. Here is his version of this classic "soup".

4 tbsp. butter
2 small carrots, peeled and finely diced
2 medium yellow onions, peeled and finely chopped
2 leeks, white part only, washed and finely chopped
4 cloves garlic, peeled and minced
3 tomatoes, peeled, seeded, and diced
1 lb. white potatoes, peeled and diced
3 lbs. assorted fish, such as cod, halibut, red snapper, or monkfish, cut into pieces about 2" square
2 sprigs fresh thyme
1 sprig fresh dill
¼ tsp. saffron threads
1 tbsp. grated orange zest
1 tbsp. grated lemon zest
6 cups fish stock (see page 62)
Salt and freshly ground black pepper
2 cups dry white wine
2 medium shallots, peeled and finely chopped
2 dozen mussels, scrubbed and debearded
½ lb. jumbo shrimp, peeled and deveined
6 small crabs, cleaned (optional)

1. Melt butter in a large pot over medium-low heat. Cook carrots, onions, leeks, and garlic until soft, about 15 minutes. Add tomatoes and potatoes, and cook until potatoes are slightly tender, about 8 minutes.

2. Place fish on top of vegetables, thicker pieces on bottom, thinner pieces on top. Add thyme, dill, saffron, orange zest, lemon zest, and fish stock. Season with salt and pepper, increase heat to medium-high, bring to a simmer, then cover, and cook for 10 minutes. Remove fish and vegetables and set aside, reserving broth.

3. Meanwhile, add white wine and shallots to a large pot. Bring to a boil over medium-high heat and add mussels, shrimp, and crabs (if using). Cover and cook, shaking pan occasionally, until mussels open, shrimp turn pink, and crabs turn red, about 4 minutes. Remove shellfish with a slotted spoon, reserving liquid. Discard any mussels that don't open and set pan aside for about 10 minutes so that any sand in the liquid will settle to the bottom.

4. Ladle shellfish broth into fish broth, then strain through a fine sieve lined with cheesecloth, discarding solids. Season broth to taste with salt and pepper. Divide fish, vegetables, and shellfish between 6 warmed soup bowls and ladle broth on top. Serve with additional broth on the side.

Cauldrons of Seafood

The word *cotriade* is thought by some to derive from the Breton *kaoter* (cauldron) and *iad* (contents): Breton contract fishermen used to be paid in fish—the lesser varieties—and their wives would toss whatever they brought home into the pot. Since at least the beginning of the 18th century, when large fishing boats began setting out from ports along the coast of Brittany on expeditions that could last for weeks, even months, fishermen have been making cotriade themselves on shipboard. It was an ideal dish under the circumstances, based on easily stored, long-lived ingredients like garlic, onions, and potatoes (with leeks and carrots added when possible) and whatever lesser seafood was caught—for instance, mackerel, conger eel, and sometimes red mullet. Saffron may seem like an atypically luxurious ingredient under the circumstances, but in fact this costly spice has been cultivated in France since the 16th century, and has been used in Brittany as early as the 19th century—when it may well have been incorporated into cotriade.

Sailor Food

In French culinary terminology, à la marinière (or just "marinière") means seaman's style, and usually refers to shellfish cooked with onions or shallots, white wine, and herbs. Here are some other nautically inspired food terms:

À LA BATALIÈRE: In the style of a boatman or ferryman; a garnish of mushrooms, onions, fried eggs, and crayfish, or pastry boats filled with seafood in a white sauce.

À LA CANOTIÈRE: Also "boatman's style" (a *canot* is a small open boat), in this case meaning freshwater fish poached in white wine.

À LA CORSAIRE: Literally corsair- or pirate-style—not a fish dish at all, but an ancient chicken dish from St-Malo in Brittany, probably using assorted spices.

MATELOTE: "Sailor style", a term usually associated, gastronomically, with the Loire region, where it means a stew of mixed freshwater fish, especially eel, carp, pike, perch, or barbal, cooked in wine (sometimes red) with onions, mushrooms, and perhaps crayfish tails and fried bread.

À LA NAGE: Literally "swimming", and meaning shellfish that is poached in an aromatic broth of white wine, herbs, shallots, and usually cream.

Moules Marinière

(Mussels with White Wine)

SERVES 4–6

ON THE PROMENADE in the seaside town of Trouville, in Normandy, the bistro called Le Central is famous for its moules marinière (right), and this is their recipe. Local fishmongers will tell you that salt isn't necessary (the seawater-drunk mussels are salty enough) and that pepper "tue le goût"—kills the flavor—of these delicious bivalves.

½ lb. unsalted butter
4 medium yellow onions, peeled and chopped
¾ bottle dry, acidic white wine, preferably muscadet
8–9 lbs. mussels, scrubbed and debearded
1 bunch fresh parsley, finely chopped
Freshly ground black pepper (optional)
1 baguette (optional)

1. Melt butter in a large, deep skillet with a lid over medium heat. Add onions and sauté until soft and golden, about 15 minutes. Add wine and mussels and cover. Shake the skillet regularly, holding the lid down firmly, and continue to cook until mussels open, about 10 minutes. (Discard any mussels that don't open.)

2. Divide mussels and their broth between 6 warmed soup bowls. Sprinkle generously with parsley and, if using, with pepper. Serve with fresh crusty bread, if you like, to soak up the broth.

Le Central.
Trouville
Sur mer.

Homard à l'Armoricaine

(Lobster in Tomato Sauce)

SERVES 4

EVERY CHEF in Brittany has a favored version of this controversially named—and possibly Parisian-born—lobster specialty (see sidebar, right). We learned this interpretation from Breton chef Patrick Jeffroy (see page 242).

2 3-lb. live lobsters
¼ cup olive oil
1 medium yellow onion, peeled and finely chopped
3 medium shallots, peeled and minced
1 clove garlic, peeled and minced
2 carrots, peeled, trimmed, and finely diced
2 tomatoes, chopped
2 tbsp. tomato paste
2 cups dry white wine
3 tbsp. butter, softened
½ tsp. cayenne
2 tbsp. crème fraîche
2 tbsp. minced fresh parsley

1. Cook lobster in a large pot of boiling water for 10 minutes. When cool, split open, remove meat, and cut into large pieces. Reserve tomalley, coral, and shells.

2. Heat oil in a large skillet over medium-low heat. Add onions, shallots, and garlic and cook for 15 minutes. Add carrots, tomatoes, tomato paste, wine, and 1 cup water. Reduce heat to low, and simmer for 8 minutes.

3. Wrap shells in a dish towel and crush with a rolling pin. Add to sauce and cook until sauce is reduced by half. Strain through a fine sieve, and return to heat. Mix together tomalley, coral, and butter in a small bowl, then stir into sauce. Add lobster, season to taste with cayenne, and cook 2 minutes. Stir in crème fraîche. Serve over rice. Garnish with parsley.

Lobster à la What?

The most famous Breton seafood dish of all—made with cut-up lobster sautéed with shallots, tomatoes, and cayenne, sometimes with white wine, cognac, and/or a dash of cream added—is homard à l'armoricaine, the name derived from Armor, the ancient Celtic word for Brittany's coastal region. Or is it homard à l'américaine? *Larousse Gastronomique* says so, proposing that the dish was invented in Paris in the 1860s by a French chef named Pierre Fraisse, who had worked for a time in Chicago and, supposedly improvising it for last-minute customers one night, named it in honor of his American experience. Other sources suggest that "à l'américaine" was simply a menu misprint for à l'armoricaine, or even that the dish came from Minorca (known for its spiny lobster and its tomatoes), and was originally "à la minorcaine". We like to think, as the Bretons do, that it belongs to Brittany, to Armor.

Dorade Farcie Grillée

(Grilled Stuffed Sea Bream)

Serves 4

Sea bream is one of the Mediterranean's tastiest fish. Striped bass may be substituted in this recipe from Joël Guillet of Le Mas du Langoustier on the Île de Porquerolles.

1 large red bell pepper
4 plum tomatoes, halved lengthwise and seeded
6 tbsp. olive oil
Salt and freshly ground black pepper
2 large shallots, peeled and minced
12 niçoise olives, pitted and coarsely chopped
2 anchovies, finely chopped
4 1-lb. sea bream, porgy, or striped bass, deboned, with heads removed and reserved for stock
6 small leeks, trimmed, washed and thinly sliced lengthwise
¼ cup fresh lemon juice
½ cup dry white wine
¼ tsp. saffron threads
8 tbsp. chilled butter, cut into small pieces

1. Preheat broiler. Place pepper and tomatoes on a baking sheet, drizzle with about 2 tbsp. of the oil, and broil, turning the pepper 3–4 times, until pepper is charred and tomatoes are soft, 12–15 minutes. Remove from broiler, set tomatoes aside, and transfer pepper to a small bowl. Cover bowl with plastic and set aside. When pepper is cool, halve, remove and discard seeds and veins, then peel, coarsely chop, season to taste with salt and pepper, and set aside.

2. Coarsely chop tomatoes, season to taste with salt and pepper, and set aside separately from peppers. Heat 2 tbsp. of the oil in a large skillet over medium-high heat. Add half of the shallots and cook, stirring, until fragrant, about 2 minutes. Add olives, anchovies, and peppers and cook, stirring, for 30 seconds. Add tomatoes, cook for 30 seconds more, season to taste with salt and pepper, then set aside to cool.

3. Preheat oven to 400°. Heat a grill pan over high heat. Lay fish out flat, butterfly fashion, then brush skin with oil, season to taste with salt and pepper, and fold closed into original shape. Grill fish in pan, turning once, about 1 minute per side, then transfer fish to a clean surface. Open fish, then spoon a quarter of the tomato mixture into each one. Fold each fish closed and transfer to a large baking dish. Bake until fish flake easily, about 7 minutes, then remove from oven, cover with foil, and keep warm.

4. Meanwhile, heat remaining 2 tbsp. oil in large skillet over medium heat. Add leeks and 2 tbsp. water. Cook, stirring frequently, until leeks are soft and pan almost dry, 5–8 minutes. Season leeks to taste with salt and pepper and set aside.

5. Combine lemon juice, wine, and remaining shallots in a medium saucepan. Bring to a boil over high heat and reduce liquid by three-quarters, about 5 minutes. Lower heat to medium-low, crumble in saffron, gradually whisk in butter, and season to taste with salt and pepper. Divide leeks between 4 plates. Arrange fish over leeks, then spoon sauce around it.

The Real Thing

The Romans admired the daurade royale, or gilthead bream, so much that they farmed it in Lake Lucrino, near Naples, fattening the fish on a diet of oysters—which were opened fresh for them day and night. The modern French agree. There are said to be as many as 22 varieties of bream in the Mediterranean alone, as well as a dozen or so close relatives, known as porgies, in North American waters (and more still in the Caribbean), but the gilthead is widely regarded to be the regal head of the family. Fished from May to October, and weighing as much as seven pounds, it bears a golden crescent on its forehead, and has firm, white, delicately flavored flesh. The French sometimes call it la vraie daurade, the real one, and even give it the honor of its own spelling: Lesser varieties of the fish are commonly called dorade instead. Another very good fish is the pagre, or couch's sea bream, which is the only Mediterranean bream also found on the American side of the Atlantic (it is sometimes sold as red porgy in the U.S); it is this variety that chef Joël Guillet at Le Mas du Langoustier on the Île de Porquerolles (proprietors Georges Richard and Marie Caroline Le Ber, above) likes to use for the dish [facing page, right]. Other bream consumed in France include the denté, or dentex (literally "toothy"; its prominent lower jaw boasts as many as six canine teeth); the sar doré, or two-banded bream; the dorade rose, or red sea bream (also known as fausse daurade, or false daurade, and as gros yeux, or big eyes); and the dorade grise, or black sea bream. All of these can be quite delicious, and all are less expensive than the daurade royale.

Sole Meunière

(Sole Sautéed in Butter)

SERVES 4

GABRIEL BISCAY, the chef at Prunier in Paris, whose recipe we've adapted here, doesn't use flour in his sole meunière; we do, because it's traditional, and helps brown the fish. To filet sole, trace backbone with a knife, cutting through to bone, then lift flesh off. Gently lift out bone.

FOR CLARIFIED BUTTER:
1 lb. unsalted butter

FOR SOLE:
4 14-oz. whole dover sole
Salt and freshly ground black pepper
Flour
1 cup clarified butter; see step 1
1 large russet potato, peeled and thickly sliced
16 tbsp. (2 sticks) butter
Juice of 2 lemons

1. For clarified butter, put butter in a small heavy saucepan over very low heat. Do not stir or allow to come to a boil. When butter has melted, completely skim off foam and carefully pour yellow fat into a clean container, discarding milky sediment on the bottom of the pan. Keep refrigerated.

2. For sole, cut off head and fins with sharp kitchen scissors. Scrape scales from the white-skinned side (bottom) of the fish with a large wide knife. On dark side of fish, score skin just above the tail with a sharp knife, then, holding the fish by the tail with one hand, use the other to peel off the dark skin all at once. If the skin catches, use a sharp knife to free it from the flesh. (There is no need to skin the other side.) Wipe fish thoroughly with a damp kitchen towel, taking care to wipe away any blood. (To save these steps, ask your fishmonger to give the fish to you pan-ready.) Pat dry, season to taste with salt and pepper, and dredge in flour, shaking off any excess.

3. Pour ½ cup clarified butter in each of 2 large skillets set over medium-high heat. When butter is just smoking, about 3 minutes, place 2 fish, white side down, into each pan. Immediately place a slice of raw potato under tail of each fish to raise thin end of sole up from the heat and help prevent overcooking. Brown fish, about 3–4 minutes on each side, pressing down on fish with a spatula and basting continually with butter. Add 2 tbsp. of the regular butter to each pan, season to taste with salt and pepper and baste for 1 more minute. Transfer to serving platter and keep warm.

4. Melt remaining 12 tbsp. butter in a small skillet over high heat. Swirl pan over heat until butter foams and turns light golden. Whisk in lemon juice and pour over sole, coating them completely. Serve fish on a platter garnished with lemon and fresh herbs, if you like.

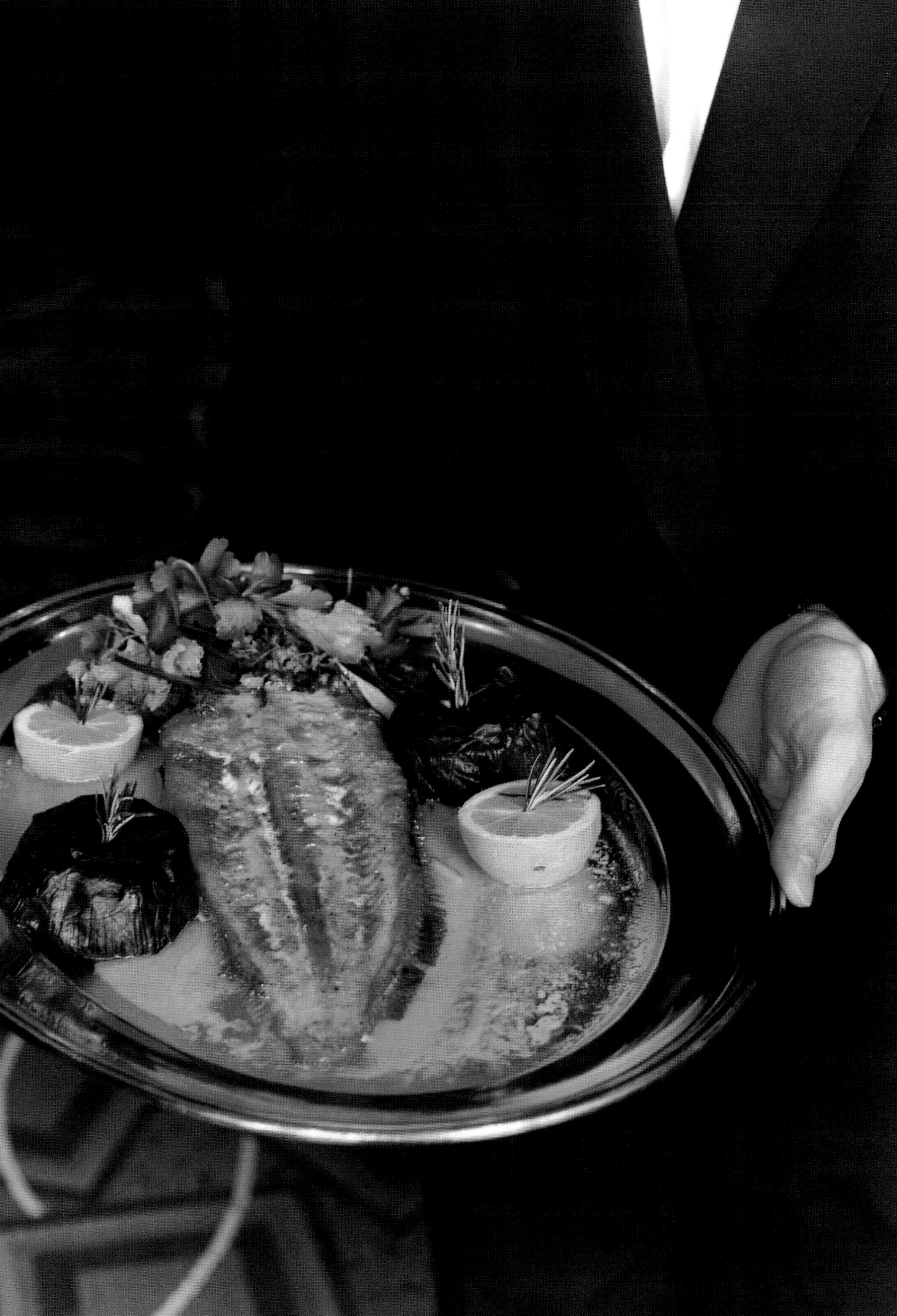

Mosaics and Oyster Shells

Prunier, on the corner of the rue Traktir and the avenue Victor Hugo in Paris, is an excellent seafood restaurant and also an extraordinary testament to the glories of the Art Deco era in France. The establishment was opened by Émile Prunier in 1925, the year of the capital's famous Art Deco salon and exhibition, and some of the style's most celebrated architects and designers contributed to the design: Auguste Labouret undertook the mosaic façade; Louis-Hippolyte Boileau created the dining room, with its blue-black marble-encrusted walls; Gaston Le Bourgeois sculpted the area behind the bar to evoke the world beneath the sea. Sadly, Prunier, whose father had run the original Prunier in Paris, died the year his new restaurant opened—but his daughter Simone took the place over and made it a success, known especially for its oysters and other shellfish, including a definitive version of lobster thermidor. Today, Prunier is under the management of Jean-Claude Vrinat, proprietor of the three-star Taillevent (see page 221)—and remains one of the best seafood restaurants in Europe.

Cigars and Sea Sows

The French tend to give their fish and shellfish imaginative nicknames—which can color one's perception of the seafood in question. Here are some of the more colorful monikers:

◆ Bécasse de mer (woodcock of the sea): red mullet, so named because, like the famous game bird, it can be cooked ungutted ◆ Cigare (cigar): grey mullet, so named for its shape ◆ Cochon de mer (pig of the sea): triggerfish, a brightly colored Mediterranean species ◆ Coq de mer (sea rooster): box crab ◆ Crapaud (toad), diable de mer (sea devil), or truie de mer (sea sow): the notoriously ugly scorpion fish (above), which goes by the more dignified name of rascasse at the fishmonger's ◆ Estrangle belle-mère (mother-in-law strangler): a Provençal term for scad or horse mackerel, different from ordinary mackerel and not as good ◆ Ivrogne de mer (sea drunkard): a small fish with red scales ◆ Langue d'avocat (lawyer's tongue): a Bordelais name for small sole ◆ Sauterelle de mer (sea grasshopper): mantis shrimp ◆ Tomate de mer (sea tomato): red sea anemone.

Loup de Mer Rôti aux Herbes

(Whole Sea Bass Roasted with Herbs)

Serves 4

Farm-raised striped bass, increasingly available in America, makes a good substitute for the loup de mer, or sea bass, used in Corsica (below) for this exquisitely simple dish.

4 1½-lb. farm-raised striped bass, cleaned and scaled
Salt and freshly ground black pepper
3 medium tomatoes, cored and sliced into rounds
2 medium lemons, sliced into rounds
3 cloves garlic, peeled and sliced
½ bunch fresh rosemary
½ bunch fresh thyme
½ bunch fresh mint
3–5 bay leaves
Extra-virgin olive oil

1. Preheat oven to 450°. Arrange fish on a large baking sheet. Season fish cavities with salt and pepper to taste, then divide the tomatoes, half the lemon slices, and a little of the garlic, rosemary, thyme, and mint between them, stuffing the cavities loosely. Scatter bay leaves and remaining lemons, garlic, rosemary, thyme, and mint over fish. Drizzle with olive oil and season to taste with salt and pepper.

2. Roast fish until skin is crisp and flesh is just cooked through, about 20 minutes. Allow fish to rest 5 minutes before serving.

APICIUS
APICIUS
M. VIGATO

Raie Raide au Beurre Clarifié

(Skate in Clarified Butter)

SERVES 4

AT APICIUS, a highly original Parisian two-star, chef Jean-Pierre Vigato is famous for unlikely combinations of ingredients and the inspired use of modest ones, as in this recipe.

- *1 tbsp. extra-virgin olive oil*
- *¼ tsp. fresh lemon juice*
- *Salt and freshly ground black pepper*
- *2 cups baby spinach leaves, trimmed and washed*
- *6 tbsp. butter*
- *3 ½ tbsp. aged sherry vinegar*
- *1 tbsp. ketchup*
- *¼ cup finely diced peeled granny smith apple*
- *2 tbsp. finely diced peeled red bell pepper*
- *2 tbsp. finely diced peeled celery, blanched*
- *1 tbsp. finely diced peeled pithed lemon flesh*
- *1 tbsp. capers*
- *2 tbsp. minced fresh parsley*
- *4 6-oz. skate filets*
- *3 tbsp. clarified butter (see page 156, step 1)*

1. Pour oil and lemon juice into a mixing bowl and whisk together. Season to taste with salt and pepper. Toss spinach in vinaigrette and set aside.

2. Melt butter in a small skillet over medium heat, then cook until it turns deep brown, about 4 minutes. Meanwhile, heat sherry vinegar in a medium skillet over medium heat until skillet is almost dry, about 2 minutes. Stir in browned butter and ketchup. Add apples, peppers, celery, lemon, capers, and parsley, and cook, stirring continually, until just heated through, about 10 seconds. Season to taste with salt and pepper and set aside.

3. Season skate on both sides with salt and pepper to taste. Heat clarified butter in a large skillet over medium-high heat, add fish, and cook until crisp and golden, about 2 minutes per side.

4. To serve, divide spinach between 4 plates, arranging in little piles. Place a skate filet on top of each pile of spinach, then spoon some of the fruit and vegetables with their sauce over skate.

Mouth Music

"The seafood pavilions at Rungis, the immense wholesale food market outside Paris," reports writer Thomas McNamee (facing page, upper right, tasting sauce), "cover indoor acres, and are full of glistening rascasses, john dories, conger eels, spiny lobsters, and about a thousand other things. Everything looks fresher than anything I have ever seen, but the fish brokers prod, sniff, argue, reject. The pickiest of them will bring his haul to the likes of Jean-Pierre Vigato [facing page, upper right, at right], chef at the two-star Apicius in Paris. In his kitchen, I watch as Vigato's fish chef scrapes meat from tiny frogs' legs one by one. The pastry chef brings silky sheets of pasta to a young guy who scores them into squares, centers clumps of raw lobster and chopped vegetables in each, and ties them with threads of leek green into a pouch for steaming. For me, the American, Vigato wants to make his "ketchup dish". A thick chunk of skate wing sizzles in clarified butter while he reduces old sherry vinegar to almost nothing, then adds butter. Into that goes the spoonful of Heinz. Vigato grins. In go minutely diced red peppers, apple, lemon, celery, capers, parsley. Vigato slides the fish on top of a little spinach salad, drizzles the chunky sweet-and-sour sauce over and around it. Oh, Lord! The intensity of that super-reduced vinegar, the vivid sweetness of pepper—this is a Bach counterpoint."

Of Cod and Man

As fish go, cod doesn't get much respect; it isn't sexy like salmon, trendy like tuna, handsome like striped bass. But historically, cod is the most important sea creature in the world: Because it lends itself superbly to preservation, through salting or drying, it became a nonpareil article of commerce as long ago as the 10th century, linking northern and southern Europe financially, spurring and provisioning sea journeys of exploration (Basque sailors who may have reached the shores of Canada were looking for new cod grounds), aiding the spread of Catholicism (it provided fast-day fare), and making it possible for protein-starved communities all over Europe, and later Africa, Asia, and the Caribbean, to survive. It is a tribute to the sheer gustatory value of both salted and dried cod that even today, when fresh fish is widely available around the world, these preserved varieties are still greatly appreciated—especially in parts of Spain, Portugal, Italy, and the south of France.

Brandade de Nîmes

(Puréed Salt Cod)

Serves 6–8

The ancient Provençal capital of Nîmes was on the trade route between Scandinavia and southern Europe, and thus knew salt cod well. Its claim to have invented this simple preparation of the fish puréed with olive oil—eaten in similar form all over the Mediterranean—seems credible.

1 lb. salt cod
1 cup plus 2 tbsp. extra-virgin olive oil
¾ cup milk
Salt and freshly ground white pepper
1 loaf country bread, sliced and toasted

1. Put cod in a large bowl, cover with cold water, and refrigerate for 5 hours, changing the water 2–3 times.

2. Put soaked cod in a large pot with 6 cups cold water and bring to a simmer over high heat, about 12 minutes. Remove from heat and drain.

3. Heat 6 tbsp. of the oil in a heavy-bottomed skillet, add cod, and sauté, breaking up the fish with the back of a wooden spoon, for 2–3 minutes. Transfer to the bowl of a food processor fitted with a metal blade.

4. Heat milk and remaining ¾ cup oil in a heavy saucepan over medium-high heat until it just comes to a simmer. Drizzle milk and oil mixture into salt cod as you process for 1 minute. Season to taste with salt and pepper, then transfer cod to a gratin dish, spreading it to fill the dish but leaving surface uneven. Broil in a preheated broiler until golden brown on top, 5–10 minutes. Serve with toasted bread.

The Master

He may be Swiss, but Frédy Girardet (facing page) is widely considered to be the greatest French (-style) chef in the world—the master, the Pope of cuisine. Unfortunately for the world's diners, he sold his three-star establishment in Crissier, near Lausanne, in 1997, and retired with his family to his roomy, art-filled villa above the wine-producing village of Féchy. It was here that Girardet cooked dinner for us one post-retirement evening, offering us a dazzling repast that included sesame seed-coated fried langoustines with curry sauce; wild Scottish salmon filets roasted in butter in a very slow oven, then served warm over an emulsion of fennel (see recipe, right); young pigeon stuffed with foie gras and truffles and encased in a crust of parsley and more truffles; and a local traditional specialty, a very thin tarte à la crème vaudoise. After such a meal, we couldn't help but regret his retirement. Girardet seemed to regret it, too. "I was a chef for 45 years," he said as we finished. "To stop, after so long, has not been easy."

Saumon Sauvage Juste Tiède

(Warm Wild Salmon Filets)

SERVES 4

WILD SALMON (i.e., not farm-raised) from the Pacific Northwest is sometimes available at premium fish markets in this country. It's well worth the search. Frédy Girardet won't make this dish, or any other, with farmed salmon.

1 tomato, peeled, halved, and seeded
2 tbsp. extra-virgin olive oil, preferably Provençal
6 loosely packed cups fennel tops
1 ¼ cup fish stock (see page 62)
3 tbsp. heavy cream
1 tsp. pastis (optional)
8 tbsp. butter, softened
4 6-oz. skinless center-cut salmon filets
2 tbsp. lemon juice
1 tsp. Chinese chili oil
Salt and freshly ground black pepper
1 tbsp. peeled and minced red bell pepper
3 tbsp. minced fresh dill
Coarse sea salt

1. Preheat oven to 275°. Place tomato halves on a baking sheet, drizzle with 1 tbsp. of the oil, and bake for 3½–4 hours. Finely dice and set aside.

2. Reduce oven heat to 225°. Place fennel in a pot with salted water to cover and boil over high heat for about 10 minutes. Drain well, transfer to a blender, add ¼ cup fish stock, and blend until smooth. Pass through a fine sieve set over a bowl. Whisk in heavy cream and pastis (if using) and set aside.

3. Spread 1 tbsp. butter over each salmon filet, and put salmon, rounded side up, in an ovenproof dish. Cover dish with aluminum foil and bake for about 20 minutes. (Salmon should be barely cooked, just warm but still translucent.)

4. Meanwhile, in a small saucepan, reduce remaining cup of the fish stock by half over medium heat. Whisk in lemon juice, remaining 1 tbsp. olive oil, and chili oil and season to taste with salt and pepper. Whisk in remaining 4 tbsp. butter, 1 tbsp. at a time, until sauce thickens a bit. Stir in tomato, bell pepper, and dill.

5. Divide fennel sauce between 4 plates, leaving a 1½" border all around. Place a salmon filet, rounded side up, in the middle of each plate, on top of fennel sauce, and spoon dill sauce around the edges. Sprinkle coarse sea salt and pepper over salmon.

Sandre au Pinot Noir

(Pike Perch Braised in Pinot Noir)

Serves 8

In Alsace, rich, aromatic white wines like riesling and gewürztraminer are often served with hearty game dishes—and the region's light, fragrant pinot noir might end up in sauce for delicate pike perch (related to America's northern pike), as in this recipe from the Husser family's Le Cerf.

- *1 5½-lb. whole northern pike or walleye, cleaned*
- *Salt and freshly ground black pepper*
- *5 tbsp. butter*
- *3 small carrots, peeled and thinly sliced*
- *3 stalks celery, chopped*
- *2 small yellow onions, peeled and chopped*
- *3 small leeks, white parts only, washed and sliced*
- *1 lb. white mushrooms, trimmed and quartered*
- *1 bottle of Alsatian pinot noir or other light red wine*
- *1 tsp. tomato paste*
- *5 bay leaves*
- *4 sprigs fresh thyme*
- *½ cup heavy cream*

1. Rinse fish, pat dry, and season generously inside and out with salt and pepper.

2. Preheat oven to 350°. Place a metal roasting pan large enough to hold fish (about 18" x 14") spanning two burners. Melt butter over medium-low heat, add carrots, celery, onions, and leeks, and cook, stirring occasionally, until vegetables are soft, about 20 minutes. Add mushrooms and cook, stirring often, for 5 minutes more.

3. Stir wine, tomato paste, bay leaves, thyme, and 1 cup water into roasting pan. Spread out vegetable mixture evenly, then put fish on top of vegetables. Cover pan with aluminum foil, and braise fish in oven, without turning, until fish flakes easily, about 30 minutes.

4. Remove pan from oven. Using two spatulas, carefully transfer fish to a large serving platter and cover with aluminum foil to keep warm while you finish sauce.

5. Place pan spanning two burners. Bring vegetable mixture to a simmer over medium-high heat, and cook, stirring often to prevent vegetables from scorching, until liquid is reduced by half, about 15 minutes. Reduce heat to medium, stir in cream, and simmer, stirring, until sauce thickens enough to coat the back of a spoon, about 2 minutes. Remove bay leaves. Season to taste with salt and pepper, then spoon vegetables and sauce over fish.

Family Continuity

In Alsace," reports writer David Downie, "family ties are strong—and Alsatian restaurants, from the simplest to the most exalted, tend to be family-run and rich in family tradition. Three generations of the Husser family, for instance, run the acclaimed Le Cerf in Marlenheim [below, from left, Marcelle and Robert; Robert's mother, Irmgard; and Marcelle and Robert's daughter-in-law, Cathy, and son, Michel]. Michel Orth is the sixth-generation chef at the venerable Hostellerie à L'Écrevisse in Brumath; the family's sprawling, cluttered restaurant has occupied the same spot since the 1840s. Vintner Martin Gaertner opened a country auberge called Aux Armes de France in the wine-growing village of Ammerschwihr, just outside Colmar, in 1920. Philippe Gaertner, Martin's grandson, is the chef today. Émile Jung serves adaptations of his chef-father's recipes at his elegant three-star Au Crocodile in Strasbourg. He might be speaking for most Alsatian restaurants when he says 'Our heritage is never lost. The soul of the family is passed down with the generations.'"

CHAPTER

7

POULTRY

"ONE EVENING, I was guest of honor at a dinner attended by a large contingent of the Grande Confrérie du Cassoulet de Castelnaudary, a gastronomic brotherhood devoted to that epic French dish, at a restaurant called Hostellerie Étienne in the village of Labastide-d'Anjou, about five miles west of Castelnaudary. Connoisseurs distinguish between the cassoulets of Carcassonne, Toulouse, and Castelnaudary—but generally acknowledge that the dish was born in the last of these. Celebrated turn-of-the-century chef Prosper Montagné wrote that cassoulet was the God of southern French cuisine, with three incarnations, of which Castelnaudary's was God the Father. Anatole France, in his *Histoire comique*, spoke with great warmth of a restaurant in Paris where a Castelnaudary-style cassoulet had been simmering in the same pot for 20 years—but added, this 'must not be confused with cassoulet in the style of Carcassonne, a simple leg of mutton with beans'. When I arrived at the Hostellerie Étienne, many of the Confrérie were already there, dressed in flowing brown robes with yellow trim and sporting large hats shaped like a *cassole*—the dark brown earthenware bowl, resembling a squashed flowerpot, for which cassoulet is named. In the kitchen, I could see a short man with white hair and glasses. 'That's Étienne Rousselot,' one of the brothers told me. 'He's the champion.' As I shoveled forkfuls of sumptuous, perfectly cooked beans, crispy duck confit, and spicy sausage into my mouth, I was more than happy to agree. After the meal, I asked the 71-year-old chef when he planned to retire. 'Never,' he said. 'My dream is to die with an oven full of cassoulet.'" —MICHAEL BALTER

RECIPES

CASSOULET, page 172; CONFIT DE CANARD *(Duck Confit)*, page 175; CANARD EN CROÛTE D'HERBES ET DE SEL *(Duck Baked in a Crust of Herbs and Salt)*, page 176; CANARD RÔTI AU CIDRE AVEC NAVETS *(Roast Duck with Cider and Turnips)*, page 178; MAGRET DE CANARD À LA CHEMINÉE *(Duck Breast Cooked on the Coals)*, page 181; POUSSIN VALLÉE D'AUGE *(Baby Chicken with Calvados and Cream)*, page 182; COQ AU VIN *(Rooster in Red Wine Sauce)*, page 185; PÂTES FARCIES DE COQ AU VIN *(Coq au Vin "Cannelloni")*, page 186; VOLAILLE FERMIÈRE AU VINAIGRE *(Farmhouse Chicken in Vinegar Sauce)*, page 189; POULET AUX ÉCREVISSES *(Chicken with Crayfish)*, page 190; CHAPON FARCI RÔTI *(Roast Capon with Stuffing)*, page 193; PINTADE AU CHOU *(Guinea Hen with Cabbage)*, page 194; LAPIN À LA MOUTARDE *(Rabbit with Mustard Sauce)*, page 197; CIVET DE LAPIN *(Rich Rabbit Stew)*, page 198.

Cassoulet
Véritable Cassole
Véritable Cassole
Grand choix à L'intérieur
Je passe au Four
Véritable Pla
à Cassoulet

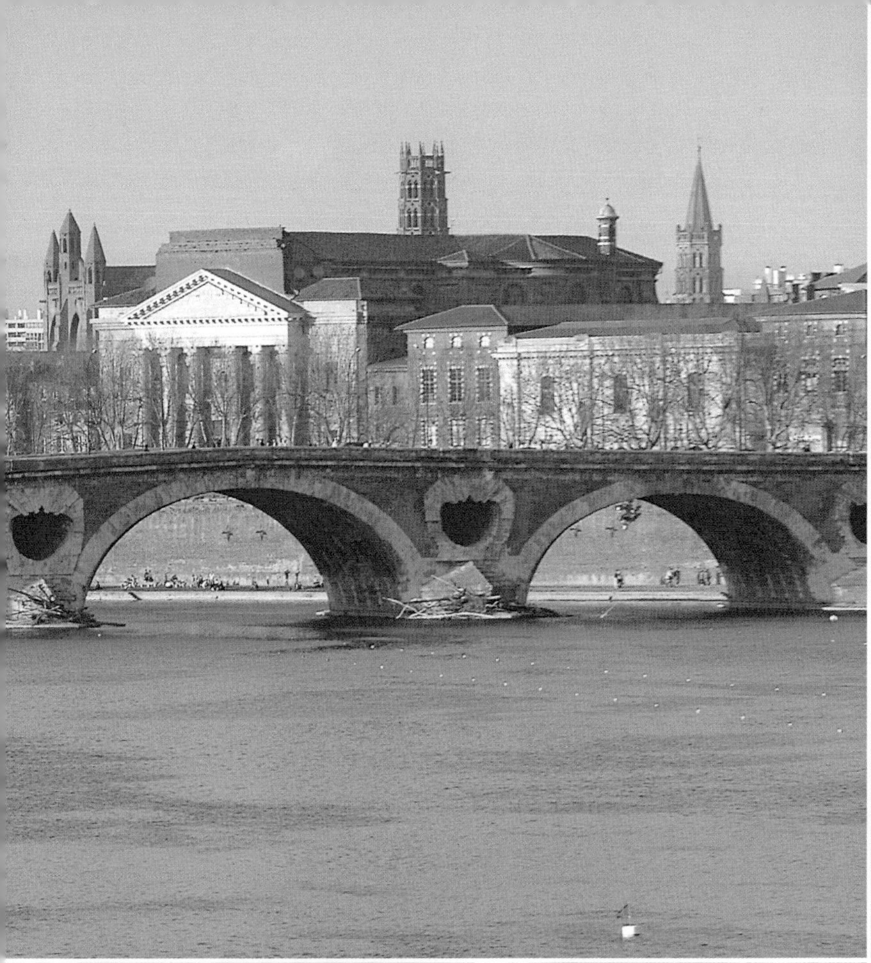

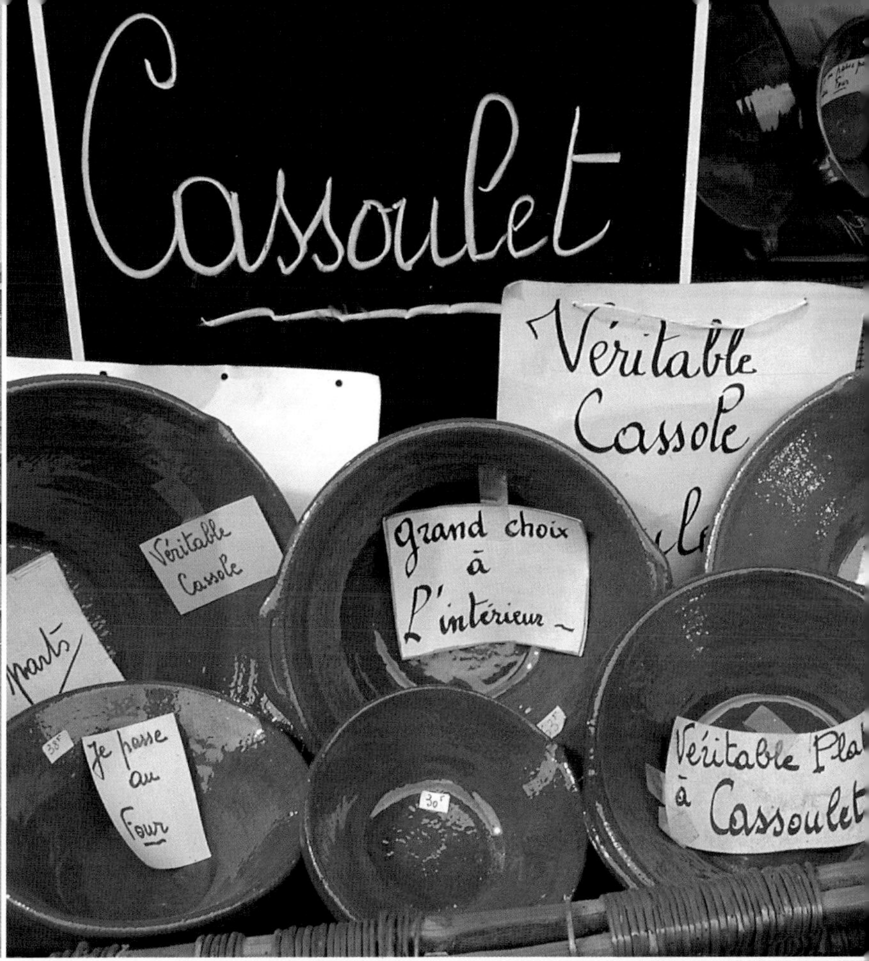

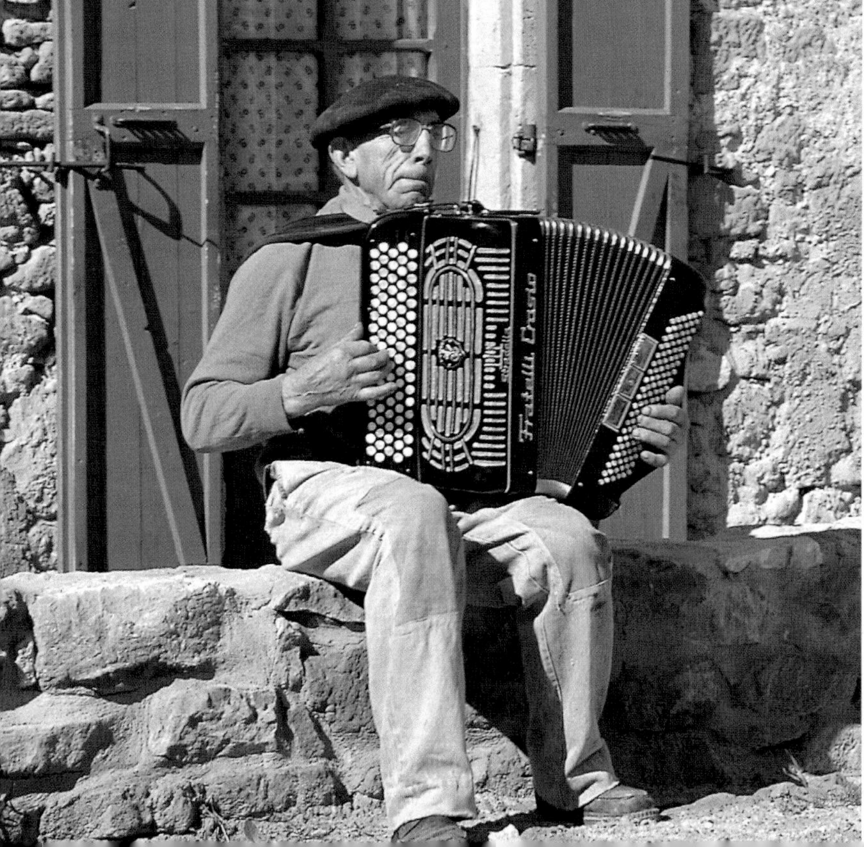

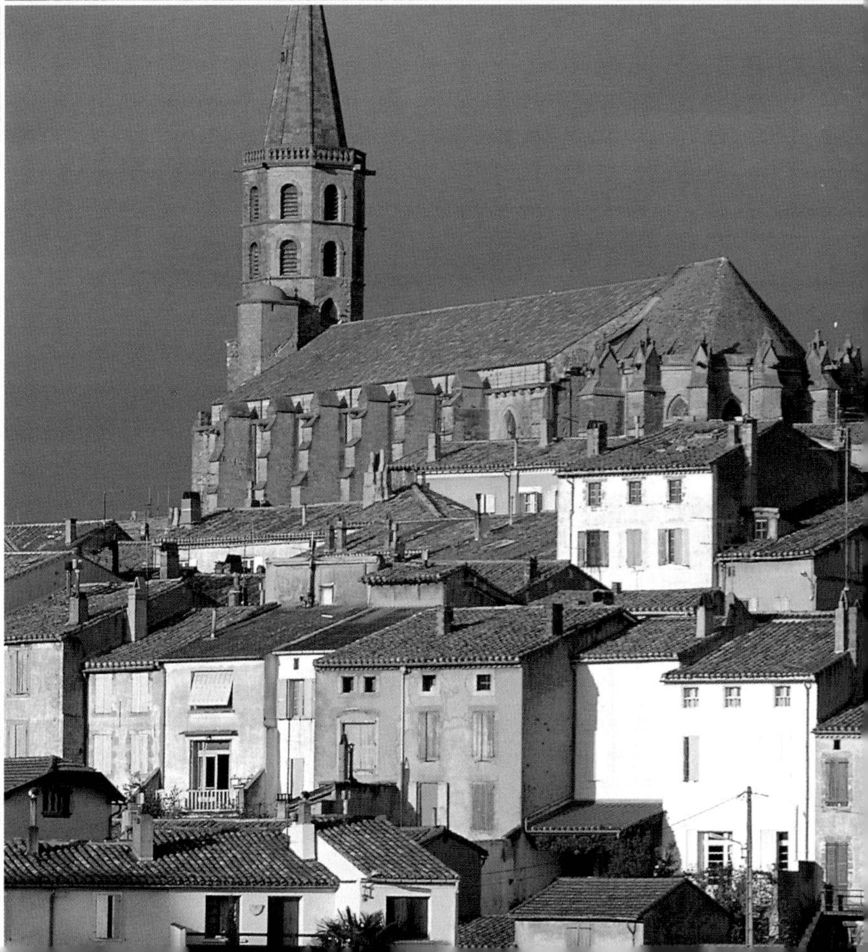

Cassoulet

SERVES 8–10

THOUGH IT CONTAINS pork and sometimes lamb, cassoulet is usually defined by the presence of duck or goose confit. Beyond that, disputes abound, about what kind of beans to use, how long to cook the dish—and how often the cassoulet's top crust should be broken and pushed down. Étienne Rousselot, whose recipe we adapted here, recommends doing it often enough to keep the beans moist—at least four times; others counsel breaking the crust hourly.

4 cups dried great northern or other small white beans
4 fresh ham hocks (about 1 lb. each)
3 large yellow onions, peeled and quartered
5 sprigs fresh thyme
Salt and freshly ground black pepper
⅓ lb. fresh pork rind, cubed
1 ham bone
1 tbsp. duck fat
1 lb. unseasoned fresh pork sausage (about 4 links), cut into 2" pieces
1 large head garlic, separated into cloves and peeled
Confit of 1 quartered duck or 4 whole legs (see page 175)
¼ tsp. ground nutmeg

1. Rinse beans thoroughly, pick through and discard stones. Set beans aside.

2. Put ham hocks in a large pot. Add 1 onion, thyme, and season to taste with salt and pepper. Cover with water and bring to a boil over high heat. Reduce heat to low and simmer, partially covered, for 2 hours. Remove from heat, allow to cool for 15 minutes, then drain ham hocks, discarding onion and thyme. Cut meat from each hock into 2 pieces. Discard bones and set meat aside.

3. Meanwhile, put pork rind and 1 onion in a large heavy-bottomed pot. Cook over medium heat, stirring frequently, until pork rind is rendered, about 20 minutes. Add beans, ham bone, and 4 quarts of water. Bring to a simmer, then reduce heat to low, and cook until beans are tender, about 1½ hours. Season to taste with salt, then set beans aside to cool. Remove and discard ham bone and onion from beans with a slotted spoon (it's all right if some pieces of onion remain).

4. Heat duck fat in a large skillet over medium-high heat. Add sausages and cook, turning to brown on all sides, for about 10 minutes. Put garlic, remaining 1 onion, and ½ cup water in a blender and purée until smooth. Add garlic paste to sausages and reduce heat to medium-low. Cook, turning sausages occasionally, for 10 minutes more.

5. Preheat oven to 350°. Assemble cassoulet in layers: Using a slotted spoon, transfer about half the beans with pork rind to a heavy wide-mouthed 5–6-qt. cast-iron, clay, or earthenware pot. Place the meat from the ham hocks on top of the beans and cover with sausages and garlic paste. Divide duck confit into 8 pieces, then arrange duck on sausages. Spoon in remaining beans with pork rind. Season with nutmeg and add just enough reserved bean cooking liquid to cover the beans (about 3 cups), reserving remaining liquid. Bake, uncovered, until cassoulet comes to a simmer and a crust begins to form, about 1 hour.

6. Reduce heat to 250° and cook for 3 hours, checking every hour or so to make sure cassoulet is barely simmering (a little liquid should be bubbling around edges). If cassoulet appears dry, break crust by gently pushing it down with the back of a spoon, allowing a new layer of beans to rise to the surface. Add just enough reserved bean cooking liquid (or water) to moisten beans.

7. Remove cassoulet from oven. Allow to cool completely, then cover with a lid or aluminum foil and refrigerate overnight.

8. Remove cassoulet from refrigerator and allow to warm to room temperature for at least 45 minutes. Meanwhile, preheat oven to 350°. Bake for 1 hour. When cassoulet begins to simmer, break crust and add enough warm water to just cover beans (about 1 cup). Reduce heat to 250° and bake, breaking crust and adding water as needed, for 3 hours. Remove cassoulet from oven and allow to rest for 15–20 minutes. Serve cassoulet from the pot, breaking the crust at the table.

Confit de Canard

(Duck Confit)

SERVES 6

IN AMERICA, the duck most often eaten is the long island (or white pekin), which is mild in flavor and inexpensive—but not very highly regarded by French chefs. For confit, they (and we) prefer the fatty moulard, a cross between pekin hen and muscovy drake bred for foie gras, often available from specialty butchers (or see page 33).

1 8-lb. moulard duck (see page 33)
4 tbsp. coarse sea salt

1. Preheat oven to 350°. Remove skin and all fat from duck and set duck aside. Cut skin and fat into 1½" x 4" strips. Put in a baking pan and bake until skin is golden and crisp, about 3½ hours. Drain skin on paper towels and use to garnish salads. Strain fat through fine sieve. (Rendered fat can be stored in the freezer for up to 6 months.)

2. Meanwhile, cut duck into 2 legs with thighs attached, 2 wings with tips removed, and 2 breasts. Put duck pieces in a nonreactive pan and sprinkle salt on all sides of the bird. Cover with plastic wrap and refrigerate overnight.

3. The next day, brush away as much salt as possible with a paper towel (some will have dissolved). Melt rendered duck fat in a tall heavy pot over low heat. When fat reaches 200° on a kitchen thermometer, barely simmering, add duck and simmer, completely submerged, until very tender, about 2 hours. Remove pan from heat. Transfer duck and fat to a container, and cover. Make sure that the duck is completely submerged in the fat. Refrigerate; the flavor will improve for a week. Confit will keep for at least a month.

Goodness Preserved

The French culinary term *confit* can apply to foods preserved in different ways—by coating them in sugar syrup (as with, for instance, candied fruit), by bottling them in alcohol (commonly done with cherries and grapes, among other things), by curing them in vinegar (various pickles), and, as in the case of duck and goose (and also pork), by cooking them and then storing them in their own fat. The confit process was known to the ancient Greeks and Romans, and the latter probably introduced it to southwestern France—along with the production of foie gras, which it parallels: When birds are force-fed to fatten their livers, they simultaneously develop an ample layer of subcutaneous fat—and when they are slaughtered for their livers, that same fat is the perfect medium in which to preserve their meat. There's more to the notion of confit than mere preservation, though. Marinating the meat in salt and sometimes other spices (cloves are typical) and then simmering it in its own fat turns it rich and succulent without—believe it or not—making it fatty. Though it is commonly used in cassoulet, incidentally, confit is also eaten by itself as a meat course, often with a salad on the side.

Canard en Croûte d'Herbes et de Sel

(Duck Baked in a Crust of Herbs and Salt)

SERVES 4

ROBERT LALLEMAN, chef at his family's acclaimed Auberge de Noves near Avignon, makes this dish with the famous ducks from the town of Challans, in the Vendée, in western France; muscovy ducks make a good substitute.

3 cups flour
1 ½ cups kosher salt
10 egg whites
Freshly ground black pepper
2 tbsp. finely chopped fresh rosemary
2 tbsp. finely chopped fresh thyme
¼ cup finely chopped fresh cilantro
1 5-lb. muscovy duck (see page 33)
Salt
1 tbsp. olive oil
2 tbsp. white wine vinegar
½ cup dry white wine
1 shallot, peeled and minced
Bouquet garni (see sidebar, page 59) with ½ tsp. coriander seeds added
1 tbsp. acacia honey
½ cup chicken stock (see page 56)
½ cup veal stock (see page 60)

1. Combine flour, salt, egg whites, 2 tbsp. pepper, rosemary, thyme, and cilantro in a large bowl and mix until dough holds together. Turn dough out onto a lightly floured surface and knead until smooth and elastic, about 2 minutes. Form dough into a ball, wrap in plastic, and refrigerate for 30 minutes.

2. Preheat oven to 450°. Prick duck skin all over with a fork. Season inside and out with salt and pepper. Heat oil in a large ovenproof skillet over medium-high heat. Add duck and brown on all sides, turning as it browns, about 15 minutes in all. Put the skillet with the duck in the oven for 15 minutes. Remove duck from pan and set aside to cool.

3. Turn dough out onto a lightly floured surface and roll into a 10" x 14" rectangle. Place cooled duck in center of dough, breast side down, then wrap dough around duck, pinching to seal. Place duck, seam side down, on a baking sheet and bake for 30 minutes. Remove from oven, leaving oven on.

4. Meanwhile, put vinegar, wine, shallots, and bouquet garni into a sauté pan and cook over medium-high heat until reduced by three-quarters, about 7 minutes. Add honey, chicken stock, and veal stock. Cook until sauce is slightly thickened, about 5 minutes more, then strain, season with salt and pepper, and keep warm.

5. To serve, use a sharp knife to cut through dough crust, then peel away and discard. Thinly slice breast meat and arrange on 4 plates. Spoon warm sauce over meat. Cut legs (with thighs) from duck and return them to oven, until skin is crisp, 15–30 minutes. Serve legs as second course.

Cooking for Provence

Robert and Suzanne Lalleman opened the Auberge de Noves, about nine miles southeast of Avignon, in 1955. Their son André, today a charming gentleman with a thick white mustache and a ready smile, took over management of the place in 1972, and now runs it with his wife, Jacqueline. Their son, another Robert, a good-looking, rangy young man who worked at Pic, Troisgros, and Chapel, among other temples of French gastronomy, is now in charge of the kitchen, and the food is confident, sophisticated, and unmistakably Provençal. "All the things I learned in other restaurants," says Robert, "I transformed when I came back here, to use local products and develop stronger flavors. When people eat in Provence, they expect strong flavors. This is not Paris."

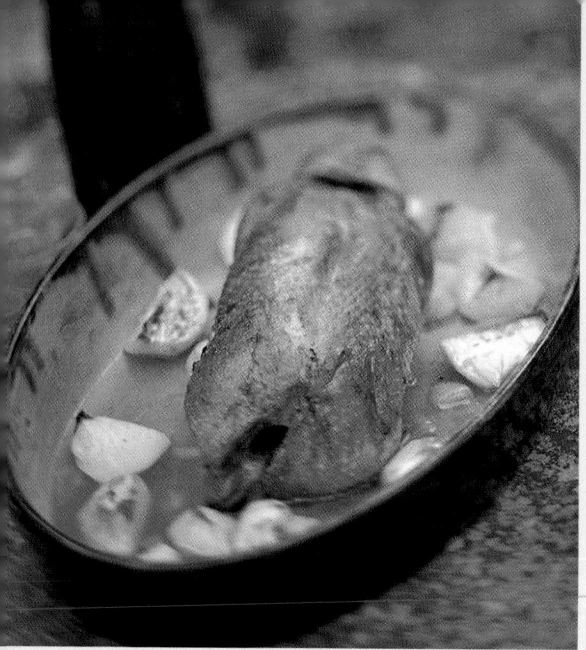

Wine from Apples

To anyone who thinks cider is just apple juice, the handcrafted ciders Eric Bordelet makes at Château de Hauteville, his family's farm in the département of Mayenne, about 150 miles southwest of Paris, are a revelation. (His deluxe cuvée is sold in the U.S. under the name Sydre Argelette.) Cidermaking is thought to have been introduced here from Spain in the 13th century. By the 16th century, orchards had replaced grapevines in the region, and cider began appearing on the best local tables. Louis XIV sometimes even served it instead of champagne. By the 19th century, it had become France's second most popular alcoholic beverage—after wine but ahead of beer. Today, notes Bordelet—who left his job as sommelier at the trendsetting Arpège restaurant in Paris in 1991 to move back to the farm and make cider of his own—"Cider is underestimated because most of it is mass-produced or poorly made. Wine has continued to evolve but cider has stagnated, if not regressed. It will take ten years to restore its nobility." Bordelet may well be the first farmhouse cider producer to have studied winemaking before returning to the farm to make cider. "I'm not there yet," he admits, "but when my ciders are offered at auction at Christie's, I will have arrived."

Canard Rôti au Cidre avec Navets

(Roast Duck with Cider and Turnips)

SERVES 4

CIDERMAKER Eric Bordelet's family (his father and mother, Roger and Claudine Bordelet, are at far right) cooks duck with sweet potatoes in cider sauce, and serves it with more cider. We adapted the recipe to use turnips and a shot of that other great French apple product, calvados.

1 5-lb. muscovy or long island duck (see page 33), fat trimmed
Salt and freshly ground black pepper
5 shallots, peeled
5 cloves garlic, crushed and peeled
1 tbsp. butter, softened
2 tbsp. calvados
2 lbs. turnips, peeled and quartered
1 ¼ cups Sydre Argelette or other good-quality French hard cider
1 cup chicken stock (see page 56)

1. Preheat oven to 400°. Season cavity of duck with salt and pepper. Stuff duck with shallots and garlic and truss with kitchen string. Rub with butter, season with salt and pepper, and place duck, breast side down, on a rack in a medium roasting pan.

2. Pour calvados over duck and put turnips in pan around it. Roast duck, basting frequently, for 20 minutes, then turn duck breast side up and continue roasting until juices run clear, about 30 minutes more. Remove duck from oven, transfer to a serving platter and set aside to rest for 15 minutes. Return pan to oven and continue cooking turnips until tender, about 10 minutes more.

3. Arrange turnips around duck. Pour any accumulated juices from duck's cavity into roasting pan and bring to a boil over medium-high heat on top of the stove. Skim fat from pan juices, add cider, and simmer, stirring constantly until pan is almost dry, about 10 minutes. Reduce heat to medium, add stock, season with salt and pepper, and cook for 3–5 minutes more. Carve duck, and serve with turnips and pan juices.

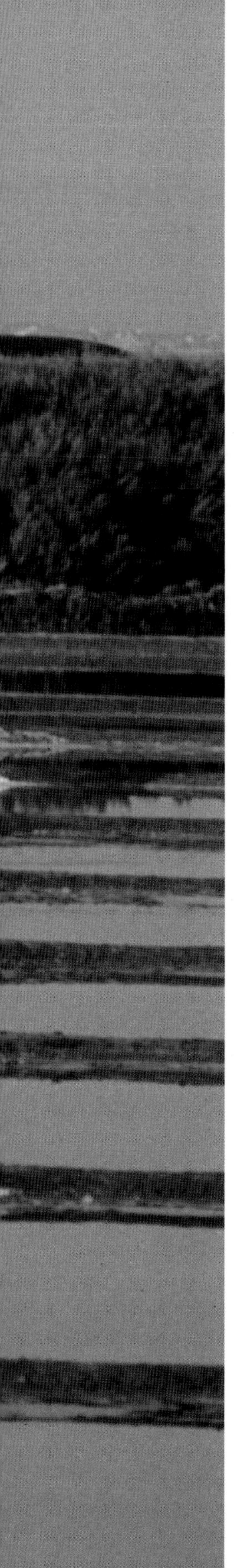

Magret de Canard à la Cheminée

(Duck Breast Cooked on the Coals)

SERVES 4

IT IS NOT UNCOMMON to find Jean-Pierre Xiradakis (see page 273) cooking magret in the hearth—the oversize fireplace—at his La Tupiña in Bordeaux. "For centuries," he explains, "the hearth was the heart of the home." A magret is the lean breast of a fat duck, which in France is usually a moulard or muscovy that has been fattened for foie gras.

2 1-lb. moulard duck breast halves (see page 33)
Sel de Guérande (see sidebar, right)
Freshly ground black pepper

1. Light wood or charcoal in a barbecue and wait until the fire dies down and the coals are uniformly glowing and hot. Trim skin (with fat attached) from duck breasts, leaving a lengthwise strip about ½" wide across the middle of each.

2. Put duck breasts on grill, skin side down, and grill until brown, about 3 minutes. Turn and cook on the other side until brown, about 2 minutes. (Duck breasts should be crisp on the outside and rare in the middle, like a steak.)

3. Transfer duck breasts to a cutting board and set aside to rest for 5 minutes, then slice thinly, and arrange on a warm serving platter. Season generously with sel de Guérande and pepper.

Salient Thoughts

Sel de Guérande, one of the most respected of French condiments, is nothing more than gray sea salt from a small peninsula on the Brittany coast. It is swept by the movement of the tides into a series of natural pools, stretching across 5,000 acres, and then harvested manually, from mid-June to mid-September, by *paludiers*, or salt-marsh farmers (facing page). They gather two types of salt: coarse, darkish gros sel, detached from pool bottoms with long wooden rakes; and fleur de sel, or flower of salt, snowy flakes that float to the water's surface. The latter is the caviar of salt, usually sprinkled over finished dishes, not used for cooking. Both kinds are high in magnesium and potassium—but contain less sodium than other salts—and are available here in the U.S.

Poussin Vallée d'Auge

(Baby Chicken with Calvados and Cream)

Serves 6

From the Vallée d'Auge in Normandy comes the famed apple brandy called calvados (see page 225). This simple, classic, calvados-flavored Norman preparation can be adapted to larger chickens, other fowl, and pork.

6 poussins or cornish hens
Salt and freshly ground black pepper
4 tbsp. unsalted butter, softened
2 cups pearl onions
½ cup calvados
¾ cup heavy cream

1. Preheat oven to 400°. Rub poussins inside and out, generously, with salt and pepper.

2. To truss poussins, fold wing tips back beneath shoulders (drumsticks should fit snugly against the tip of breastbone) and hold in place by tying legs together with kitchen string.

3. Rub birds with butter and arrange in a roasting pan so they do not touch. Scatter unpeeled onions around birds, then place pan in lower third of oven and cook for at least 45 minutes, basting several times. Prick fat part of drumstick on 1 bird after 45 minutes; if juice runs clear the birds are done.

4. Transfer poussins and onions to a serving platter. Place the roasting pan on top of the stove and bring the pan drippings to a boil over medium-high heat, scraping with a wooden spoon to loosen any browned bits stuck to the bottom of the pan. Warm calvados in a small pot, then add to pan juices, and carefully ignite with a kitchen match, keeping a large pan lid nearby to extinguish flames if necessary. When flames die out, stir in cream, and continue to reduce sauce until thickened, about 5 minutes. Adjust seasonings as needed. Untie string and discard. Pour sauce over and around poussins.

Bird Talk

In France, where chickens are classified according to weight, method of rearing, and age at slaughter, a poussin is a chicken that is killed at an age of about four weeks, and weighs about a pound. It has delicately flavored flesh and is ideal for broiling, grilling, or roasting. (Longer cooking methods, like stewing, tend to turn poussins dry and stringy.) Poussins are now available in the U.S., but if you can't find them, the best substitute would be the small North American rock Cornish game hen—bred from the Plymouth rock hen and the white Cornish game cock. It is killed slightly later than the poussin, and is larger than that bird, both because of its age and because of its accelerated feeding program. It can weigh up to two pounds, and cooking time must be adjusted accordingly.

Coq au Vin

(Rooster in Red Wine Sauce)

Serves 6

Coq au vin isn't chicken cooked in cheap red wine; it's rooster cooked in something good enough to drink. But it is hard to find even in France today, and all but impossible in the U.S. (unless you know a poultry farmer); a roasting chicken or a large capon is the best substitute.

1 6-lb. roasting chicken, capon, or rooster, cut into 10 pieces
2 large yellow onions, peeled and chopped
3 shallots, peeled and chopped
2 large carrots, peeled and chopped
3 large cloves garlic, peeled
Bouquet garni (see sidebar, page 59)
1 ½ bottles good, rich red burgundy or California pinot noir
Salt and freshly ground black pepper
¼ cup vegetable oil
2 tbsp. flour
¼ cup good cognac
1 ½ tbsp. unsweetened cocoa powder
6 oz. salt pork, diced
¾ lb. small white mushrooms, stems trimmed and caps peeled

1. Put chicken, onions, shallots, carrots, garlic, and bouquet garni in a large bowl and add wine. Mix all the ingredients together with your hands, then cover bowl with plastic wrap and refrigerate for 24 hours.

2. Remove chicken from marinade, reserving marinade, and dry well on paper towels. Season to taste with salt and pepper. Heat oil in a large heavy pan over medium-high heat. Working in batches to avoid crowding pan, add chicken and brown on all sides, turning as pieces brown, about 15 minutes in all. Remove pieces as done and set aside. Add flour to the pan and cook, stirring constantly for 2 minutes. Return chicken to pan and add cognac. Remove pan from heat and carefully ignite cognac with a kitchen match, keeping pan lid nearby to extinguish flames if necessary. Return pan to stove top, add marinade, and bring to a boil over high heat, scraping up browned bits from bottom of pan. Reduce heat to low and simmer, partially covered, until chicken is tender, about 1½ hours.

3. Remove chicken from pan and set aside. Strain sauce through a sieve, discard solids, and return sauce to pan. Put cocoa in a small mixing bowl and whisk in ½ cup of strained sauce, whisking until smooth. Stir cocoa mixture into pan, then reduce sauce over medium heat to about 4 cups, 15–20 minutes. Reduce heat to low and return chicken to pan.

4. Meanwhile, sauté salt pork in a skillet over medium heat until crisp, about 10 minutes, then remove from skillet with a slotted spoon and add to chicken. Add mushrooms to the same skillet and sauté in salt pork fat until golden, about 10 minutes. Drain and add mushrooms to chicken, stirring them in gently. Serve finished dish with croutons (rounds of lightly toasted French bread) if you like.

Patriotic Chicken

The squawks are varied, loud, and constant at the Monday poultry market in Louhans, in southern Burgundy (above)—where fowl of every sort, from gawky geese to tiny pigeons, are offered for sale. The stars of the market are the famed poulets de Bresse, a unique breed of chicken, grain-fattened in the region. Acclaimed by gastronomes since the mid-19th century, these birds are considered a quintessential symbol of la cuisine française—not least because their blue feet, white feathers, and red wattles echo the colors of the French flag.

Celestial Carrots

"One afternoon not long ago in Burgundy, I bit into a carrot. It was tiny and neatly beveled, lightly steamed and glazed in butter...[and] I thought for a moment that it was perhaps the most perfect thing I had ever tasted...." SAVEUR editor Colman Andrews wrote those words 16 years ago, in an article about an unassuming country inn called l'Hostellerie du Vieux Moulin, in the hamlet of Bouilland, near the Burgundian wine capital of Beaune. The proprietors were Jean-Pierre and Isabelle Silva, a young couple then in the process of developing a style of food and service (and a wine list) that would eventually make their establishment an essential stop on any gastronomic tour of Burgundy. At the time, Jean-Pierre (facing page, at the market in Chalon-sur-Saône, and above, left foreground, enjoying a market breakfast with friends and colleagues, including three-star chef Jacques Lameloise, in red sweater) cooked in a relatively straightforward, then-inescapably "nouvelle" way. Over the years, his style grew both more sophisticated and more demonstrably expressive of the region—even when it took off on such flights of fancy as cannelloni stuffed with shredded coq au vin; sweetwater pike perch in vinegar sauce with lentils cooked in veal reduction (a particularly successful example of Burgundian-rustic lily-gilding); and roast lamb from a nearby farm with a bouquet of exquisite, simply cooked local vegetables—perfect carrots assuredly among them.

Pâtes Farcies de Coq au Vin

(Coq au Vin "Cannelloni")

SERVES 4

THIS ITALIAN-accented specialty of Bouilland's Hostellerie du Vieux Moulin is a delicious illustration of the way chef Jean-Pierre Silva reinterprets Burgundian traditions.

4 cups leftover coq au vin (see recipe, previous page) with sauce, meat shredded and bones removed and discarded
4 carrots, peeled and finely chopped
1 large yellow onion, peeled and finely chopped
12 pasta sheets, 4" square
Salt
1 cup shelled fresh peas
2 cups chicken stock (see page 56)
2 tbsp. heavy cream
6 tbsp. butter, cut into pieces
1 tsp. minced fresh rosemary
Fresh rosemary sprigs for garnish

1. Combine coq au vin (with sauce), carrots, onions, and 1 cup water in a heavy pot. Cook over medium heat until sauce has reduced and thickened, about 30 minutes.

2. Cook pasta in a large pot of boiling salted water over high heat until tender, about 8 minutes. Drain on a kitchen towel. Divide coq au vin mixture between pasta sheets, roll up, arrange on a platter, cover, and keep warm.

3. Meanwhile, cook peas in a medium pot of boiling salted water until just cooked, about 4 minutes. Drain and set aside.

4. Combine stock, cream, butter, and minced rosemary in a small pot and bring to a boil over medium heat. Cook, whisking constantly, until slightly thickened. Pour over pasta. Garnish with rosemary sprigs and peas.

Volaille Fermière au Vinaigre

(Farmhouse Chicken in Vinegar Sauce)

Serves 4

Philippe Gaertner, chef—like his father and grandfather before him—at the respected Aux Armes de France in the Alsatian town of Ammerschwihr, prefers to make this classic dish with the local honey-perfumed melfor vinegar. In the absence of this strictly regional product, he recommends using cider vinegar sweetened with a bit of honey.

- *1 3½-lb. chicken, cut into 8 pieces*
- *Salt and freshly ground black pepper*
- *2 tbsp. olive oil*
- *6 tbsp. butter*
- *8 cloves garlic, peeled and minced*
- *4 shallots, peeled and minced*
- *½ cup cider vinegar*
- *1 cup Alsatian riesling or other dry but fruity white wine*
- *1 tbsp. honey*
- *1 tbsp. tomato paste*
- *1 cup chicken stock (see page 56)*
- *1 tbsp. finely chopped fresh parsley*

1. Rinse chicken, pat dry, and season to taste with salt and pepper. Heat oil and 2 tbsp. of the butter in a large skillet over medium-high heat. Working in batches to avoid crowding pan, add chicken and brown on all sides, turning as pieces brown, for about 15 minutes in all. Remove pieces as done and set aside. When all chicken has browned, pour off most of the fat from the skillet, leaving just enough to thinly coat it.

2. Reduce heat to medium, add garlic and shallots, and cook, stirring frequently, until slightly soft, about 5 minutes. Deglaze skillet with vinegar and wine, add honey and scrape browned bits off bottom with a wooden spoon. Reduce by about one-third, 3–5 minutes, then stir in tomato paste. Return chicken to skillet, pour in stock, and simmer for 10–15 minutes. Turn chicken and continue cooking until juices from chicken run clear, about 15 minutes.

3. Remove chicken from skillet and set aside. Increase heat to medium-high, and continue cooking until sauce is thick and glossy, about 5 minutes. Cut remaining 4 tbsp. butter into small pieces. Remove skillet from heat and whisk butter into sauce. Adjust seasonings. (Sauce should be smooth but tart; add additional vinegar if you like.) Return chicken to skillet, turning to coat evenly with sauce and serve, sprinkled with parsley.

Vins d'Alsace

The hilly vineyards of Alsace (facing page) produce some of France's best white wine—fragrant, flavorful dry riesling and gewürztraminer most notably, but also muscat, pinot gris, sylvaner, and pinot blanc (as well as a bit of light red wine from pinot noir). Very good sweeter wines, labeled vendange tardive or sélection de grains nobles, are also made. Granted appellation contrôlée status only in 1962, Alsatian wines are labeled not according to subregion, but by grape variety—which made them immediately attractive to American consumers, used to the varietal labeling of California wines. Look for the wines of Trimbach and Hugel or, for a real treat, those of Domaine Weinbach, Zind-Humbrecht, or Gustave Lorentz.

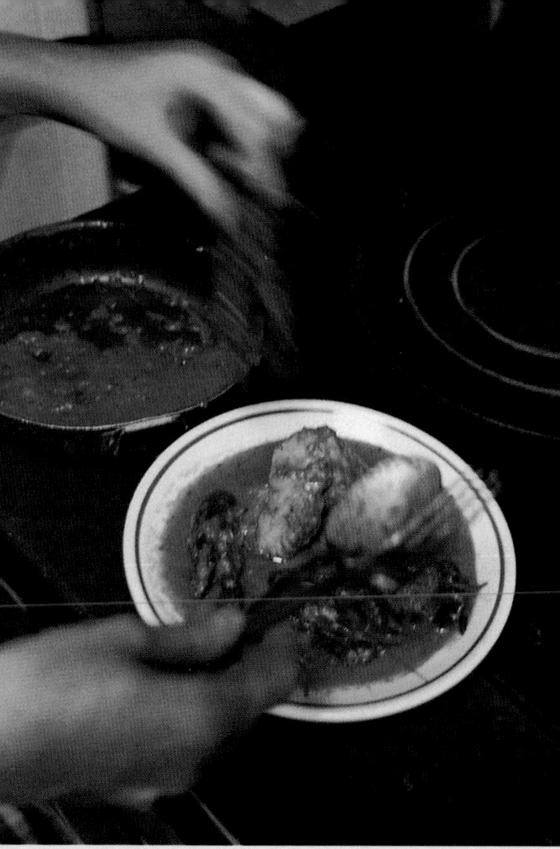

Mixed Metaphors

Students of the American psyche might well speculate on the impulse behind the creation of that much-(and justly) maligned American/Continental restaurant classic called surf and turf—which is usually steak and lobster on the same plate. Was it an expression of plenty? A way of showing off? A misguided attempt to make a really great dish by combining a couple of very good ones? The underlying principle behind poulet aux écrevisses, a specialty of the French département of the Rhône-Alpes, is clearer: The best chickens in France come from the nearby plains of Bresse (see page 185), and crayfish thrive in the Alpine streams to the east of Lyon, and especially around the town of Nantua. What could be more logical than to marry these two regional treasures? It is a French tradition, after all, to let local ingredients inspire the creation of local dishes.

Poulet aux Écrevisses

(Chicken with Crayfish)

SERVES 4

LIVE CRAYFISH (see page 65), sometimes available from specialty seafood markets, are best for this dish. If you can't find them, use frozen precooked whole crayfish instead.

FOR SAUCE:
3 tbsp. olive oil
1 ¼ lbs. live or defrosted frozen crayfish, rinsed
2 tbsp. cognac
2 yellow onions, peeled and chopped
3 shallots, peeled and minced
2 carrots, peeled and chopped
4 medium tomatoes, peeled
1 tbsp. tomato paste
3 sprigs fresh thyme
1 sprig fresh tarragon
3 bay leaves
2 cups dry white wine
¾ cup heavy cream
Salt and freshly ground black pepper
Fresh parsley sprigs for garnish

FOR CHICKEN:
1 4-lb. chicken, cut into 8 pieces
Salt and freshly ground black pepper
3 tbsp. olive oil

1. For sauce, heat oil in a large skillet over medium-high heat. Add crayfish and cook, stirring, for 5 minutes (2 minutes if using precooked crayfish). Remove skillet from heat, add cognac, and carefully ignite with a kitchen match, keeping skillet lid nearby to extinguish flames if necessary. Return pan to heat and cook until flames die out.

2. For chicken, preheat oven to 350°. While sauce cooks, season chicken with salt and pepper. Heat oil in a large ovenproof skillet over medium heat. Working in batches to avoid crowding pan, add chicken and brown on all sides, turning as pieces brown, about 15 minutes in all. Remove pieces as done and set aside. Return chicken pieces to skillet and put in oven. Cook until juices run clear, about 20 minutes more. Turn off oven, transfer chicken to a large platter and cover with aluminum foil. Return chicken to oven to keep warm.

3. Remove one-third of crayfish from skillet and set aside. Reduce heat to medium, add onions, shallots, and carrots, and cook until soft, 20 minutes. Add tomatoes, tomato paste, thyme, tarragon, bay leaves, and wine. Cook for 10 minutes, then add cream and simmer, stirring occasionally, until sauce thickens, about 30 minutes. Strain through a fine sieve, season sauce with salt and pepper to taste, then spoon over chicken. Add reserved crayfish and garnish with parsley.

Chapon Farci Rôti

(Roast Capon with Stuffing)

Serves 4

When meaty force-fed capons aren't in season—they're a year-end specialty in France—Jean-Pierre Xiradakis uses chicken instead for this dish at his La Tupiña in Bordeaux.

1 6–7-lb. capon
Olive oil
Salt and freshly ground black pepper
1 loaf country-style white bread
1 head garlic, cloves separated, peeled and slightly crushed
1 tbsp. butter
1 medium yellow onion, peeled and chopped
2 shallots, peeled and chopped
6 oz. mushrooms, trimmed and chopped
1 ½ lbs. pork sausages, removed from casings
1 carrot, peeled and chopped
1 turnip, peeled and chopped

1. Preheat oven to 400°. Rinse capon, pat dry with paper towels inside and out, rub all over with 1–2 tbsp. oil, then generously season with salt and pepper and set aside. Slice bread into thick slices. Rub both sides of one of the crusty heels of the bread with 1 garlic clove, then discard garlic. Brush bread generously with oil, then stuff into the bird's cavity. Arrange the rest of the bread in a shallow roasting pan and scatter remaining cloves of garlic on top of bread.

2. Put capon, breast side down, directly on an oven rack set in the middle of the oven. Set the roasting pan with the bread on a rack under the capon so that the fat and juices will drip onto the bread. After 15 minutes pour 2 cups of water over bread. Add another 2 cups water after 15 minutes more. After 40 minutes turn capon breast side up. Roast until the skin turns crisp and golden, about 35 minutes more.

3. Meanwhile, melt butter in a large skillet over medium-high heat. Add onions and shallots and cook for 2 minutes. Add mushrooms and cook until they release their juices, about 5 minutes. Stir in sausage meat, carrots, and turnips and reduce heat to medium-low. Stir occasionally with a wooden spoon, breaking up and crumbling sausage meat. Reduce heat to low and cook until vegetables caramelize slightly, about 30 minutes.

4. When capon is done, remove from oven and allow to rest for 10–15 minutes. Spoon about ¼ cup of the pan juices into the meat and vegetables. Carve the capon and serve with the stuffing and the roasted bread.

An Edible Heritage

Jean-Pierre Xiradakis, chef-owner of the celebrated La Tupiña restaurant in Bordeaux, was brought up in the southwest of France, eating and loving its exceptional culinary raw materials. But as long ago as the 1960s, he began to worry that they were disappearing. Local farmers were increasingly mass producing for agro-industry, trucking their goods to warehouses instead of to the open-air markets of Xiradakis's childhood. Game animals were getting crowded out of their environment; migrant herdsmen, whose flocks once fertilized and weeded the fields, were becoming an endangered species. "Restaurateurs have an obligation to defend the traditions of their region," declares Xiradakis—which is why, for 30 years, he has combed the region, talking, tasting, and encouraging. In the 1970s, when France fell in love with nouvelle cuisine, Xiradakis's quest for authentic regional ingredients grew into a genuine fear for the culinary heritage. "When nouvelle cuisine took off," he says, "my God, I thought no one was going to care anymore about the real cuisine." Xiradakis started looking for products that had vanished, like the beef of Bazas, the capon of Landes, and the lamb of Pauillac, all of which he claims credit for rejuvenating. "It's imperative," he proclaims, "that we don't forget our heritage!"

Under Pressure

Every French housewife, it has been said, owns a *cocotte-minute*—a pressure cooker. Widely (and unfairly) distrusted in America, this kitchen appliance, in fact, was invented in France. It traces its origins to Denis Papin, a physicist from Blois, who, in 1675, built a machine "for softening bones and cooking meat". For some time afterward, small-scale manufacturers in France and elsewhere produced various models of the contraption (like the 19th-century example, probably French, on the facing page)—all of which had one flaw in common: Their pressure valves tended to stick, which caused the pot to explode. It was not until 1953 that the Burgundy-based Société d'Emboutissage de Bourgogne was able to solve this problem by installing a stirrup-shaped handle on the lid, which slotted under two ear-shaped side pieces. The handle was turned to seal the pot—but if the valve stuck, pressure inside the vessel would force the handle to turn, allowing steam to escape through the sides. Today, SEB is one of the world leaders in home cooking equipment, selling its wares under the SEB, Tefal, Calor, and Rowenta brands.

Pintade au Chou

(Guinea Hen with Cabbage)

SERVES 4

WHEN MARIELLE GRIVOT prepares this dish for her husband, Étienne, and their children (he helps run the family's wine estates, one of Burgundy's best), she often serves it with potatoes freshly dug from the garden.

1 2½–3-lb. guinea hen
Salt and freshly ground black pepper
2 tbsp. vegetable oil
8 oz. lean salt pork, diced
2 medium yellow onions, peeled and finely chopped
2 tbsp. butter
2 carrots, peeled and sliced into thin rounds
12 new potatoes
1 medium savoy cabbage, quartered, cored, and cut into ¼"-wide strips
1 12-oz. bottle of lager-style beer

1. Rub guinea hen inside and out with salt and pepper, then tie legs together with kitchen string.

2. Heat 1 tbsp. of the oil in the bottom of a pressure cooker over medium heat, add salt pork, and sauté until brown and crisp, about 10 minutes. Remove salt pork with a slotted spoon and set aside. Sauté onions in salt pork fat until soft, about 20 minutes. Remove with slotted spoon and set aside.

3. Add butter and remaining 1 tbsp. oil to pressure cooker. Add hen and brown all over, turning several times, for about 20 minutes. Season to taste with salt and pepper, then add salt pork, onions, carrots, potatoes, and cabbage. Pour beer over hen and vegetables. Place lid on pressure cooker, close tightly, and process according to manufacturer's instructions at a pressure of 10 lbs. or on high for 20 minutes. Remove from heat, let stand for 5 minutes, and carefully open cover.

Monsieur Mustard

There's probably not a brasserie or bistro in France that doesn't have a jar of mustard on the table—and chances are that it comes from the Burgundian capital of Dijon. The Romans brought mustard seeds to the region, and by the Middle Ages, the bright yellow blossoms of mustard plants (right) could be seen covering local hills each spring. As early as the 14th century, local ordinances in Dijon laid out rules for the manufacture of mustard, more or less as we know it; one specified the use of only "good mustard seed soaked in good vinegar". By 1634, an official alliance had been formed in Dijon to regulate the profession of the moutardier. Dijon mustard is creamy and spicier than the old-style, coarse-grained mild mustard often referred to in French as *à l'ancienne.* Like the wines of Burgundy, it is protected by an appellation contrôlée, granted in 1937—and like the wines of Burgundy, it is both definitive of the region and appreciated the world around.

Lapin à la Moutarde

(Rabbit with Mustard Sauce)

SERVES 4–6

RABBIT COOKED with mustard is a classic French grandmother's dish. This version is from Parisian-born grandmother Viviane Lago, long a resident of Rouen, who learned it from her own *grandmère*. Like her, she adds, "I cook with my heart, not my hands." (Rabbit isn't poultry, strictly speaking, but is sold in poultry shops in France and cooked similarly.)

1 large rabbit (3–4 lbs.), cut into 6–8 serving pieces
½ cup dijon mustard
Salt and freshly ground black pepper
2 tbsp. unsalted butter
1 small yellow onion, peeled and finely chopped
½ cup French chablis or other dry white wine
Bouquet garni (see sidebar, page 59)
⅓ cup crème fraîche
2 tbsp. finely chopped fresh parsley

1. Smear rabbit pieces all over with mustard, and season generously with salt and pepper.

2. Heat butter in a large skillet over medium-high heat. Add onions and cook until soft, about 10 minutes. Add rabbit pieces and cook, turning frequently, until rabbit is golden brown, about 15 minutes. Transfer to a platter.

3. Add wine to skillet and scrape up any browned bits from the bottom of the pan with a wooden spoon. Reduce heat to medium and return rabbit pieces to the skillet, along with bouquet garni. Cover and cook until rabbit is tender, about 35 minutes.

4. Remove skillet from heat. Discard bouquet garni and stir in crème fraîche. Garnish with parsley.

The Red and the Black

The Romans introduced winemaking to the region of Cahors—a handsome medieval walled town on the Lot River in Quercy, in southwestern France—and Caesar reportedly exported its "black" red wine to Rome. In medieval times, the reputation of cahors spread across Europe; its biggest promoter was Pope John XXII, the former bishop of Cahors, who made it the communion wine when he became the second Avignon pope during the 14th-century schism with the Vatican. Cahors gets its intensity and dark color mostly from the sturdy malbec grape (though some tannat and an increasing measure of merlot is also used), and from the dry limestone soils that predominate in the region's vineyards—which encourage the retention of heat and moisture. In the Middle Ages, when the wines of Bordeaux were a literally paler version of their current selves, cahors was often blended in to lend body and color. By the 18th century, though, bordeaux's fame had eclipsed that of cahors—and around 1880, the vine pest phylloxera wiped out the region's vineyards. Cahors began rebuilding its wine industry after World War II (the fact that the town doctor, Bernard Pons, was appointed minister of agriculture in the early '70s—and promptly got Cahors its own appellation contrôlée—didn't hurt), and today cahors has become something approaching fine wine.

Civet de Lapin

(Rich Rabbit Stew)

Serves 6

Jean-Louis Palladin, chef at Napa in the Rio Hotel Las Vegas and at his own new Palladin in New York City, grew up and began cooking not far from Cahors. He created this variation on a classic dish for SAVEUR.

4 tbsp. butter
3 tbsp. olive oil
2 2½-lb. rabbits, each cut into 6 pieces, with hearts, kidneys, and livers reserved
Salt and freshly ground black pepper
1 medium yellow onion, peeled and finely chopped
4 cloves garlic, peeled and minced
1 leek (white part only), washed and chopped
2 carrots, peeled and chopped
1 turnip, peeled and chopped
2 celery stalks, chopped
3 sprigs fresh rosemary
6 sprigs fresh thyme
1 bay leaf
3 ⅓ cups cahors or other rich, dry red wine
4 cups chicken stock (see page 56)
1 lb. pearl onions, blanched and peeled
1 tbsp. sugar
¼ lb. pancetta, julienned
1 lb. small white mushrooms

1. Melt 2 tbsp. butter and 2 tbsp. oil in a large, deep skillet over medium-high heat. Season rabbit with salt and pepper, then, working in batches to avoid crowding pan, add to skillet and brown for about 3 minutes on each side. Remove pieces and set aside. Reduce heat to medium, add chopped onions and garlic, and cook until slightly softened, about 5 minutes.

2. Add leeks, carrots, turnips, celery, rosemary, thyme, and bay leaf to pan. Cook, stirring occasionally until vegetables begin to brown, 7–10 minutes. Add wine and cook until reduced by two-thirds, about 30 minutes. Add stock and rabbit, reduce heat to medium-low, cover, and cook for 25 minutes more.

3. Remove rabbit from skillet with a slotted spoon and set aside. Increase heat to medium-high and simmer, skimming occasionally, until liquid is reduced by half, about 15 minutes. Add hearts, kidneys, and livers. Simmer until firm to the touch, about 5 minutes, then transfer to a food processor with a slotted spoon. Strain cooking liquid into food processor (discard vegetables and herbs) and purée until smooth. Season sauce with salt and pepper and set aside.

4. Wipe out skillet, then add pearl onions, sugar, remaining 2 tbsp. butter, and 1 cup water. Bring to a boil over high heat, reduce heat to medium, and simmer until most of the liquid evaporates, about 15 minutes. Stir to coat onions in syrup, and continue to cook, stirring, until onions begin to caramelize, 3–5 minutes. Heat remaining 1 tbsp. oil in another skillet over medium heat, add pancetta, and cook until crisp, about 8 minutes. Remove with a slotted spoon and drain on paper towels. Increase heat to medium-high, add mushrooms, and sauté until golden, about 5 minutes.

5. To assemble, pour sauce through a fine sieve into large skillet. Add rabbit and warm over medium heat. Add pearl onions, pancetta, and mushrooms and heat through.

CHAPTER

8

MEATS

"YOU SEE THEM all over Burgundy—sturdy, impassive, off-white cattle, browsing in the fields and pastures. These are the charolais, which yield the finest beef in France. The breed is thought to have prehistoric origins, but in its present form was probably developed in the 18th century, around the town of Charolles, not far from Mâcon in southeastern Burgundy. The full-flavored, well-marbled, famously tender meat of the charolais was first shipped to the markets of Paris in 1747, and by the late 19th century it had earned its reputation as the most prized of all meats sold in Parisian boucheries. Though charolais cattle are now seen all over France—and, increasingly, in other countries as well (even the U.S.; the rangeland of Texas, and the Midwest, is crowded with them)—they remain emblematic of Burgundy. As much as the region's immense plantings of sunflowers and rapeseed, its fecund orchards, its patchwork grids of market gardens full of vegetables and herbs, its lush meadows accented with trees (said to be the model for the formal gardens of the region's great estates)—as much even as its world-famous vineyards—the charolais are an integral part of the Burgundian landscape. They are mythic animals, edible symbols of a way of life. Anyone who seeks to understand why Burgundy produces so much hearty, honest cooking, and why that cooking is linked so intimately to the earth, would do well to stop and appreciate, visually as well as gastronomically, these mighty beasts." —COLMAN ANDREWS

RECIPES

1995
Mercurey
PREMIER CRU
"Les Champs Martin"
CHATEAU

Boeuf à la Bourguignonne

(Beef Stew Burgundy-Style)

Serves 4–6

When we asked Burgundian chef Marc Meneau, of the estimable l'Espérance in St-Père-sous-Vézelay, where we could find simple, classic Burgundian cooking, he sent us down to the little town of Planchez, in the southwestern reaches of the Morvan, Burgundy's most rural region, to sample boeuf à la bourguignonne as made by Millette Coquillon at her popular Chez Millette. This is her recipe.

3 lbs. beef chuck, cut into large pieces
1 large yellow onion, peeled and finely chopped
2 carrots, peeled and finely chopped
2 cloves garlic, peeled
Bouquet garni (see sidebar, page 59)
1 bottle good, rich red burgundy or California pinot noir
6 oz. lean salt pork, diced
Salt and freshly ground black pepper
1/3 cup flour
1 lb. small white mushrooms, stems trimmed and caps peeled

1. Put beef, onions, carrots, garlic, and bouquet garni into a large bowl and add wine. Using your hands, mix all the ingredients together, then cover bowl with plastic wrap and refrigerate for 24 hours.

2. Remove beef from marinade, reserving marinade, and dry meat well on paper towels. Fry salt pork in a large pot over medium heat until crisp, about 7 minutes. Season beef with salt and pepper to taste. Add to pot and brown on all sides, about 7 minutes. Sprinkle in flour, and cook, stirring constantly, for 3 minutes. Add marinade and 2 cups water and bring to a boil over high heat, scraping up browned bits from bottom of pan with a wooden spoon. Reduce heat to low, cover, and cook until meat is tender, about 3 hours. Add mushrooms and cook for 30 minutes more. Remove bouquet garni before serving.

Rural Soul

The Morvan is a mountainous region defined by a distinct topography—an ecology, if you will. It isn't one of the four départements that compose Burgundy, but occupies corners of all of them—lying mostly in the Nièvre, spilling over into the Yonne, the Côte-d'Or, and the Saône-et-Loire. The Morvan is wild Burgundy, repository of the region's rural soul. The terrain can be mountainous, and the Morvan is recognizable even from a distance, as the Michelin guide notes, "by its vast and sombre forests". Much of the region, in fact, is designated as a nature park by the French government. There are no vineyards to speak of; the autoroute seems a world away, and roads run past not vast panoramas of open farmland, but small fields divided by hedgerows. The physical characteristics of the Morvan have shaped the personality of its inhabitants, who are known for being tough and self-reliant. They have also shaped local eating habits: This is the domain of pork, wild mushrooms, snails, and honey. It is also the place to eat big, hearty, winter-beating dishes like boeuf à la bourguignonne—as prepared, for instance, by Millette Coquillon and her daughter Giselle Morin (below, from left) at their Chez Millette in the Morvan village of Planchez.

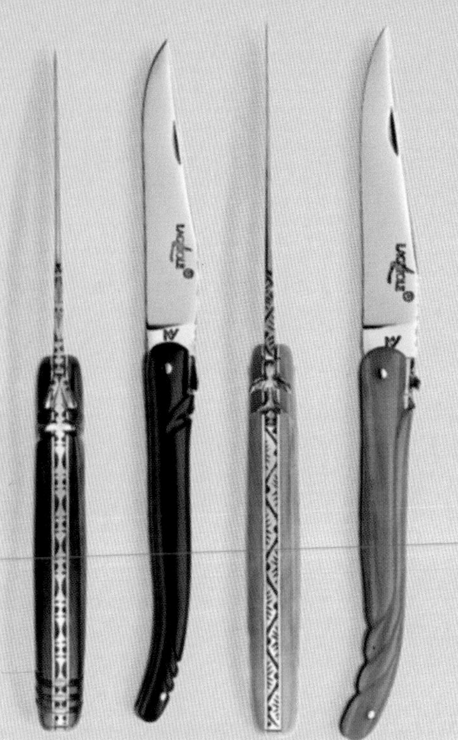

Pointed Elegance

The small French mountain town of Laguiole (pronounced "lie-yole"), about 350 miles south of Paris, is famous for its cattle, its cheese, and above all its cutlery. The Laguiole knife exists in numerous forms. The original, dating from the early 19th century, was a farmer's tool, sometimes with a corkscrew and an awl set into the handle. A refinement is the Laguiole steak knife (above)—common today, among other places, on the tables at French three-star restaurants, where it is the meat-cutting tool of choice. The knife's form is elegance itself, with a gently curving blade, an elongated pistol-grip handle, and a small stylized bee or fly (no one is quite sure which, or why) set into the bolster. Put them together and you've got a knife that bears as much resemblance to the usual chophouse slicer as a Baccarat goblet to a souvenir-shop coffee mug.

Filet de Boeuf au Vin de Marcillac

(Filet of Beef with Marcillac Wine Sauce)

SERVES 4

MARCILLAC IS A SMALL, isolated wine region in France's Massif Central, producing spicy, aromatic reds (and a few rosés) based on a grape called mansois. Other full-bodied French red wines may be substituted. This recipe comes from the Grand Hôtel Auguy, on Laguiole's main square.

Olive oil
2 medium carrots, peeled and chopped
2 stalks celery, chopped
1 small yellow onion, peeled and chopped
3 tbsp. cognac
1 cup red wine vinegar
3 cups marcillac, cahors, or other hearty red wine
3 cups veal stock (see page 60)
Cracked black pepper
4 6-oz. beef filets, each about 1 ½" thick
Coarse salt
2 tbsp. cold butter, cubed

1. Heat 1 tbsp. oil in a heavy pot over medium heat. Add carrots, celery, and onions, and sauté until browned, about 5 minutes. Add cognac and carefully ignite with a kitchen match, keeping pot lid nearby to extinguish flames if necessary. When flames die out, add vinegar, wine, veal stock, and 1 tbsp. pepper. Reduce heat to low and cook until sauce is reduced by three-quarters, about 1½ hours. Strain, discard solids, and set sauce aside.

2. Season filets to taste with salt. Heat 1 tbsp. oil in a heavy skillet over high heat until hot but not smoking. Add filets and cook for 7 minutes on each side, then transfer to 4 plates. Reduce heat to medium, add sauce to skillet, whisk in butter, then spoon sauce over filets.

Daube de Boeuf

(Beef Braised in Red Wine)

SERVES 4

DAUBE MIGHT be called a more rustic cousin of boeuf à la bourguignonne, typically made with heartier red wine and perfumed with earthy dried cèpes (porcini mushrooms). In Nice, it is usually served with plain buttered noodles or polenta. This is an adaptation of Franck Cerutti's recipe.

½ oz. dried porcini mushrooms
2 lbs. beef chuck, cut into 2" pieces
Salt
1 tbsp. butter
1 tbsp. olive oil
1 medium yellow onion, peeled and diced
2 medium carrots, peeled and diced
2 cloves garlic, peeled and chopped
2 large plum tomatoes, peeled, seeded, and roughly chopped
1 stalk celery, diced
Bouquet garni (see sidebar, page 59)
1 tbsp. flour
2 cups red côtes-de-provence or other dry, hearty red wine
Freshly ground black pepper

1. Put mushrooms in a bowl, cover with boiling water, and set aside. Generously season beef with salt.

2. Heat butter and oil in a large, heavy pot over medium-high heat. Working in batches to avoid crowding pan (pieces shouldn't touch), add beef to pot and brown on all sides, turning pieces as they brown, for about 15 minutes in all. Remove pieces as done and set aside.

3. Lower heat to medium-low and pour off all but a small amount of oil and butter. Add onions, carrots, garlic, tomatoes, and celery and cook for about 5 minutes, stirring with a wooden spoon to scrape browned bits from the bottom of the pot and coat vegetables with oil.

4. Return meat to pot and add bouquet garni. Mix together flour and half the wine with a fork in a small bowl, making sure there are no lumps. Stir into pot, then add remaining wine. Cover and simmer over low heat for 2 hours.

5. Drain mushrooms, reserving soaking water, then rinse and roughly chop mushrooms. Strain mushroom water through a coffee filter, then add mushrooms and strained soaking water to pot. Simmer for 1 hour more, then remove bouquet garni and season to taste with salt and pepper.

Elusive Perfection

In many ways, Don Camillo—a small family-owned establishment just off the Promenade des Anglais in Nice—was the perfect French restaurant: With young Franck and Véronique Cerutti (below) in the kitchen and dining room, respectively, and with her parents helping out, it ignored fads and trends and dug deep into regional culinary tradition—but with a contemporary sensibility and a top chef's regard for the integrity of raw materials. Every town in France ought to have had a place like this. In 1996, though, with business at the restaurant increasingly erratic, Cerutti left his sous-chef in charge of the kitchen and went back to work for an old boss—celebrity chef Alain Ducasse—at the three-star Le Louis XV, in the Hôtel de Paris in Monte Carlo. Don Camillo stayed as good as ever for a couple of years...until the Ceruttis sold it to new proprietors, who have kept the name, but not the wonderful food.

Dining with Claude

"I met Claude Caspar-Jordan," recalls SAVEUR editor Colman Andrews, "in 1966, on my first night in Paris. Claude [above, with wife, Pepita, and facing page, lower right, getting fed at a reception] was 60 at the time, and I was 21. When he'd been about 21 himself, he'd worked in America for a year on the *Chicago Daily News*, where my father was an editor. The two became fast friends, but lost touch after Claude returned to Paris; in 1963, by chance, they rediscovered each other, and when I headed off to discover Europe, it seemed natural that I'd look Claude up. He and I got along pretty well—I suppose I was the son he'd never had, and he provided an amiable personal entree into the heart of a culture I loved—and over the next 28 years, we must have shared hundreds of meals. We dined at his house (Pepita was a great cook), at Parisian bistros like Aux Amis du Beaujolais and Allard, in three-star restaurants from Alsace to Burgundy, in rural Provençal cafés. We talked, we enjoyed our food and drink, we learned (I think) from each other. The last time I saw him, in his hospital bed, we talked about the next meal we were going to have together."

Boeuf à la Mode aux Carottes

(Braised Beef with Carrots)

SERVES 6

BERNARD PICOLET of Aux Amis du Beaujolais in Paris still delights his regular customers (like those pictured at near right) with old-fashioned bistro classics like this one.

1½ lb. veal knuckle, cracked
2½–3 lbs. chuck roast, larded and tied by butcher
Salt and freshly ground black pepper
3 tbsp. lard or vegetable oil
1 medium yellow onion, peeled and roughly chopped
1 head garlic, halved
8 carrots, peeled, 4 roughly chopped, 4 cut into 1" pieces
2 stalks celery, roughly chopped
¼ lb. pork rind
3 cups dry white wine
3 cups beef stock (see page 59)
1 tbsp. white wine vinegar
Bouquet garni (see sidebar, page 59)
1 tbsp. butter
1 tbsp. sugar
1 tsp. arrowroot (optional)
Fresh parsley for garnish

1. Preheat oven to 400°. Put veal knuckle in a roasting pan and roast, turning to brown on all sides, for about 1½ hours.

2. Season beef liberally with salt and pepper. Melt lard in a large pot (with a cover) over medium heat. Add beef and brown on all sides, turning as it browns, for about 15 minutes in all, then remove beef from pot, reduce heat to medium, and add onions, garlic, the 4 roughly chopped carrots, and celery. Cook, stirring occasionally, until vegetables caramelize, 12–15 minutes.

3. Meanwhile, put pork rind in a medium saucepan with enough water to cover. Bring just to a boil over high heat, then drain. Return beef to pot with vegetables, add veal knuckle, pork rind, wine, beef stock, vinegar, and bouquet garni. Bring to a boil over medium-high heat, then reduce heat to low, cover, and simmer, turning beef occasionally, until meat is easily pierced with a kitchen fork, 2½–3 hours.

4. Remove beef and set aside. Increase heat to medium and simmer broth to concentrate flavor for 15 minutes. Remove and discard veal knuckle, pork rind, and bouquet garni. Strain broth through a fine sieve, pressing vegetables with the back of a spoon, then return liquid to pot and skim fat.

5. Add remaining 4 carrots to broth, cover, and cook over low heat until tender, 15–20 minutes. Melt butter in a medium saucepan over medium heat and stir in sugar. Transfer carrots from pot to saucepan with a slotted spoon. Cook, stirring occasionally, until carrots are caramelized, about 10 minutes. Taste sauce, season to taste with salt and pepper, and, if necessary, thicken with arrowroot. Remove string from beef, cut beef into thick pieces, and return to sauce to heat through. Serve with carrots and, if you like, boiled potatoes. Garnish with parsley.

Pot-au-Feu

(French Boiled Beef Dinner)

SERVES 8

FRENCH-BORN Alice Tunks, whose recipe is adapted here, offers this pot-au-feu advice: Use both lean and fatty meats; cook potatoes separately so the broth doesn't cloud; and make enough so that there's some left for the next day.

11 medium leeks, trimmed and washed
12 carrots, peeled and halved crosswise
12 celery stalks, trimmed and halved crosswise
1 large yellow onion studded with 3 cloves
Bouquet garni (see sidebar, page 59) with 1 clove peeled garlic added
1 4-lb. rump roast, tied by butcher
2 1-lb. beef shanks, about 1½" thick
2 1-lb. beef short ribs
Coarse sea salt
1 2-lb. beef marrow bone, cut into 2" pieces (ask your butcher)
4 medium turnips, peeled, trimmed, and cut into quarters
16 baby new potatoes, scrubbed
Freshly ground black pepper
8 slices toasted country bread

1. Put 3 leeks, 6 carrot pieces, 6 celery pieces, onion, and bouquet garni in a large stockpot. Place rump roast, beef shanks, and short ribs on top of vegetables. Press about ½ tsp. salt into each end of 2 marrow bone pieces and add to pot, tucking them between meats. Add enough cold water to cover meats (about 7 quarts), and bring to a boil over high heat. Reduce heat to medium and simmer for 3 hours, skimming foam. Press about ½ tsp. salt into each end of remaining bones and place in pot along with turnips and remaining leeks, carrots, and celery. Cook, partially covered, until vegetables are very tender, about 1 hour more.

2. Meanwhile, put potatoes in a medium pot and cover with cold water. Add a generous pinch of salt and bring to a boil over medium-high heat. Lower heat to medium and simmer until potatoes are easily pierced with a knife, about 20 minutes. Drain water from pot and set aside, covering pot to keep potatoes warm.

3. Carefully remove top layer of vegetables from stockpot and arrange on a large, warm serving platter. Remove bones from pot and set aside. Remove meats, cut off and discard strings from rump roast, carve meats, and arrange on serving platter with vegetables and potatoes. Cover to keep warm. Strain broth through a colander, discarding remaining vegetables and bouquet garni. Return broth to pot and skim off fat. Season to taste with salt and pepper and keep warm over medium-low heat.

4. To serve: For the first course, ladle about 1 cup broth into each of 8 large soup bowls. Pass marrow bones at the table and serve with toasted country bread for spreading with marrow scooped from bones. For the second course, ladle some of the remaining stock over the meat and vegetables, and serve with additional sea salt, cornichons, and mustard, if you like.

The Eternal Pot

My mother's pot-au-feu," SAVEUR research editor Marina Tunks Ganter tells us, "was more than just a rustic meal; it was an ode to joy. Unlike chicken soup meant to soothe a variety of ills, pot-au-feu turned a meal into a rich and glorious feast, representing qualities the French have held dear throughout their turbulent history: resourcefulness, common sense, resilience, boldness, and most of all, joie de vivre." Literally "pot on the fire", pot-au-feu dates back to the Middle Ages and is now unarguably the national dish of France. And though adaptations abound from household to household and region to region, it has remained basically unchanged since its creation. "My mother likes to point out," Ganter continues, "that the oldest French cookbooks didn't even bother including a recipe for pot-au-feu; it was simply assumed that it was inscribed in our genes. So it must be. The pot-au-feu I grew up with is the same one my great grandmother Hélène (below center, with daughter Caroline, left, and grandaughter Alice, right) enjoyed as a child."

Tripes à la Niçoise

(Nice-Style Tripe)

SERVES 4

TRIPE MUST be cooked long and very slowly to tenderize it properly. At La Merenda in Nice, the Giustis always served this dish with the savory chickpea-flour "fries" called panisses, but polenta goes well with it, too.

- *2 lbs. beef tripe, cut into 2" x ½" strips*
- *¼ cup white vinegar*
- *¼ cup extra-virgin olive oil*
- *2 cups dry white wine*
- *4 tomatoes, peeled, seeded, and roughly chopped*
- *4 cloves garlic, peeled and finely chopped*
- *2 medium yellow onions, peeled and sliced*
- *Bouquet garni (see sidebar, page 59)*
- *1 small dried red chile (optional)*
- *Salt and freshly ground black pepper*
- *Freshly grated parmigiano-reggiano*

1. Rinse tripe very well in several changes of cold water. Bring a large pot of water to a boil over high heat and add vinegar. Blanch tripe for 20 seconds in boiling water, then drain.

2. Heat oil in a medium pot over medium heat and add tripe. Cook for about 2 minutes, stirring frequently. Stir in wine, tomatoes, garlic, onions, bouquet garni, chile (if using), and salt and pepper to taste.

3. Cover, reduce heat to very low, and simmer for at least 8 hours. Adjust seasoning and serve with grated parmigiano-reggiano and panisses, if you like.

C'est Fini

Jean and Christiane Giusti were the owners of La Merenda—a tiny, one-of-a-kind restaurant on the edge of Vieux Nice—and, respectively, its chef and its waitress/hostess/manager. A blackboard in the window of the place spelled out the house rules to prospective customers: pas de chèques, pas de cartes de crédit, pas de téléphone. It was open only Tuesday through Friday, reservations were not (officially) accepted, and when all the seats were taken, Christiane hung a sign on the door—with a certain satisfaction, one suspects—reading C'EST FINI. The Giustis—(right, standing in center) who sold the restaurant several years ago to Dominique Le Stanc, former chef at the elegant Chantecler in Nice's first-class Hôtel Négresco (it remains La Merenda, but not quite the Giustis' La Merenda)—were famous for their uncompromising Niçois specialties: the defining local classic called estocaficada (a kind of ragoût of stockfish, or dried cod), squash-blossom beignets (which were called the best in France), a classic daube, unctuous pâtes au pistou—and tripes à la niçoise so succulent that even tripe haters were converted.

"Blanquette" de Veau

(Veal Stew)

Serves 4

By definition, the meat in a blanquette is simmered but never browned. Arlette Hugon (behind bar, left), however—who runs the wonderful Lyonnais bouchon called Chez Hugon with her husband, Henri (seated, left) and son Éric (in chef's whites)—redefines the dish on her own terms: She likes the heartier flavor browning lends—so she browns.

2½ lbs. boneless veal shoulder, trimmed and cut into 2"–3" pieces
Salt and freshly ground black pepper
1 tbsp. flour
2 tbsp. vegetable oil
1 yellow onion, peeled and chopped
2 cloves garlic, peeled and minced
2½ cups dry white wine
1 small leek, white part only, washed and chopped
3 sprigs fresh thyme
3 bay leaves
1 cup beef stock *(see page 59)*
1 lemon, halved
1 cup heavy cream
2 tbsp. capers, drained

1. Season veal with salt and pepper, then dust with flour. Heat oil in a large pot over medium-high heat. Working in batches to avoid crowding pan, add veal and brown on all sides, turning pieces as they brown, for about 5 minutes in all. Remove pieces as done and set aside. When all veal is browned, return to pot, add onions and garlic, and cook, stirring frequently, until vegetables are golden, about 10 minutes.

2. Add wine, leeks, thyme, and bay leaves to pot. Reduce heat to medium-low and simmer for 10 minutes, then add stock. Cover pot and continue simmering until veal is tender, about 1½ hours.

3. Remove veal from pot with a slotted spoon and set aside. Squeeze juice from both lemon halves into sauce, then add squeezed-out shells. Stir in cream and simmer, stirring occasionally, until sauce thickens, about 30 minutes. Remove and discard lemon halves, bay leaves, and thyme. Transfer sauce to a food processor and purée until smooth. Strain through a fine sieve and return to pot. Season sauce to taste with salt and pepper, then return veal to pot and heat through for about 10 minutes. Serve garnished with capers.

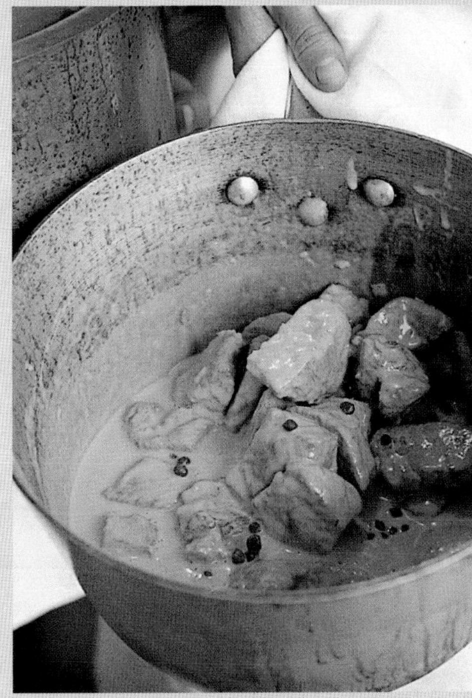

Corking Good

Bouchons, the informal, usually family-run little eating places native to Lyon," reports political and gastronomic analyst R.W. Apple, Jr., "are bistros of a sort, but with even more limited menus. Their decor tends to be modest to the point of austerity. Some have paper tablecloths, and some don't change the cutlery between courses—but the food and ambience of any good bouchon will warm the coldest heart. The food is almost always based on humble ingredients—not foie gras, lobster, and truffles, but things like cocks' combs, calves' feet, cardoons, lentils, and swiss chard. The first bouchons were 19th-century Lyonnais equivalents of our truck stops—taverns where grooms and coachmen paused for a glass and a bite after brushing down their horses. Since *bouchon* means 'cork', I had always assumed these places took their name from the many bottles that were uncorked inside. But a bouchon is also the handful of straw used for rubbing down horses, and a more likely explanation is that taverns with facilities for horses hung bundles of straw over their doors as insignia, the way bakeries hung out pretzels."

Organ Music

Liver is one of the many *abats de boucherie,* or variety meats, with which the French create culinary masterpieces. (In English these are known as *offal,* from "off-fall", meaning the parts that virtually fall out when the butcher opens an animal's carcass.) The most famous liver in French kitchens, of course, is the fattened kind from ducks and

geese—foie gras. Bresse chicken liver, called foie blond, is also highly regarded, and used often in terrines. The next most appreciated liver is certainly that of the calf—like the one displayed on the facing page by Jean-Pierre Mouton (!) at his Triperie Mouton in Paris. In traditional Chinese medicine, liver is thought to engender strength and courage. In French gastronomy, it engenders pleased palates.

Foie de Veau Poêlé

(Sautéed Calf's Liver)

SERVES 4

IN FRANCE, where offal of every kind is appreciated, calf's liver is often served in thick, rosy-pink slabs instead of the thinner, crisper scallops Americans seem to prefer. For mild flavor and tender texture, look for young calf's liver—and soak the meat in milk for at least an hour before cooking.

½ cup flour
4 6-oz. slices calf's liver
Salt and freshly ground black pepper
3 tbsp. vegetable oil
⅔ cup butter
4 shallots, peeled and thinly sliced
½ cup cognac
¾ cup minced fresh chives

1. Pour flour into a shallow dish. Dredge slices of calf's liver in flour, coating well on both sides. Shake off excess and season with salt and freshly ground black pepper. Warm oil in a skillet over medium heat until hot but not smoking. Add liver and cook, turning once, until medium rare, about 3 minutes per side. Remove liver and cover loosely with aluminum foil to keep warm.

2. Pour off and discard oil from skillet, then wipe out skillet with paper towels. Melt butter in skillet over medium heat. Add shallots and cook until golden, about 5 minutes. Add cognac, cook for 1 minute, then stir in chives and adjust seasoning. To serve, spoon sauce over liver.

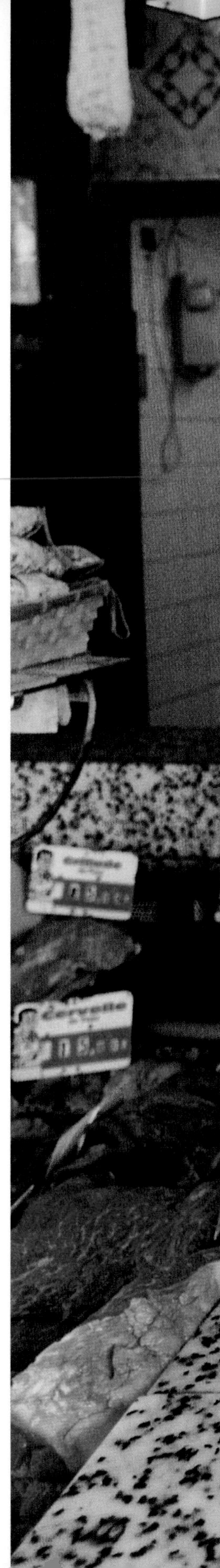

LUTRANA
Foie
de Veau
1 kg
150,
RIPES A LA
MODE DE CAEN
40,

Ris de Veau à l'Ancienne

(Veal Sweetbreads in the Old Style)

SERVES 8

SWEETBREADS are the thymus or the pancreas gland of (usually) calves or lambs. Thymus glands are long and irregular in shape; pancreas glands may be larger and rounder.

4 9-oz. pieces veal sweetbreads, halved
Salt
Juice of half a lemon
24 asparagus tips, trimmed
½ cup fresh peas
¼ lb. haricots verts, trimmed
16 pearl onions, peeled
¼ lb. baby carrots, peeled and trimmed
¼ cup peanut oil
8 tbsp. butter
Freshly ground black pepper
¼ cup dry vermouth
1 cup veal stock (see page 60)
2 tbsp. minced fresh flat-leaf parsley

1. Wash sweetbreads in cold water, then put them in a large bowl, cover with ice water, and refrigerate for 2 hours, changing the water several times. Next, put sweetbreads in a saucepan, cover with cold salted water, add lemon juice, and bring to a boil over medium heat. Boil for 1 minute. Drain, then transfer sweetbreads to a bowl of ice water to cool them. When cool, clean sweetbreads by removing and discarding all fat and sinew. Blot dry with a kitchen towel, wrap in plastic, and refrigerate overnight.

2. Preheat oven to 325°. Bring a large pot of salted water to a boil over medium-high heat. Cook asparagus, peas, and haricots verts separately for 3–4 minutes each, removing each from water when done with a slotted spoon, and setting aside. Cook onions and carrots separately for 6–8 minutes each, removing from water and setting aside as above.

3. Heat oil and 4 tbsp. butter in a large ovenproof skillet over medium heat until butter begins to sizzle. Generously season sweetbreads with salt and pepper, then sauté until just browned, about 5 minutes per side. Add 3 tbsp. butter and transfer skillet to oven for 20 minutes. Remove skillet from oven, transfer sweetbreads to a heated platter, cover loosely with foil, and set aside. Pour off and discard fat, then add vermouth to same skillet. Cook for 1 minute over high heat, stirring with a wooden spoon to loosen any browned bits stuck to the bottom of the pan. Add stock and reduce by half, about 5 minutes.

4. Melt remaining 1 tbsp. butter in a large sauté pan over medium heat, pour in ¼ cup of reduced stock, then add vegetables, season to taste with salt and pepper, and cook until heated through. Arrange vegetables around sweetbreads on platter. Spoon remaining reduced stock over sweetbreads and sprinkle with parsley.

Easy to Love

The gougères and champagne arrive almost immediately, fueling the diner as he tackles the pleasantly difficult task of deciding between the snails braised with sorrel and the crabmeat cannelloni in sauce ravigote, and then perhaps between the truffled pig's foot sausage, the sautéed foie gras in gingerbread crumbs, and the sweetbreads à l'ancienne (see recipe, left). The wine list, conveniently printed right on the menu itself, offers a similarly vexing embarrassment of riches. But never mind. The attentiveness of the staff—which goes beyond mere "service"—is so remarkable and reassuring, and the elegantly paneled dining room is so calmly attractive that the whole experience is absolutely unintimidating, a veritable breeze. And that's why Taillevent in Paris (above) really is quite possibly the best, most perfect restaurant in the world.

Potluck Dinner

Potée, according to *Larousse Gastronomique*, is any dish cooked in an earthenware pot, but the term usually applies to a mixture of meat (mainly pork) and vegetables—especially cabbage and potatoes—cooked in stock and served as a single course. Potée is a very old dish and is found throughout rural France, often under other names—among them hochepot, garbure, and oille. Recipes vary with region: Potée alsacienne, for instance, is made with smoked bacon fat, white cabbage, celery, carrots, and haricots verts—the vegetables sweated in goose fat before liquid is added; potée auvergnate includes fresh or salt pork, sausages, half a pig's head, cabbage, carrots, and turnips; potée bourguignonne uses bacon, pork shoulder, ham hocks, cabbage, carrots, turnips, leeks, and potatoes (plus peas and haricots verts in spring); potée bretonne's ingredients include lamb shoulder, duck, sausages, and various vegetables (an eel potée is also made in Brittany); potée lorraine contains lean bacon, filet or shoulder of pork, cabbage, carrots, haricots verts, dried or fresh white haricot beans, peas, turnips, leeks, celery, potatoes, and sometimes lentils; and potée champenoise, or grape pickers' potée, is a mix of unsmoked bacon, salt pork, cabbage, turnips, celeriac, potatoes, sometimes sausages or smoked ham, and perhaps chicken.

Potée

(Savoyard Pork and Vegetable Stew)

Serves 10

This version of potée, from the mountains of the Savoie region of southeastern France, is considered one of the most traditional of all. You'll need a 24-quart stockpot.

1 3-lb. pork shoulder, rolled and tied
2 smoked ham hocks
3 lbs. smoked kielbasa
6 medium yellow onions, peeled, each studded with 1 clove
4 cloves garlic, peeled
Coarse salt
5 black peppercorns
3 bay leaves
6 leeks, trimmed and washed
10 whole carrots, peeled
10 small turnips, scrubbed
10 small potatoes, scrubbed
1 head savoy cabbage, cored and quartered
Freshly ground black pepper

1. Put pork, ham hocks, kielbasa, 1 onion, garlic, 1 tsp. salt, peppercorns, and bay leaves in a 24-quart stockpot with water to cover. Bring to a boil over medium-high heat. Reduce heat to low and gently simmer for 2 hours, skimming fat and foam.

2. Add leeks, carrots, turnips, potatoes, and remaining 5 onions, increase heat to medium, and bring back to a simmer. Cook until vegetables are almost tender, about 30 minutes. Add cabbage and cook for 10 minutes more.

3. Transfer meat and vegetables from pot to a large platter and keep warm in a low oven. Increase heat under stockpot to high and reduce stock by one-quarter, about 15 minutes. Season to taste with salt and pepper.

4. Slice meat and sausages and place in the center of a deep platter; surround with vegetables. Ladle some broth over the dish and sprinkle with salt and pepper. Serve with remaining broth in bowls with toasted bread, if you like.

Rôti de Porc aux Pommes

(Pork Loin with Apples, Cider, and Calvados)

Serves 8–10

Inspired by the celebrated apples of Normandy, we developed this recipe to use apples in three forms, two of them liquid. Though pork has been eaten by the French since the time of the Gauls, it was long regarded as the meat of the common people; this preparation ennobles it.

1 4½-lb. pork loin roast
1 tbsp. flour
Salt and freshly ground black pepper
2 tsp. finely chopped fresh rosemary
4 tbsp. butter
3 medium yellow onions, peeled and chopped
2 cloves garlic, peeled and chopped
4 stalks rosemary (optional)
5 baking apples, cored and quartered
½ cup Sydre Argelette (see sidebar, page 178) or other good-quality French hard cider
¼ cup good-quality calvados

1. Preheat oven to 325°. Tie pork loin every 2" with kitchen string so that it holds a cylindrical shape. Mix together flour, salt and pepper to taste, and chopped rosemary in a small bowl. Rub the flour mixture all over the pork loin, coating evenly and well.

2. Heat 2 tbsp. butter in a large heavy skillet and sear meat over high heat, turning often, until browned on all sides, about 15 minutes. Transfer meat with pan juices to a large baking pan and scatter onions and garlic around it. Cut up remaining butter and distribute evenly over onions. Add rosemary stalks (if using) to pan. Cover pan with foil.

3. Put in oven and cook for 45 minutes, then add apples and hard cider to pan. Baste pork and apples with pan juices. Re-cover and cook for 30 minutes more. Raise oven temperature to 400°, remove foil, baste, and cook for another 15 minutes.

4. Transfer roast to a cutting board, remove string, and allow to rest for 10 minutes before slicing. Meanwhile, transfer onions and apples to a platter. Put pan on top of the stove over medium-high heat and reduce pan juices by half, about 5 minutes. Warm calvados in a small pan, add to the pan juices, and carefully ignite with a kitchen match, keeping pan lid nearby to extinguish flames if necessary. Simmer sauce while you slice the pork loin. Arrange meat over apples and onions and serve with the sauce.

Apple Spirits

There is no secret to making good calvados, says Claude Camut. "All you need is the *bonne fortune* of being in the right place, on the right farm, with the right apples, for 800 years." Calvados, of course, is Normandy's famed apple brandy, distilled from cider just as cognac is from wine. At the turn of the century, 90 percent of all calvados was made by farmers. Today, it's a mere 2 percent, with the rest turned out by large companies. Farmer Camut grows all his own apples, makes and distills his own cider, and ages it himself. Each of the 25 traditional apple varieties he grows, says Camut, contributes something distinctive to his calvados. "In Paris," he says, laughing, "they think it is very funny we can make such a marvelous spirit with such horrible-looking apples."

Cutting Cabbage

The word *choucroute* has also come to mean the show-stopping dish, definitive of Alsatian cuisine, of sauerkraut topped with copious portions of pork in myriad

forms—but it translates simply as fermented cabbage. The earliest reference to sauerkraut in Alsace dates from the 15th century. For hundreds of years, until the early 1900s, Sürkrüt-schniders, or sour-cabbage cutters, toured the countryside, shredding cabbage to order. Today, the process is left to professionals. "You could make it at home," says Xavier Schaal, managing director of the Choucroutal cooperative in Geispolsheim, "but you'd need at least a hundred kilos of raw cabbage at a time."

Choucroute Garnie à l'Alsacienne

(Sauerkraut Garnished with Smoked, Cured, and Fresh Pork)

SERVES 6–8

NO OTHER dish shows off the richly varied charcuterie of Alsace quite like choucroute. This recipe was adapted from one of eight varieties served at Maison Kammerzell, Guy-Pierre Baumann's legendary choucroute institution in Strasbourg.

1 ½ lbs. fresh ham hocks
¼ cup goose fat
3 small yellow onions, peeled and finely chopped
4 ½ lbs. sauerkraut, drained and rinsed
3 ¼ cups Alsatian riesling or other dry but fruity white wine
1 ½ lbs. boneless pork loin
1 lb. smoked ham
½ lb. slab bacon
Bouquet garni (see sidebar, page 59) with 1 head garlic, 3 whole cloves, 6 juniper berries, and 5 coriander seeds added
Salt and freshly ground black pepper
12 medium red bliss potatoes, peeled
6 fresh pork sausages, such as saucisses de Strasbourg
3 blood sausages (optional)
1 tbsp. peanut oil
6 smoked pork sausages

1. Place ham hocks in a large pot. Cover with water and simmer over medium heat for 1½ hours. Drain and set aside.

2. Preheat oven to 350°. Melt goose fat in a dutch oven, or a large heavy pot with a lid, over medium heat. Add onions, cook until soft, 10–15 minutes, then add sauerkraut, wine, ham hocks, pork loin, ham, bacon, and bouquet garni. Season with salt and pepper, cover, and cook in oven until meats are tender, about 1½ hours.

3. About 35 minutes before serving, place potatoes in a pot of salted water over medium-high heat and cook until tender, 20–25 minutes. Drain and keep warm.

4. Prick fresh and blood sausages, if using, with a fork, then place in a skillet, cover with water, and simmer over medium heat for 10 minutes. Drain. Dry skillet, add oil, and heat over medium heat. Brown fresh and blood sausages (if using), turning occasionally, then remove. In the same oil, adding more if necessary, brown smoked sausages, turning occasionally, then remove. To serve, spoon sauerkraut onto a large platter, discarding bouquet garni. Slice pork loin, ham, and bacon, and arrange on platter with ham hocks, potatoes, and all sausages.

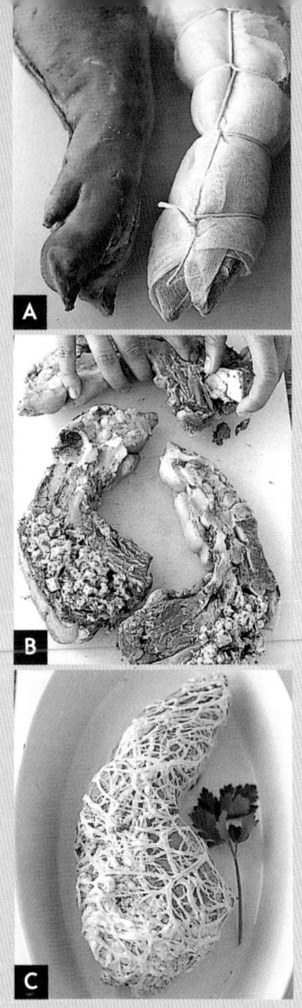

Good Food Afoot

Americans eat about 16 billion pounds of pork annually—but pork "parts" like pigs' feet remain largely unappreciated. Making the Lyonnais classic (facing page, bottom) is a good way to get acquainted with this delicacy. Ask your butcher to halve pigs' feet lengthwise, then reassemble them, wrap tightly in cheesecloth, and tie with kitchen string (**A**). After cooking, unwrap, remove any bones, and fill with stuffing (**B**), then wrap in caul fat (**C**) before roasting.

Pieds de Cochon Farcis

(Stuffed Pigs' Feet)

SERVES 4–8

CAUL FAT is a lacy, netlike pork membrane, often used in France as casing for homemade sausages and other ground meat dishes. Though not readily available in the U.S., it can usually be special-ordered from your butcher.

- *⅓ cup red wine vinegar*
- *3 sprigs fresh thyme*
- *3 bay leaves*
- *1 tsp. black peppercorns*
- *4 pigs' feet, split in half lengthwise (ask your butcher)*
- *2 cups finely chopped soft white bread*
- *⅔ lb. boiled ham, finely chopped*
- *2 large shallots, peeled and minced*
- *½ cup finely chopped fresh parsley*
- *¼ cup milk*
- *1 egg yolk, lightly beaten*
- *½ cup dry white wine*
- *Salt*
- *1 lb. caul fat, rinsed*

1. Combine vinegar, thyme, bay leaves, and peppercorns in a pot large enough to accommodate 4 whole pigs' feet. Reassemble split pigs' feet, wrapping each foot in cheesecloth, then tying with kitchen string. Add enough water just to cover, weight with a heavy plate, then cover and slowly simmer over medium-low heat for 4 hours. Cool, then refrigerate pigs' feet in cooking liquid overnight.

2. Preheat oven to 375°. Combine bread, ham, shallots, parsley, milk, egg yolk, and ¼ cup of the wine in a medium bowl. Mix well and season with salt. Unwrap and separate pigs' feet. Using your fingers, remove and discard leg bone down to ankle joint and discard (foot bones should remain in place). Divide stuffing between feet, spooning about ¼ cup into each cavity. Rinse caul fat and cut into four pieces, each about 12" x 12". Reassemble pigs' feet, wrap each in caul fat, then fit snugly in a roasting pan in a single layer. Add remaining ¼ cup wine and roast until golden, about 45 minutes. Separate halves again and serve warm.

Informal Gourmand

Gérard Oberlé (above)—a rare-book dealer born in Alsace but Burgundian by choice—is a kind of profane cherub of a man with a generously beaming face and an unapologetic gourmand's lust for good food. When he invited us to lunch one day at his house in Montigny-sur-Canne, a hamlet near Château-Chinon, the Morvan's main town, he promised us an informal meal. As we arrived, he introduced us to "a colleague"—Marc Meneau, chef-proprietor of l'Espérance in St-Père-sous-Vézelay, arguably the best restaurant in Burgundy—who had collaborated with him on the informality. Our main course was the definitive coq au vin, and there were wonderful cheeses and homemade apple and rhubarb tarts for dessert—but the most memorable dish was our first course, a veritable culinary monument composed of potatoes and the sweet meat of pigs' snouts encased in perfect pastry. Was it unexpected? Yes. Daunting? No, surprisingly. Delicious? *Absolument!*

Tourte de Groins de Porc

(Torte of Pigs' Snout)

Serves 8

If pigs' snouts are unavailable from your butcher, says Marc Meneau—who gave us the recipe for this uncompromising Burgundian specialty—substitute pigs' feet.

2 lbs. pigs' snouts, soaked in water overnight, or 3 pigs' feet (5–6 lbs. total)
Salt
1 cup dry white wine
2 tbsp. flour
1 medium yellow onion, peeled
2 cloves
1 carrot, trimmed and halved
1 leek, trimmed, halved and washed
1 celery stalk, trimmed and halved
Bouquet garni (see sidebar, page 59)
5 waxy potatoes
3 tbsp. butter
1 shallot, peeled and minced
4 cloves garlic, peeled and minced
2 tbsp. minced fresh tarragon leaves
2 tbsp. minced fresh chervil leaves
2 tbsp. minced fresh parsley leaves
1 ½ tbsp. dijon mustard
¼ cup white wine vinegar
Freshly ground black pepper
2 sheets Dufour or other good-quality prepared puff pastry
1 egg, lightly beaten

1. Put meat into a large pot, cover with cold salted water, and bring to a boil over high heat. When foam rises to the top, drain, rinse meat and pot, then return meat to pot. Add wine to flour in a small bowl, whisking until smooth, pour over meat, then add salted water to cover. Stud onion with cloves and add to pot with carrots, leeks, celery, and bouquet garni. Bring to a boil over high heat, reduce heat to low, and simmer, partially covered, until meat is tender, 4–5 hours. Remove meat from pot and allow to cool. Discard vegetables and stock from pot. When meat has cooled, finely chop. (Debone pigs' feet if using them.)

2. Preheat oven to 400°. Put potatoes in a large pot of cold salted water, then bring to a boil over high heat. Cook until tender, about 25 minutes. Allow to cool, then peel and thinly slice. Set aside.

3. Melt 2 tbsp. butter in a sauté pan over medium heat. Add shallots and garlic and cook until soft, about 5 minutes, then combine with meat, tarragon, chervil, parsley, mustard, and vinegar in a large bowl. Season to taste with salt and pepper.

4. Roll out pastry sheets on a lightly floured surface into 2 16" rounds. Set a buttered and floured 8" x 2½" vacherin mold on a parchment-lined baking sheet. Fit 1 pastry sheet into ring, leaving 1" overhanging edge. Layer in a third of potatoes, then add half the meat mixture (**A**). Repeat layers, finishing with potatoes. Fold pastry over potatoes (**B**) and place second pastry sheet over it. Trim pastry, leaving 1" overlap, then tuck overlap inside ring with a dinner knife. Insert a 2" parchment tube in center of torte as a steam vent and cut decorative slits in the center of the pastry (**C**). Mix together egg and 1 tbsp. water, then brush over top of torte. Bake for 40 minutes. Let rest for 20 minutes before slicing (**D**).

A
B
C
D

1994
PARIS
AMERICAN EXPRESS

Haricot d'Agneau

(Lamb Stew with White Beans)

Serves 6–8

Despite the white beans (haricots blancs) in this dish from À Sousceyrac in Paris, the name *haricot* probably derives from the verb *halicoter*, "to cut into small pieces".

1 lb. dry emergo or other large white beans
½ cup goose or duck fat
3 lbs. stewing lamb, trimmed and cut into 2½" pieces
Salt and freshly ground black pepper
3 medium yellow onions, peeled
4 medium carrots, peeled
2 whole heads of garlic, halved
2 sprigs fresh thyme
1 bay leaf
3 medium tomatoes, seeded and diced
5 cloves
¾ cup dry bread crumbs
¼ cup melted butter

1. Soak beans overnight in the refrigerator in a large bowl with cold water to cover.

2. Heat 3 tbsp. of fat in a large dutch oven over medium heat. Season lamb with salt and pepper. Working in batches to avoid crowding pan, add lamb and brown on all sides, turning as pieces brown, for about 10 minutes in all per batch. Remove pieces with a slotted spoon as done and set aside.

3. Coarsely chop 2 onions and 3 carrots, then add to dutch oven with 1 head garlic, 1 sprig thyme, and bay leaf. Cook, stirring occasionally, over medium heat for 12–15 minutes. Add tomatoes and cook, stirring, for 1 minute, then add lamb and enough water to cover (about 6 cups). Bring to a boil, then reduce heat to low, cover, and simmer, skimming fat, until lamb is tender, about 2 hours. Liquid should not fall below half the height of lamb; add more water if necessary.

4. Meanwhile, drain beans. Heat remaining 5 tbsp. fat in large saucepan over medium heat, add beans, and cook, stirring frequently, for 7–10 minutes. Stud remaining onion with cloves, halve remaining carrot, and add both to beans with remaining garlic and thyme and enough water to cover (about 8 cups). Reduce heat to low, and simmer until beans are tender, about 45 minutes. Remove onion, carrots, garlic, and thyme from beans and discard.

5. When lamb is done, remove meat from liquid with a slotted spoon and set aside. Discard bay leaf and thyme sprig. Purée vegetables and lamb broth together in a blender or food processor. Strain through a fine sieve and adjust seasoning.

6. Preheat broiler. Drain beans, reserving cooking liquid. Transfer beans to dutch oven, layer lamb on top, then pour in strained sauce and, if necessary, enough reserved bean cooking liquid to come up just to the level of the lamb. Combine bread crumbs and butter in a bowl, spread evenly over lamb, and broil until brown, about 5 minutes.

Serious Eaters

"My friends Claude and Pepita Caspar-Jordan," SAVEUR editor Colman Andrews recalls (see sidebar, page 210), "took me to À Sousceyrac, one Christmas Eve in the early 1970s, for the first of many visits. I shocked them a bit, I think, by arriving with an Older Woman, about a dozen years my senior, whom I had brought to Paris for the holidays. But Pepita was always *très correcte*, and Claude, as usual when addressing my foibles, displayed something closer to avuncular bemusement than to parental disapproval—so the evening went well, full of chatter and champagne. My companion might even have impressed Claude a bit by the way she held her own at a table fairly heaped with foie gras, grilled boneless pigs' feet, whole braised sweetbreads, and the restaurant's famous lièvre à la royale—an elaborately old-fashioned dish of hare stuffed with foie gras, truffles, and its own innards and stewed in wine. À Sousceyrac—under the direction of brothers Patrick and Luc Asfaux, who run the kitchen and the dining room, respectively [their father, Gabriel, facing page, still cooks at lunchtime], is a restaurant for serious eaters only."

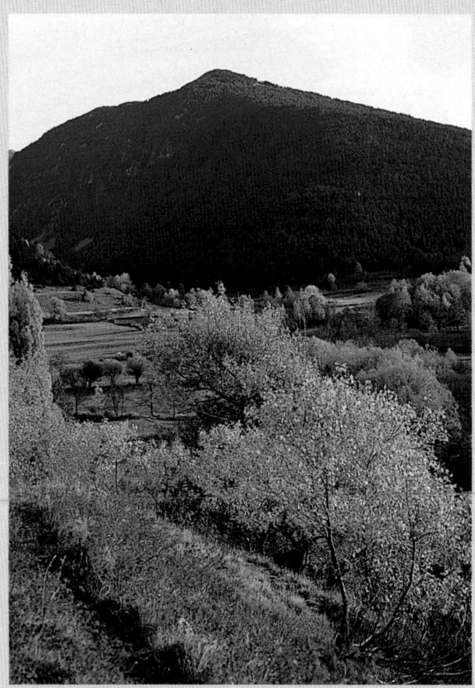

Border Food

"Meitat França, meitat Espanya, no hi ha altra terra com la Cerdanya," goes the refrain in the Catalan language—half France, half Spain, there is no other country like the Cerdanya. This wide and luminous valley in the eastern Pyrenees—solomonically sliced in two in the 17th century by the Treaty of the Pyrenees—straddles the border about 75 miles north of Barcelona and 95 south of Toulouse. In the end, food and language (i.e., Catalan) seem to be the ties that bind. One of the region's best cooks is unquestionably Françoise Massot. For her hearty, memorable meals, she grows or buys the best meat, fowl, and produce she can procure high in the Pyrenees between France and Spain. But she also forages daily in the woods around Cal Pai, her bucolic inn overlooking the 6,000-foot-high Pic Carlit, highest in the Pyrénées-Orientales. Locals call her "Framboise"—and indeed she seems to know the whereabouts and quality of every wild framboise (raspberry) in her part of the mountains—as well as every strawberry, blueberry, églantine (wild rose hip), chanterelle, morel, asparagus, plum, pear, and apple. All of these seem to end up on her table.

Épaule d'Agneau à la Catalane

(Catalan-Style Shoulder of Lamb)

SERVES 8–10

AT HER INN in the Pyrenees, Françoise Massot makes this dish with banyuls, a fortified wine from the town of the same name on the French Catalan coast, on the Spanish border. If you can't find it, substitute a good ruby port.

3 lemons
1 7–8 lb. boneless lamb shoulder, trimmed
Salt and freshly ground black pepper
10 cloves garlic, peeled
2 sticks cinnamon
1 lb. ripe tomatoes, peeled and seeded, or 1 28-oz. can whole peeled tomatoes with their juice
1 bottle sweet banyuls or ruby port
2 sprigs fresh thyme
2–3 bay leaves

1. Bring a medium pot of water to a boil over high heat, then add lemons and blanch for 2 minutes. Drain, then cut each lemon into 8 pieces lengthwise and set aside.

2. Season lamb generously with salt and pepper. Set a large, heavy roasting pan over 2 burners on top of the stove. Add lamb and cook, without additional fat, over medium-high heat, turning once, until well browned on both sides, about 20 minutes in all. Remove lamb and set aside, then pour off and discard excess fat and return pan to stove.

3. Add lemons to roasting pan and cook over medium heat, stirring and crushing lemons with a wooden spoon and scraping up any browned bits stuck to the bottom of the pan, about 2 minutes. Add garlic and cinnamon and cook for about 3 minutes. Add tomatoes, wine, thyme, and bay leaves and cook for 1 minute longer. Season to taste with salt and pepper, then return lamb to the pan. Reduce heat to low, cover pan tightly with foil, and slowly braise until lamb is tender, about 1¾ hour. Remove cinnamon, thyme, and bay leaves before serving.

Cabri à la Corse

(Corsican-Style Kid)

Serves 6

GOAT MEAT is little appreciated in mainstream American cooking, but its sweet, flavorful, pork-plus-lamb-like meat is widely available in Hispanic and Greek markets.

6 lbs. boneless shoulder of kid (baby goat), cut into medium-size pieces (ask your butcher)
Salt and freshly ground black pepper
Olive oil
4 small yellow onions, peeled, halved, and thinly sliced
3 cloves garlic, peeled and minced
3 medium tomatoes, peeled, seeded, and diced
3 tbsp. tomato paste
2 cups red wine
½ bunch fresh parsley, minced
6 sprigs fresh thyme, minced
1 tbsp. flour
1 bay leaf

1. Generously season kid with salt and pepper. Heat 3 tbsp. oil in a large heavy pot over medium-high heat. Working in batches to avoid crowding pan, add meat and brown on all sides, about 10 minutes per batch. Transfer meat to a bowl and set aside.

2. Reduce heat to medium-low, add more oil if needed, and cook onions and garlic, stirring constantly, until soft, about 5 minutes. Increase heat to medium and add tomatoes, tomato paste, wine, parsley, and thyme, scraping with a wooden spoon to loosen any browned bits stuck to bottom of the pot. Cook until alcohol has evaporated, about 5 minutes.

3. Return meat with accumulated juices to pot. Sprinkle in flour, season to taste with salt and pepper, and cook, stirring often, for 5 minutes. Add 3 cups water and bay leaf, bring to a simmer, and cook until meat is tender and sauce has thickened, about 1 hour, basting and turning the meat as it cooks. Remove bay leaf and adjust seasonings before serving.

Flavor in the Air

Corsica's maquis, or scrub—a dense, fragrant underbrush of oak, juniper, thorn, heather, and wild herbs and flowers that covers much of the island—yields up a bittersweet lemon-pepper aroma; Napoleon Bonaparte, the island's most famous son, was so enamored of it that he dreamed of the maquis during his days on Elba. In addition to its perfume, the scrub provides ideal grazing for wild game and for free-range pigs, cows, sheep, and goats. This means especially flavorful meats—which Corsica's industrious cooks utilize to the fullest—usually in simple, sturdy preparations.

The Deer Farmer

Unless you're a hunter or a hunter's friend, the venison you eat in America today is likely to be farm-bred (put out to pasture to feed on planted grasses) or ranched (allowed to range free over large expanses of land). About 80 percent of the venison sold here comes from New Zealand; another 15 percent is domestic, raised or harvested primarily in New York and Texas. The remainder comes mostly from Scotland. Whatever their origin, these deer are usually the Eurasian species—most commonly red, fallow, and sika—as America's native white-tailed deer do not breed well in captivity. The animals' managed diet also gives their meat (everything from chops to the shoulder meat and sausage at right) a slightly milder flavor than that of their wild cousins.

Civet de Chevreuil

(Rich Venison Stew)

SERVES 6

A HEARTY GAME STEW, civet is traditionally thickened with the blood of the animal used; our venison stew substitutes flour, for a lighter, more easily accomplished version.

3 lbs. boneless venison shoulder, cut into large pieces
1 medium carrot, peeled and diced
1 medium yellow onion, peeled and diced
3 cloves garlic, peeled
12 sprigs fresh parsley
2 sprigs fresh thyme
2 bay leaves
15 black peppercorns
1 bottle côtes-du-rhône or other dry, hearty red wine
¼ lb. bacon slices, julienned
Salt and freshly ground black pepper
2 tbsp. olive oil
2 tbsp. flour
12 small boiling onions, peeled
1 tsp. sugar
4 tbsp. butter
½ lb. white mushrooms, trimmed and sliced
2 tbsp. cognac

1. Combine venison, carrots, diced onions, garlic, 2 sprigs of the parsley, thyme, bay leaves, peppercorns, and wine in a large bowl. Cover and refrigerate for 24 hours to tenderize venison.

2. Fry bacon in a heavy pot or dutch oven over medium heat until crisp, 8–10 minutes. Remove with a slotted spoon and drain on paper towels, leaving fat in pot.

3. Remove venison from marinade and blot dry with paper towel. Strain liquid into a bowl, discarding herbs and vegetables. Generously season meat with salt and pepper. Add oil to bacon fat in pot and increase heat to medium-high. Working in batches to avoid crowding pan, add venison and brown on all sides, turning as pieces brown, for about 10 minutes in all per batch. Remove pieces with a slotted spoon as done and set aside. When all meat is browned, return to pot, sprinkle flour over meat, then add bacon. Cook, stirring, until flour turns a nut-brown color, about 1 minute. Add marinade, bring to a simmer, then reduce heat to medium-low, cover, and cook until venison is tender, 2–2½ hours.

4. Meanwhile bring a medium pot of salted water to a boil. Add small whole onions and sugar and simmer over medium heat until tender, 25–30 minutes. Drain and set aside. Heat 2 tbsp. butter in a medium skillet over medium-high heat. Add mushrooms and cook, stirring, until golden, about 3 minutes.

5. Remove venison from pot to finish sauce. Increase heat to medium-high, add cognac, and cook for 5 minutes. Remove pot from heat and whisk in remaining butter. Return venison to sauce, add onions and mushrooms, and mix thoroughly. Chop remaining 10 sprigs of parsley and sprinkle on top. Garnish with slices of toasted country bread, if you like.

CHAPTER

9

VEGETABLES

"THE BOUNTY of Brittany—which is the westernmost portion of France—is displayed every Saturday in the bustling open-air market in Morlaix, a river port in the département of Finistère. Though

Finistère means 'end of the earth', there is no feeling of desolation or privation here. Fish of many varieties, just pulled from the neighboring sea, are laid out on ice; also on view is pork and pork sausage, as well as succulent lamb raised on nearby salt marshes. Dairy farmers sell fresh milk and the region's famous butter. But the most glorious stalls of all are those brimming with produce grown in the golden belt of rich farmland that curves around the coastline—leeks, cauliflower, onions, peas, cabbages, the especially plump and tasty local artichokes, apples from orchards in the Argoat (as the Breton interior is called), strawberries from Plougastel, tiny new potatoes from the sandy flats just inland from the sea.... And in the middle of the market, most Saturday mornings, you're liable to see chef Patrick Jeffroy (facing page, lower left)—perhaps plucking a couple of leaves from an artichoke and rubbing them together near his ear. Jeffroy, proprietor of an acclaimed hotel-restaurant (called simply Patrick Jeffroy) in nearby Plounérin, grew up just a few steps from the marketplace, and has been coming here since he was a boy. He remembers vividly and with great affection the days he spent on his grandmother's farm not far away. And he recalls her tricks: 'My grandmother, who shopped at this market before I was born, taught me how to "hear" if an artichoke was really fresh. When you rub the leaves together, they should sing.'" —JUDY FAYARD

RECIPES

POIREAUX TIÈDES EN VINAIGRETTE *(Warm Leeks with Vinaigrette)*, page 245; TARTARE DE LÉGUMES *(Marinated Vegetable and Herb Salad)*, page 246; ASPERGES BLANCHES AU SABAYON À L'HUILE D'OLIVE *(White Asparagus with Olive Oil Sabayon)*, page 249; RATATOUILLE, page 251; BEIGNETS DE FLEURS DE COURGETTES *(Deep-Fried Zucchini Blossoms)*, page 252; FARCIS À LA NIÇOISE *(Nice-Style Stuffed Vegetables)*, page 255; TIAN DE LÉGUMES *(Mediterranean Vegetable Casserole)*, page 256; GRAND AÏOLI *(Vegetables and Salt Cod with Garlic Sauce)*, page 259; RAVIOLIS DE BOURRACHE *(Borage Ravioli)*, page 260; TRINXAT *(Catalan Cabbage and Potatoes)*, page 262; CARDONS À LA "BAGNA CAUDA" *(Cardoons with Anchovy-Garlic Sauce)*, page 265; PETITS POIS AUX MORILLES *(Ragoût of Peas and Morels)*, page 266; POMMES SOUFFLÉES *(French Potato Puffs)*, page 269; GRATIN DAUPHINOIS *(Potatoes Baked in Milk and Cream)*, page 271.

Poireaux Tièdes en Vinaigrette

(Warm Leeks with Vinaigrette)

SERVES 4

"THERE ISN'T a day of the year that we don't use leeks in one form or another," says Claude Cornut of the venerable Paris bistro Chez Clovis (see page 51). In spring, the leeks are always dressed with vinaigrette—for one of the simplest, most delicious of all French vegetable dishes.

---

4 large winter leeks
6 cups chicken stock *(see page 56)*
2 large shallots, peeled and sliced
2 tsp. dijon mustard
1 tbsp. red wine vinegar
3 tbsp. peanut oil
Salt and freshly ground pepper
Pinch freshly grated nutmeg
8 sprigs fresh flat-leaf parsley

1. Remove roots and outer leaves from leeks. Trim off greens to 2" above the white part. Slice leeks in half lengthwise, not quite all the way through so that you can open the leek like a book. Wash leeks under cold running water to remove all sand and dirt, and set aside.

2. Bring chicken stock to a simmer over medium heat in a large skillet. Lay leeks, all facing in the same direction, in the simmering stock. Reduce heat to medium-low, cover and cook until leeks are soft but not mushy, 10–15 minutes. Transfer leeks to a rack to drain. Add shallots to the simmering stock and cook until soft, about 3 minutes, then remove shallots from stock with a slotted spoon and set aside. Reserve stock for another use.

3. Whisk together mustard and vinegar in a small bowl and gradually drizzle in peanut oil. Season to taste with salt and pepper, then continue whisking until vinaigrette is smooth and creamy.

4. Arrange leeks in circles on a platter or on individual plates and scatter shallots on top. Drizzle vinaigrette over leeks, season with nutmeg, and garnish with parsley.

Cuisine or Not?

There are those who will tell you that Brittany has no real cuisine of its own. Even Patrick Jeffroy, one of the region's best chefs, admits that "Old-fashioned Breton cooking is simple. It's not belabored or particularly polished. We don't want to cover up the flavor of the ingredients." Indeed, in Brittany, the quality of the ingredients that go into a dish has always been more important than any complicated techniques or fancy sauces that might be applied to them. So maybe it's not a cuisine. Maybe it's just a panoply of fresh, unpretentious, full-flavored things to eat.

The Essential Olive

The département of the Alpes-de-Haute-Provence, northeast of Marseille and northwest of Nice, is unknown Provence—a rugged land of steeply terraced mountains and vast rocky plains softened here and there by water (like the Lac de Ste Croix, facing page). The soil is poor, and if those ancient Provençal crops, the vine and the olive tree, endure, it is only because their roots are deep. The olive tree, though, is the ideal metaphor for Haute Provence: It is as thrifty, modest, and hardworking as the people whose needs it serves. It doesn't ask for much—just meager earth and a little rain—yet it generously provides a great deal in return. It shelters the land with a delicate year-round shade that protects plants growing beneath its foliage. Its twigs and branches are carved into useful implements or burned for cooking fuel. An herbal tea is made from olive sprouts, and olives themselves are splendid food. And as for olive oil, well, it's impossible to imagine Provençal cuisine without it (see page 115).

Tartare de Légumes

(Marinated Vegetable and Herb Salad)

Serves 6

As chef at the Hostellerie de la Fuste in Manosque, in Haute Provence, Dominique Bucaille served this salad to show off the region's wealth of fresh summer vegetables.

FOR SALAD:
Salt
Hearts of 2 small artichokes, diced
1 small bulb fennel, diced
2 small carrots, peeled and diced
2 small turnips, peeled and diced
1 small zucchini, diced
1 small acorn squash, peeled, seeded, and diced
6 small asparagus stalks, trimmed and diced
1 cup fresh shelled peas
½ cup shelled fava beans
2 ripe tomatoes, seeded and diced
½ cup total of the following finely chopped fresh herbs: basil, parsley, chives, chervil, tarragon, and/or sage

FOR VINAIGRETTE:
1 tbsp. dijon mustard
2 tbsp. balsamic vinegar
⅔ cup extra-virgin olive oil
Salt and freshly ground black pepper

Additional fresh herbs for garnish
Extra-virgin olive oil

1. For salad, bring a large pot of salted water to a boil over medium-high heat. Cook artichokes, fennel, carrots, and turnips separately for 2 minutes each, removing each from water when done with a slotted spoon and plunging into a large bowl of ice water. Cook zucchini, squash, asparagus, and peas for 30 seconds each, removing each from water with a slotted spoon as before and adding to the bowl of ice water. Cook fava beans for 30 seconds, removing them from water as above, then slip them out of their tough outer skins before adding to bowl of ice water. Drain vegetables first in a colander, then on paper towels, so that they are as dry as possible. Set aside.

2. For vinaigrette, whisk mustard and vinegar together in a large salad bowl, adding olive oil in a thin stream. Season to taste with salt and pepper. Add cooked vegetables, tomatoes, and chopped herbs. Mix together gently but thoroughly. Cover bowl and refrigerate overnight.

3. To serve, garnish with fresh herbs and a drizzle of olive oil.

Asperges Blanches au Sabayon à l'Huile d'Olive

(White Asparagus with Olive Oil Sabayon)

SERVES 4

THE COOKING TIME for white asparagus depends on the age and thickness of its stalks, but is always considerably longer than for the green variety—particularly since, unlike its green cousin, white asparagus is never eaten crisp.

1 cup dry white wine
⅓ cup white wine vinegar
2 egg yolks, lightly beaten
⅓ cup extra-virgin olive oil
Salt and freshly ground white pepper
1 lb. white asparagus, peeled

1. Combine wine and vinegar in a saucepan and bring to just below the boiling point over medium-high heat. Continue cooking until liquid is reduced by three-quarters, about 15 minutes, then allow to cool and transfer to the top of a double boiler.

2. Whisk egg yolks into wine reduction. Set over simmering water over medium heat and cook, whisking constantly, until yolks thicken enough to fall into thin ribbons when whisk is lifted from pan. Remove top of double boiler from bottom and, off heat, gradually whisk in olive oil. Thin, if necessary, with 1–2 tbsp. water. Season to taste with salt and pepper and set aside.

3. Tie asparagus together in a bundle with kitchen string and stand upright in an asparagus cooker or a deep, narrow saucepan. Add about 4" water and bring to a simmer over medium-high heat. Reduce heat to medium, cover pan with a lid or aluminum foil, and cook until asparagus is tender, 15–30 minutes. Untie bundle, transfer to a platter, and spoon sauce over asparagus.

Underground Delicacy

Greatly prized in Germany, Holland, Italy, France, and just about everywhere else in Europe, white asparagus is grown under mounds of earth to protect its pale stalks from the sunlight-inspired chlorophyll that would otherwise turn them green. Underground, the asparagus cores often grow fibrous and woody, so they need a long cooking time; and their skins tend to toughen—which is why white asparagus is virtually always peeled before cooking. Lay the brittle spears flat on a clean dish towel to peel and drain them, suggests Robert Lalleman (facing page, standing, with his father, André)—who serves flawless white stalks from a neighbor's farm with an olive oil sabayon at the family's Auberge de Noves near Avignon.

Ratatouille

SERVES 8

WITH ALL DUE respect to Jacques Médecin, Mamé Clairette, and other experts on Niçois cuisine (see sidebar), we've found that sautéing ratatouille vegetables separately and then cooking them together yields superior results. Mamé Clairette recommends making more ratatouille than you need, so there'll be some to eat later, hot or cold.

3 medium eggplants, cut into 2" cubes
4 medium zucchini, quartered lengthwise, then cut into 2" pieces
Coarse kosher salt
½ cup extra-virgin olive oil
6 medium yellow onions, peeled and thinly sliced
4 medium green or red bell peppers, cored, seeded, and cut into 1" x 2" strips
6 small tomatoes, peeled, seeded, and quartered
8 cloves garlic, peeled and minced
20 leaves fresh basil
1 bunch fresh parsley, stems trimmed
8 sprigs fresh thyme
Freshly ground black pepper

1. Put eggplant and zucchini in 2 separate strainers and toss each with 1 tbsp. salt. Allow to drain for 30 minutes. Blot dry with paper towels.

2. Heat 2 tbsp. oil over medium-low heat in a large skillet. Add onions and sauté until translucent, about 15 minutes, then transfer to a bowl and set aside. Add 2 tbsp. oil to same skillet, increase heat to medium-high, add eggplant, and sauté until golden, about 20 minutes. Transfer eggplant to a large heavy pot with a cover and spoon a thin layer of onions on top. Add 2 tbsp. oil to skillet, then add zucchini and sauté until golden, about 10 minutes. Transfer to pot and cover with a thin layer of onions. Add 1 tbsp. oil to skillet, then add peppers and sauté until edges turn brown, about 15 minutes. Transfer to pot and cover with a thin layer of onions.

3. Add remaining 1 tbsp. oil to skillet, add tomatoes, garlic, and basil, lightly crushing tomatoes with the back of a fork, and cook until slightly thickened, about 15 minutes. Transfer to pot, add remaining onions, parsley, and thyme, and season to taste with salt and pepper.

4. Simmer, partially covered, over low heat, gently stirring occasionally, for 1½ hours. Adjust seasoning, then cook about 30 minutes more.

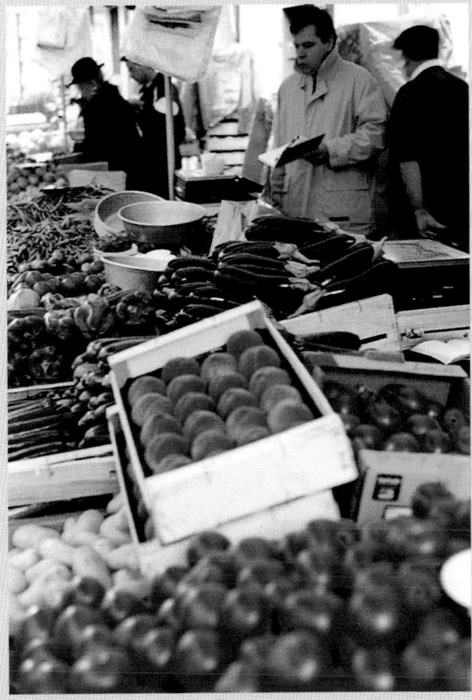

From the Experts

"Contrary to what is generally believed," writes Jacques Médecin, the late mayor of Nice and an expert on Niçois cuisine, in his *La Cuisine du comté de Nice* (Juillard, 1972), "ratatouille is a dish requiring a particularly long and difficult preparation". That's because, he insists, the ingredients of this mix of (mostly post-Columbian) Mediterranean vegetables should be cooked individually, then married together in one pot just before serving. Mamé Clairette, the Niçois grandmother interviewed by Bernard Duplessy in his *Cuisine traditionnelle en pays niçois* (Édisud, 1995), agrees, proposing that little touches like salting the eggplant and the zucchini before cooking and then using separate pots for the vegetables are "what makes the difference between the ratatouille of Nice and the mishmashes of the incompetent".

Flower Power

Although the flowers from any variety of squash can be eaten, those of the zucchini are the most popular in the south of France—where it sometimes seems as if the flowers are more genuinely appreciated than the fruit itself. The blossoms sold for frying purposes in Provence and along the Côte d'Azur are usually male—i.e., blossoms that will never yield an actual zucchini. It's easy to tell the difference between the male and female flowers on the vine: Male ones grow on long stems; female ones extend from the zucchini itself.

Beignets de Fleurs de Courgettes

(Deep-Fried Zucchini Blossoms)

SERVES 6

AT LA MERENDA, on the edge of Vieux Nice, former owner Jean Giusti made the most extraordinary deep-fried zucchini blossoms, using large pale green flowers delicately veined in egg-yolk yellow. This is our version of his recipe.

1 ½ cups flour
1 tsp. salt
1 tbsp. extra-virgin olive oil
1 egg, lightly beaten
18 large or 36 small zucchini or other squash blossoms
Vegetable oil
1 clove garlic, peeled and finely chopped
2 tbsp. finely chopped fresh flat-leaf parsley
Salt

1. Sift flour and salt together into a medium bowl. Whisk in oil, egg, and 2 cups water.

2. Remove center and discard stamens from the squash blossoms, then carefully wash and pat dry. Pour vegetable oil into a heavy skillet to a depth of 2". Heat oil over medium-high heat to 375° or until it sizzles when you drop in a little batter. (If oil isn't hot enough, squash blossoms will absorb too much of it.) Just before frying, add garlic and parsley to batter, stirring well. Dip flowers in batter, coating them inside and out. Drop into oil—working in batches and not crowding the pan—and fry until lightly golden, 1–3 minutes, turning frequently. Use a slotted spoon to transfer to paper towels, drain, and sprinkle with salt.

la Merenda

Farcis à la Niçoise

(Nice-Style Stuffed Vegetables)

Serves 6

Jacques Médecin, that most authoritative of authorities on the subject of Niçois cooking, maintains that each vegetable in this classic assortment should be stuffed with a different filling. In reality, most Niçois restaurants and home cooks alike use one all-purpose stuffing recipe like this one.

3 small eggplants
6 small green or red bell peppers
½ cup extra-virgin olive oil
Salt
3 small yellow onions, peeled
3 small zucchini
3 medium tomatoes
¼ lb. lean salt pork, diced
½ lb. ground lamb
¾ cup cooked rice
1 cup finely chopped fresh flat-leaf parsley
2 cloves garlic, peeled and minced
Freshly ground black pepper
2 eggs, lightly beaten
½ cup finely grated parmigiano-reggiano
½ cup fresh bread crumbs
1 bunch fresh thyme

1. Preheat oven to 350°. Cut eggplants in half lengthwise. Cut tops from peppers, then core and seed them. Place eggplants and peppers on an oiled baking sheet and brush lightly with oil. Bake for 30 minutes, then remove from oven and set aside to cool. When eggplants are cool enough to handle, scoop out pulp, leaving about ½"-thick shell. Chop pulp finely and set aside in a large bowl.

2. Heat a large pot of salted water over medium heat. Add onions and zucchini and simmer for about 10 minutes. Drain and set aside to cool.

3. Halve onions crosswise and remove centers, leaving a shell of about 3 outer layers. Halve zucchini lengthwise and scoop out pulp, leaving about ½"-thick shell. Halve tomatoes crosswise, then squeeze out and discard seeds and juice. Scoop pulp from tomatoes, finely chop, and add to eggplant pulp. Finely chop onion centers and zucchini pulp and add them to eggplant mixture as well.

4. Increase oven temperature to 375°. Heat 2 tbsp. oil in a large pan over low heat. Stir in vegetable mixture, salt pork, lamb, rice, parsley, and garlic. Season to taste with salt and pepper. Cook for about 15 minutes, stirring occasionally. Remove from heat, cool slightly, then stir in eggs.

5. Fill vegetable shells (don't pack too tightly), top with parmigiano-reggiano and bread crumbs, drizzle with remaining olive oil, and bake for 30 minutes on an oiled baking sheet. Serve garnished with fresh thyme sprigs.

Clever Cooking

Stuffed vegetables are eaten all along the French Riviera, and perhaps no genre of dishes more dramatically characterizes the region's legendary frugality and ingenuity. Faced with the challenge of feeding a whole family with the meager daily output of a kitchen garden, housewives along this portion of the Mediterranean coast figured out that by scooping out the flesh of vegetables they grew, mixing it with wild herbs, crumbs of hardened bread, leftover rice, and maybe a bit of meat and/or a few wild mushrooms, then packing it back into the shells, they could virtually double the volume of their produce. This kind of inventiveness is common to the region's kitchens. A little flour can be stretched into tourte dough, filled with wild greens and a bit of cheese, and served to half a dozen people; the lowly chickpea can be turned into flour and the flour into the crêpe-like socca or the fried-polenta-like panisse; a hint of dried mushrooms or dried or salted fish can perfume a huge pot of soup. Abundance sometimes yields great food, but so can impoverishment.

Name That Dish

The tian is not just something to eat, but also the shallow earthenware vessel in which it is traditionally cooked. A number of other French dishes derive their names from the vessels that contain them. **COCOTTE:** A round dish, usually ceramic or cast-iron, used for casseroles (e.g. poulet en cocotte) or, in smaller form, for dishes like oeufs (eggs) en cocotte. **DAUBE:** From *daubière*, an earthenware pot; a daube is meat, poultry, game, or fish braised in wine and stock with vegetables, etc. Used without qualification, daube means beef in red wine. **MARMITE:** A tall stew pot, and the (usually) fish and shellfish stew cooked in one. **RAMEQUIN:** An individual baking dish, or the little treat (e.g. ramequin au fromage, cheese tartlet) that fills it. **TERRINE:** A dish, usually rectangular (like those above) and traditionally made of earthenware (the name comes from the Latin *terra*, or earth), in which pâtés are cooked (see page 37)—thus becoming, at least in traditional terminology, terrines. **TIMBALE:** A round high-sided mold, originally designed to imitate pastry crust; today, timbales are usually fish or vegetable purées or small mousses, unmolded and served with a sauce.

Tian de Légumes

(Mediterranean Vegetable Casserole)

SERVES 6

THE VEGETABLE dishes (sometimes bound with eggs) called tians are popular in traditional kitchens all over the south of France. Originally, it is said, tians were constructed so that their cooking time corresponded to the time it took to bake bread in a communal oven, because housewives would make them up at home, then bring them to these once-common public facilities to share the baker's fire.

1 medium eggplant, peeled
Salt
2 medium yellow onions, peeled and chopped
3 cloves garlic, peeled and minced
½ cup extra-virgin olive oil
Freshly ground black pepper
2 medium zucchini, sliced diagonally
6 medium ripe tomatoes, sliced
Leaves from 3–4 sprigs fresh herbs, such as thyme, rosemary, or oregano
½ cup grated parmigiano-reggiano

1. Cut eggplant into 1" cubes, sprinkle with 1 tsp. salt, and place in a colander. Drain for 30 minutes, then pat dry with paper towels.

2. Cook onions and garlic in 3 tbsp. olive oil in a large skillet over medium heat until lightly browned, about 10 minutes. Transfer to a medium baking dish. Add 2–3 tbsp. olive oil to the same skillet, then add eggplant and cook until tender and slightly browned, about 10 minutes. Season to taste with salt and pepper, and stir into onion mixture.

3. Preheat oven to 400°. Arrange zucchini and tomatoes in alternating layers over eggplant mixture. Top with herbs, drizzle with remaining 2–3 tbsp. oil, season to taste with salt and pepper, and bake 30–40 minutes. Sprinkle with cheese just before serving.

Grand Aïoli

(Vegetables and Salt Cod with Garlic Sauce)

SERVES 6–8

AÏOLI IS BOTH a garlic mayonnaise and a dish of salt cod (or cold meats) and vegetables with which the sauce is served. This recipe comes from the Relais Notre-Dame (right), a family-run hotel-restaurant surrounded by wheat and lavender fields in Quinson, in the southern part of Haute Provence.

FOR SALT COD AND VEGETABLES:
2 lbs. salt cod
2 bay leaves
4 black peppercorns
9 whole small yellow onions, peeled
2 cloves garlic, peeled
Salt
Hearts of 8 small artichokes
1 whole cauliflower, separated into florets
8 whole carrots, peeled
1 lb. green beans, trimmed
8 medium potatoes, peeled
8 medium beets, trimmed, peeled, and halved
8 hard-cooked eggs

FOR AÏOLI:
6 cloves garlic, crushed and peeled
Coarse salt
2 egg yolks
2 cups extra-virgin olive oil
Juice of 1 lemon (optional)

1. For salt cod, put fish in a large bowl with cold water to cover completely and soak for 24 hours in the refrigerator, changing the water 3 or 4 times.

2. Combine bay leaves, peppercorns, 1 of the onions, and garlic in a medium pot with 4 cups water. Bring to a boil over medium-high heat, then reduce heat to low and simmer for 20 minutes. Allow to cool, then add salt cod and return to a simmer for 20 minutes. Drain fish, set aside to cool, and remove and discard any skin or bones.

3. For vegetables, bring a large pot of salted water to a boil over medium-high heat. Cook artichokes, cauliflower, and carrots separately, until tender but not overcooked, about 10 minutes each, removing each from water when done with a slotted spoon and setting aside. Cook green beans until tender but not overcooked, about 5 minutes, then remove from water and set aside as before. Cook potatoes and beets separately (making sure to cook beets last) until tender but not overdone, about 20 minutes each, then remove from water and set aside as before.

4. For aïoli, using a large mortar and pestle, pound garlic and a good pinch of salt together into a smooth paste. Work egg yolks into garlic paste with pestle or a whisk until mixture is thick and pale yellow. Drizzle in oil a few drops at a time, whisking continuously. When sauce begins to emulsify, increase flow of oil to a fine stream, continuing to whisk in until all the oil is used up. Whisk in lemon juice 1 tsp. at a time to thin, if you like. Season to taste with salt. To serve, arrange salt cod, vegetables, and eggs on platters and serve with aïoli on the side.

Divine Aïoli

Essentially a garlic mayonnaise (it takes its name from the Provençal words for oil and garlic), aïoli may have been invented by the Roman emperor Nero, who is said to have been a great connoisseur of garlic. The Byzantines favored an eggless version of the sauce, roasting garlic whole, then crushing it with olive oil and salt. Writer Léon Daudet (son of writer Alphonse, and one of the epic gastronomes of the late 19th century), considered aïoli

the finest culinary use to which garlic could be put. Mistral, the great Provençal poet, imbued it with almost spiritual power, writing "When they are seated around the divine aïoli, fragrant aïoli, deep in color as a golden thread, where, tell me where are those men who do not recognize that they are brothers."

Raviolis de Bourrache

(Borage Ravioli)

Serves 4–6

Borage is a mild Mediterranean herb that remains something of a rarity in America, though found in some specialty markets and easy to grow. Dandelion leaves may be substituted in this recipe from Le Cagnard in Cagnes.

FOR PASTA:
4 eggs, lightly beaten
2 tbsp. extra-virgin olive oil
2 tbsp. white vinegar
4 cups flour

FOR FILLING:
4 tbsp. extra-virgin olive oil
2 small yellow onions, peeled and finely chopped
1 ½ lbs. borage, cleaned and chopped
6 cloves garlic, peeled and minced
1 tbsp. minced fresh basil
1 tbsp. minced fresh sage
½ cup minced fresh parsley
2 tbsp. minced fresh thyme
Salt and freshly ground black pepper
2 oz. mild chèvre

FOR SAUCE:
2 cups chicken stock *(see page 56)*
2 tsp. demi-glace *(see sidebar, page 61)*
3 tbsp. butter
4 fresh sage leaves, julienned

1. For pasta, whisk together eggs, oil, and vinegar in a small bowl. Put flour in a large mixing bowl or food processor. Gradually work egg mixture into flour, then turn out onto a lightly floured surface and knead for about 5 minutes, until smooth and elastic. Form dough into a ball, wrap in plastic, and refrigerate for 1 hour.

2. For filling, heat oil in a large skillet over medium heat. Add onions and cook, stirring often, until they begin to soften, about 7 minutes. Add borage, garlic, basil, sage, parsley, and thyme, season to taste with salt and pepper, then cook, stirring frequently, until greens wilt, about 5 minutes. Drain and set aside to cool, then put greens in a clean kitchen towel and squeeze dry. Transfer to a large bowl. Mix in chèvre and adjust seasoning with salt and pepper.

3. Divide dough into 4 parts. Using a pasta machine, roll out dough as thin as possible, then transfer to a lightly floured surface. Cut out about 60 rounds using a 2" cutter. To assemble ravioli, spoon about 1 tsp. of filling in the center of a dough round, brush edge with water, then top with another round, pinching to seal. Repeat process, using up all pasta rounds and filling.

4. For sauce, bring stock and demi-glace to a simmer in a medium saucepan over medium heat. Reduce by three-quarters, 20–30 minutes, then whisk in butter.

5. Meanwhile, cook ravioli in batches in a large pot of boiling salted water until they rise to the surface, 3–4 minutes. Drain and divide between 4–6 small plates. Top with sauce and garnish with julienned sage.

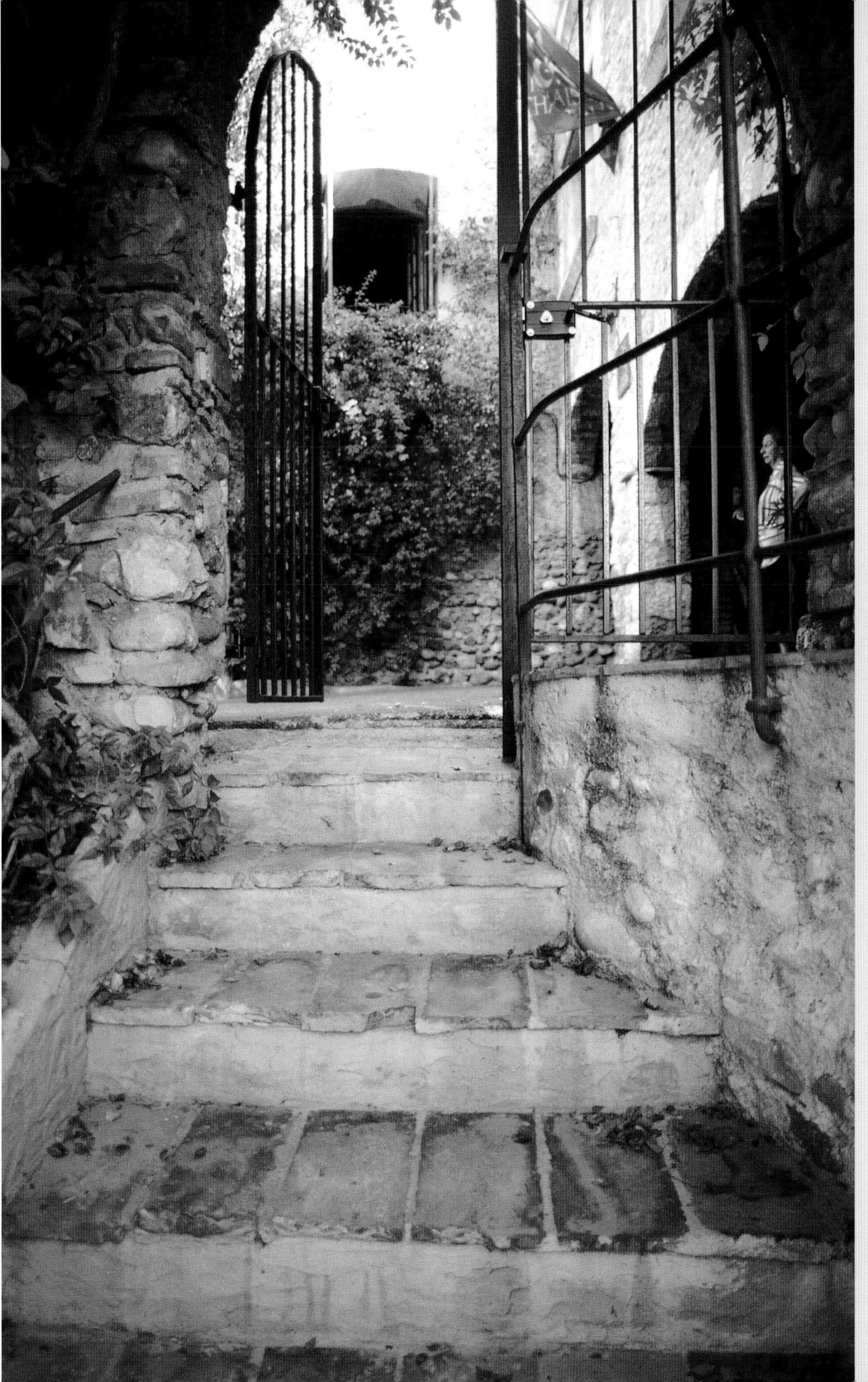

Culinary Heights

Rising above the seaside town of Cagnes-sur-Mer, just west of Nice, is the medieval hillside village of Haut-de-Cagnes (left)—once the haunt of Renoir, Modigliani, and Soutine, among other artists, and today the home of a charming hotel hideaway called Le Cagnard. Here, Jean-Yves Johanny—who must be one of the best unknown chefs in France— prepares light, pure-flavored, elegant (but not fussy) food—dishes like mushroom-stuffed squid with lobster sauce, poached veal loin with an herb and olive vinaigrette, and a remarkable borage-filled ravioli in a chicken-stock reduction. "More than anything," Johanny declares, "I look for simplicity in my cooking. I believe that cuisine *must* be simple. But it is very difficult to be simple in cuisine."

Cold Cabbage

Llívia is "in" France, but it *isn't* France: The Treaty of the Pyrenees, which established the mountain border between France and Spain over 300 years ago, gave to France all "villages" north of a certain line—but the citizens of Llívia came up with proof that they were officially a town and not a village; therefore, they still belonged to Spain. Food lovers from both sides of the frontier visit the place today for foie gras, local trout, or beef cooked on Pyrenean slate—or for reassuringly simple fare at places like the cheese shop turned restaurant called La Formatgeria de Llívia. One specialty here is trinxat, an age-old, prototypical mountain dish made of winter cabbage, potatoes, and salt pork. The cabbage, say local epicures, is best after it has semi-frozen—or at least been thoroughly frostbitten—in the fields.

Trinxat

(Catalan Cabbage and Potatoes)

SERVES 6

TRADITIONAL COOKING in the Catalan Pyrenees, on both sides of the border, is straightforward, hearty, and based on modest mountain ingredients. Trinxat (the name means "chopped" in Catalan) is a typical example. This recipe comes from Marta Pous of La Formatgeria de Llívia.

1 2-lb. savoy cabbage
Salt
2 lbs. russet potatoes, peeled
Cumin seeds (optional)
12 thick slices of salt pork or bacon
3 tbsp. extra-virgin olive oil
1 clove garlic, peeled and minced
2½ oz. fatback, rind removed, thinly sliced
Freshly ground black pepper

1. Pull off and discard tough outer leaves of cabbage. Bring two pots of generously salted water to a boil over medium-high heat. Put cabbage in one and potatoes in the other and cook both until very tender, about 30 minutes for the potatoes and 60 minutes for the cabbage.

2. Drain potatoes in a colander, then transfer to a large bowl. Drain cabbage in a colander and allow to cool slightly, then pull out and discard core and drain well, pressing cabbage to release water. Transfer cabbage to bowl with potatoes and mash together with a potato masher. Season to taste with salt, and with cumin if using.

3. Lightly brown salt pork strips on both sides in a 10" skillet over medium heat, working in batches to avoid crowding pan. Remove from skillet as done, drain on paper towels, and set aside. Pour off fat and wipe pan clean with paper towel.

4. Heat oil in same skillet over medium heat. Add garlic and cook until soft, 2–3 minutes. Stir oil and garlic into cabbage mixture.

5. In the same pan, heat half the fatback, until fat is rendered. Add half of the cabbage mixture and flatten into a ¾"-thick pancake. Cook over high heat until bottom crust has formed and pancake slides easily in the skillet, 5–10 minutes. Invert a large plate over pan and carefully flip trinxat over onto plate, then slide it back into pan, browned side up. Season to taste with salt and pepper and cook until bottom is crisp and brown. Slide pancake onto a platter and arrange 6 salt pork strips on top. Repeat process with remaining fatback and cabbage mixture to make second pancake.

Cardons à la "Bagna Cauda"

(Cardoons with Anchovy-Garlic Sauce)

SERVES 6

EUROPEAN CARDOONS can be eaten raw in preparations like this one—but the American variety needs to be cooked thoroughly to leach out its extreme bitterness.

2 lemons, 1 halved, 1 thinly sliced
3 lbs. cardoons, washed
Salt
¼ cup extra-virgin olive oil
2 tbsp. butter
1 clove garlic, peeled and minced
12 oil-packed anchovy filets, chopped

1. Squeeze juice from the halved lemon into a large pot filled with cold water, then add halves and lemon slices to the pot. Remove and discard outer stalks of cardoons, then trim off thorns (**A**) and peel off stringy fibers with a vegetable peeler (**B**). Cut into 2" pieces, and put them in the pot of lemon water as soon as they're cut to prevent discoloration (**C**).

2. Add salt to taste, and bring to a simmer over medium-high heat. Cook until cardoons are tender, about 30 minutes, then drain and dry on paper towels.

3. Heat olive oil and butter in a small saucepan over low heat. When butter is melted, add garlic and cook until fragrant, 1–2 minutes. Stir in anchovy filets, mash with a spoon, and cook, stirring occasionally, until flavors blend, about 10 minutes. Meanwhile, divide cardoons with a few lemon slices (discard halves) between 6 plates. Spoon anchovy-garlic sauce over cardoons.

Soothing Cardoons

As a child in Provence," writes Nice-born Mireille Johnston, "I viewed our big holiday meals as fraught with danger. Too many opinionated, theatrical relatives, all with nostalgic regrets—all waiting, it seemed, for lightning to strike. But at our annual *souper maigre*, the meatless meal served before midnight Mass on Christmas Eve, something interesting happened every year: The minute a basket of crisp, raw cardoon pieces was served as part of the first-course *bagna cauda*—literally 'hot bath', a Piedmontese vegetable dish adopted in Provence, featuring raw vegetables and a warm anchovy-garlic-and-olive-oil dip—conversations would shift from familial scandals to the food at hand. The process of preparing cardoons is long and messy, but they might help encourage the relatives to behave."

Petits Pois aux Morilles

(Ragoût of Peas and Morels)

SERVES 4

CANNED PEAS? The French actually prefer them for the traditional preparation of petit pois with lettuce; three-quarters of the French pea crop, in fact, ends up in cans. For this springtime ragoût, however, only fresh peas will do.

12 small dried morels
12 pearl onions
2 tbsp. butter
8 whole small carrots, peeled and trimmed
½ tsp. sugar
1 cup shelled fresh peas
Salt and freshly ground black pepper

1. Wash morels under running water and trim root ends from onions. Bring 4 cups water to a boil in a medium saucepan. Add morels and onions, cover, and remove from heat. After 1 minute, remove onions with a slotted spoon. Replace cover and soak morels until soft, about 10 minutes. Peel onions.

2. Remove morels from water with a slotted spoon and rinse well, reserving soaking liquid. Pour soaking liquid through a sieve lined with a coffee filter and return to saucepan. Bring to a boil over medium-high heat and cook until liquid is reduced to 1 cup, about 20 minutes.

3. Melt butter in a skillet over medium-high heat. Add carrots and cook until lightly browned, about 3 minutes. Reduce heat to medium-low, add onions, sugar, and ½ cup water, and simmer until liquid evaporates, about 15 minutes. Add morels and morel stock, cover, and cook for 7 minutes more. Add peas and cook for 5 minutes more. Season to taste with salt and pepper.

The Novelty of Petits Pois

Peas were eaten in France as long ago as the seventh century B.C., in the Languedoc, where archaeologists have found them fossilized in the debris left by early inhabitants. They don't seem to have entered serious French gastronomy, though, until around 1600, when the pois mange-tout, or sugar pea, arrived from Holland. And the green pea, or petit pois, as we know it today dates only from 1660 in France. In January of that year, one Sieur Audiger, sent to Italy on a confidential mission by Louis XIV, returned from Genoa to present his monarch with a hamper of them. Audiger recorded the response of the courtiers who "all declared with one voice that nothing could be more of a novelty, and that nothing like it, in that season, had ever been seen in France before". The peas were shelled and prepared for the Court—whose delight was such that the pea became the most fashionable of vegetables.

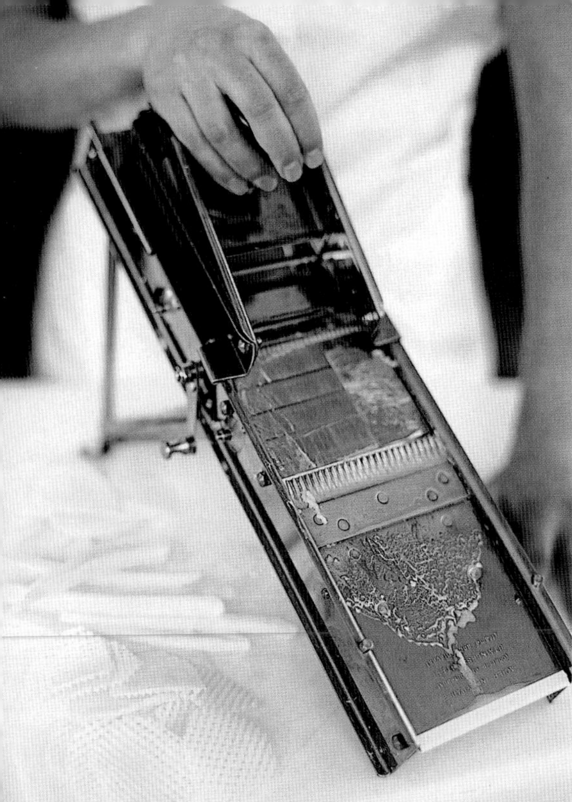

Kitchen Music

Gourmet shops are filled with work- and time-saving gizmos," notes SAVEUR executive editor Christopher Hirsheimer, "and heaven knows I've bought my fair share over the years. Most of them have ended up as drawer food. But when I decided to make pommes soufflées recently, I dug around and pulled out an old friend: my sturdy, nickel-plated stainless steel French mandoline. This super-efficient cutting tool, with its adjustable and interchangeable blades, cuts piles of potatoes in minutes. I thought it was wildly expensive when I bought it 20 years ago (it cost over a hundred bucks even then!), but it turned out to be well worth the investment. I can't imagine making pommes soufflées, or plenty of other things, without it."

Pommes Soufflées

(French Potato Puffs)

Serves 6

It's tricky to make these elegant cousins of the french fry. They must be cut evenly and to precisely the right thickness, and the (two) temperatures of the oil must be exact.

6–8 large russet potatoes (5–6 lbs.), peeled
Peanut oil
Salt

1. Shape whole potatoes into rectangles or cylinders about 2½" long and about 1½" wide, then slice potatoes evenly with a mandoline or a very sharp knife (a mandoline is better; see facing page) to a thickness of ⅛". Place slices in a nonreactive bowl and cover with water.

2. Heat about 4" oil in a cast-iron pot over medium heat. Drain potatoes, then dry very thoroughly with paper towels. Check oil temperature with a kitchen thermometer. When oil reaches 250°, cook potatoes, without browning, in small batches, turning occasionally, until they are tender and slightly blistered and their edges are slightly crisp, about 4 minutes. Drain potatoes on paper towels and allow to cool for about 20 minutes. (Potatoes may be cooked to this point several hours in advance of serving and kept in refrigerator until ready for second frying.)

3. Reheat oil. When temperature reaches 400°, fry potatoes in small batches until they puff up, which should be immediate. Continue frying until potatoes are crisp, about 1–2 minutes per batch. Serve immediately, generously salted, or recrisp for 20 seconds in 400° oil before serving and salting.

Gratin Dauphinois

(Potatoes Baked in Milk and Cream)

Serves 6

A GRATIN IS SIMPLY a dish whose top is browned in the oven. In the Dauphiné, the best-known version is made with sliced potatoes—but it may also be prepared with macaroni, ground meat, pumpkin, beets, cardoons, wild mushrooms of various kinds, or crayfish tails.

2 lbs. large russet potatoes, peeled and thinly sliced
1 ½ cups whole milk
1 ½ cups heavy cream
Salt and freshly ground black pepper
Freshly grated nutmeg

1. Preheat oven to 275°. Arrange layers of slightly overlapping potato slices in an 8-cup gratin or baking dish. Mix together milk and cream in a bowl, then pour over potatoes to cover completely (use a little more cream or milk if necessary). Bake for 1½ hours.

2. Increase heat to 400°. Remove pan from oven and generously season top of potatoes with salt, pepper, and nutmeg. Return pan to oven and cook until brown and bubbling, about 30 minutes more.

Potatoes and Cream

The Dauphiné, which stretches from Savoie to Provence—and is sometimes called "the country of the four mountains" (these being the peaks of Lans-en-Vercors, Villard-de-Lans, Autrans, and Sassenage)—is renowned for, among other things, the quality and abundance of its milk and cream. Local legend has it that around 1900, one Mère Revollet of the Hôtel Revollet in the village of St-Nizier devised a way to cook potatoes, another well-regarded specialty, that made good use of these dairy products. Later adaptations of the gratin dauphinois added garlic, butter, cheese, and/or eggs—and even, in gastronomic Lyon, slices of black truffle. Another regional variation, the gratin savoyard, uses stock in place of milk and cream, and alternates layers of potatoes and beaufort cheese, with knobs of butter throughout.

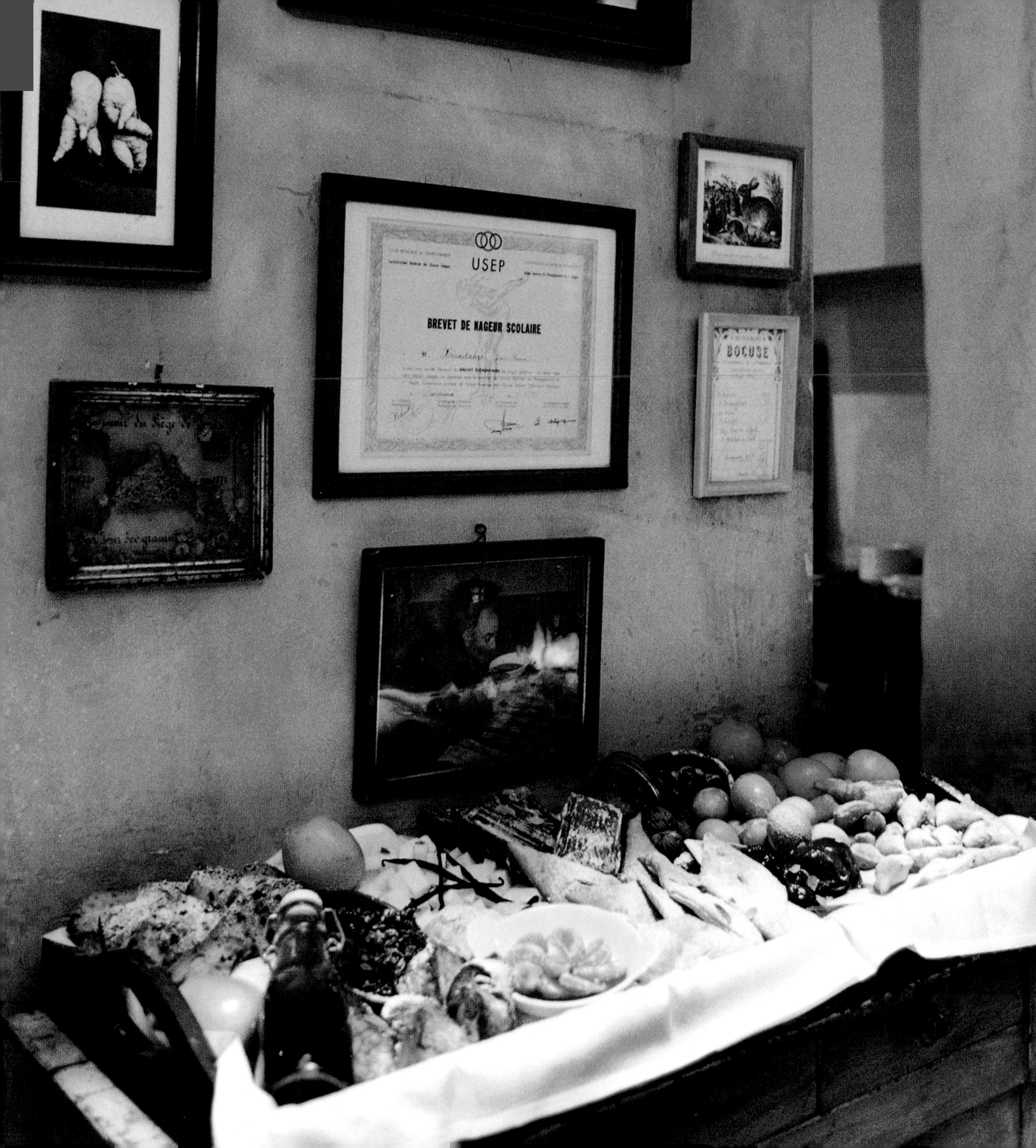
USEP
BREVET DE NAGEUR SCOLAIRE
BOCUSE

CHAPTER

10

DESSERTS

"As we step from a cobbled street in Bordeaux's old quarter through the thick stone doorway of the restaurant called La Tupiña, we see Jean-Pierre Xiradakis cook-ing before an open hearth. Wide-eyed with enthusiasm, his shirt damp from the heat, he cranks a pulley that rotates a chicken roasting on an iron spit. Xiradakis (facing page, upper left and lower right) steps back and surveys his cast-iron skillets, griddles, and caldrons. 'I started La Tupiña [itself named for a kind of cooking pot],' he tells us, 'to offer the food my mother and grandmother cooked when I was a child.' A surprising number of the old Bordelais dishes he's talking about utilize one of the great gastronomic treasures of southwestern France: the flavorful purplish plum called prune d'ente when fresh and pruneau d'Agen when dried. This modest fruit, versatile and bountiful, gets added to red wine sauces (like rabbit with dried prunes, and even the local version of coq au vin), and to all manner of confections. Xiradakis admits, however, that plums were not his favorite childhood food; his mother made her children eat them more for good health than for sheer enjoyment. Nonetheless, he uses them freely in desserts today—in, for instance, an homage to his grandmother's plum tart (see page 277); in an opulent prune ice cream; and in his remarkable pruneaux à l'armagnac, in which the prunes have spent three woozy weeks steeped in that great brandy until they have puffed up to look almost like fresh plums again. There is a saying in the region to the effect that 'The aroma of the countryside is found in a plum.' Creations like these make that easy to believe." —DAVID CASE AND MEGAN WETHERALL

RECIPES

Tarte aux Prunes Façon Grand-Mère

(Grandmother's Plum Tart)

Serves 8

France's celebrated prune d'ente was originally called the *prune datte*, or date plum, and later dubbed the *robe de sergent*, or sergeant's cloak—in reference to its purplish hue, which evoked the color of civil guards' uniforms.

FOR PASTRY:
- *1 ½ cups flour*
- *¼ cup confectioners' sugar*
- *10 tbsp. butter, cut into small pieces*
- *1 whole egg*
- *1 egg yolk*
- *½ tsp. vanilla extract*

FOR FILLING:
- *1 lb. dried pitted prunes*
- *1 cup armagnac*
- *½ cup sugar*
- *2 tbsp. butter, cut into small pieces*
- *2 egg yolks*
- *⅔ cup heavy cream*

1. For pastry, sift together flour and sugar in a mixing bowl. Add butter, and using a pastry cutter, 2 knives, or the tips of your fingers, blend butter into flour mixture until it resembles coarse meal. Beat together egg, 1 egg yolk, and vanilla in a small bowl. Add to flour mixture and mix with your hands until dough holds together. Turn dough out on a lightly floured surface and work dough by "smearing" it with the heel of your hand until it is smooth. Form into a ball, cover with plastic wrap, and refrigerate for at least 2 hours, or overnight.

2. For filling, soak prunes in armagnac and 1–2 cups hot water in a covered container for at least 2 hours or overnight.

3. Preheat oven to 400°. Roll out dough on a lightly floured surface into a 13" round. Ease dough into an 11" flan ring set on a parchment-lined baking sheet and roll the rolling pin across top to cut off excess dough. Line shell with parchment, fill with weights or dried beans, and bake for 30 minutes. Remove from oven and lift out weight-filled parchment.

4. Drain prunes, then arrange in pastry shell, sprinkle with sugar, and dot with butter pieces. Return to oven for 10 minutes to allow butter and sugar to melt into a syrup. Meanwhile, whisk together 2 egg yolks and cream in a small bowl until just mixed. Remove tart from oven and pour custard over prunes. Return to oven for another 10 minutes until custard just sets. Remove tart from oven and set aside to cool completely. Transfer tart to a serving platter by removing flan ring and lifting parchment and tart onto the platter, then gently slip parchment out from under tart.

Spirit of the Plum

Although the plum called prune d'ente is delicious to eat by itself, delicious when cooked into pastries and other desserts, and legendary in its dried form (as the pruneau d'Agen), it is appreciated in still another form by connoisseurs of southwestern French gastronomy: as vieille prune, or old plum—which is to say brandy made from the fruit. Among the best vieille prune is that produced about 90 miles south of Bordeaux, in the Pays Basque, under the Etienne Brana label. Martine Brana, daughter of the late Etienne, ferments plum juice—mostly from prunes d'ente with a soupçon of another variety, the greengage, added—in stainless steel vats, then transfers it to airtight tanks before distilling it in copper pot stills. The resulting brandy is then diluted to a strength of 100 proof and blended with older brandies. The result is a remarkable spirit, suggesting both calvados and armagnac but with an identity very much its own—characterized by an elegant bouquet and a fresh plum flavor that deepens and grows more complex as it lingers on your palate.

Upper Crusts

The French don't make "pie crust"; they make pastry dough, and in five main varieties: **PÂTE BRISÉE** is shortcrust or basic tart dough, composed of just flour, butter, salt, and water, with an egg or a bit of sugar as optional additions; it is used for savory tarts, quiches, and pâtés en croûte. **PÂTE SUCRÉE**, sweet shortcrust pastry, is the sweet, more sugary version of pâte brisée. It is the classic base for dessert tarts. **PÂTE SABLÉE** is a close relative of pâte sucrée, even sweeter; although it is delicate and thus difficult to work with, it forms a delicious base for fresh fruit tarts and for petits fours. **PÂTE À CHOUX**, which is easier to make than one might imagine, is formed from a dense white panade, or sauce, of flour, water, and butter, seasoned with salt, into which eggs are beaten; it is essential for savory delights like gougères (see page 83) and for such pastries as éclairs, profiteroles, and croquembouche (see page 308). Finally there is the revered **PÂTE FEUILLETÉE**, so difficult to make that even French housewives buy it ready-made. Fashioned from equal quantities of butter and flour plus water and salt, it is turned, rolled out, and folded back upon itself as many as eight times; when it bakes, the butter melts and steam pushes up the dough layers into the famous mille-feuille or thousand-leaf effect.

Tarte aux Pommes

(Apple Tart)

SERVES 8

AFTER LUNCH at bookseller and gastronome Gérard Oberlé's house in Burgundy (see page 230), out came thin-crust apple and rhubarb tarts made by Giles Brezol, Oberlé's friend and business partner. Oberlé's housekeeper, Lucette Malinouski, demonstrates the apple tart basics at right.

FOR PASTRY:
2 cups flour
Pinch salt
1 tbsp. sugar
9 tbsp. butter, cut into small pieces

FOR FILLING:
3–4 granny smith apples
¼ cup sugar

1. For pastry, sift flour, salt, and sugar together into a mixing bowl. Add butter, and using a pastry cutter, 2 knives, or the tips of your fingers, blend butter into flour mixture until it resembles coarse meal. Add up to 6 tbsp. ice water, 1 tbsp. at a time, mixing with a fork until dough just holds together. Cover with plastic wrap and refrigerate for 30 minutes.

2. Preheat oven to 425°. Roll out dough on a lightly floured surface into a 14" round (**A** & **B**). Fit pastry into a buttered 10" false-bottomed tart pan, taking care not to stretch dough (**C** & **D**). Roll the rolling pin across top of tart pan to cut off excess pastry. Prick the bottom of the pastry all over with a fork (**E**).

3. For filling, peel (**F**), core, and thinly slice apples. Sprinkle 1 tbsp. sugar across surface of pastry. Working from outer edge towards the center, overlap apple slices in concentric circles (**G** & **H**), then evenly sprinkle with remaining 3 tbsp. sugar (**I**). Bake until edge of tart is golden, about 40 minutes. Allow to cool before serving.

A
B
C
D
E
F
G
H
I

Tarte aux Fraises

(Strawberry Tart)

Serves 6

To avoid the flavorless-strawberry problem, buy fresh strawberries only in season, look for the best local varieties—and make this tart only when you can find those tasty fruits.

FOR STRAWBERRIES:
4 cups fresh strawberries, washed and hulled
¼ cup sugar

FOR PASTRY:
1 ½ cups flour
½ tsp. salt
1 tbsp. sugar
9 tbsp. butter, cut into small pieces

FOR PASTRY CREAM:
1 cup milk
½ vanilla bean, split lengthwise
3 egg yolks
¼ cup sugar
1 tbsp. flour

1. For strawberries, put strawberries in a bowl and sprinkle with sugar. Set aside to macerate for at least 30 minutes at room temperature.

2. For pastry, preheat oven to 400°. Sift flour, salt, and sugar into a bowl. Rub butter into flour mixture with your fingers until it resembles coarse crumbs. Sprinkle in 3 tbsp. ice water. Work dough on a floured surface until it just holds together. Form into a ball, wrap in plastic, and refrigerate for 30 minutes.

3. For pastry cream, put milk and vanilla bean in a medium heavy saucepan. Bring milk just to a boil over medium heat. Cool slightly, remove vanilla bean, scrape seeds into milk, then discard the pod. Whisk egg yolks and sugar together in a bowl until blended, then sprinkle in flour, continuing to whisk the mixture. Gradually whisk in milk, then return mixture to saucepan. Cook over low heat, stirring, until thickened, about 10 minutes. Remove from heat and set aside to cool.

4. Roll out pastry dough on a floured surface into a 12" round then fit into a 9" tart pan, taking care not to stretch the dough. Roll the rolling pin across top of tart pan to cut off excess pastry. Prick the bottom of the pastry all over with a fork. Cover dough with foil and fill with dried beans. Bake for 15 minutes, then remove foil and beans and continue baking until shell is golden, 10–15 minutes. Allow to cool.

5. Stir juice from berries into pastry cream, then spread mixture evenly in tart shell. Arrange strawberries upright atop mixture. Serve at once.

Drunken Strawberries

Appealing though a homemade strawberry tart may be, there's an even easier and no less delicious way to present good berries: as fraises au vin rouge, strawberries in red wine. To serve 4, wash and hull 4 cups fresh, ripe strawberries, then halve them lengthwise. Sprinkle berries with 2–3 tbsp. sugar, mix gently, then set aside to macerate for about 1 hour. Divide berries between 4 large wine goblets, then pour in enough red wine—preferably a fruity young pinot noir or beaujolais—to cover berries. (Certain elegant Parisian restaurants used to offer fraises au Lafite, made with guess what wine—but that may be overdoing things a bit.) Serve topped with a dollop of crème fraîche, if you like.

Tarte Tatin

(Upside-Down Apple Tart)

Serves 8

IN HONOR of the role played by Maxim's in popularizing this classic tart, we asked Jean-Yves de Charme (right), the restaurant's present-day chef-pâtissier, for this recipe.

FOR APPLES:
2 ½ sticks (20 tbsp.) butter, cut into small pieces
1 ½ cups sugar
9 golden delicious apples, peeled, cored, and halved

FOR PASTRY:
1 cup flour
½ tsp. salt
1 tbsp. sugar
6 tbsp. butter, cut into small pieces

1. For apples, preheat oven to 400°. Scatter butter pieces and sprinkle sugar evenly in a 9–10" copper tatin pan or a heavy baking pan. Tightly pack 14 apple halves around inside edge of pan, standing upright, nestled against one another, with round side tilted down. Place 4 remaining halves in similar position in center of pan. (Apples will shrink as they cook and slip round side down into pan.) Bake for about 2 hours.

2. Transfer pan from oven to stove top and cook over medium-high heat until butter and sugar caramelize to a rich brown, 15–20 minutes. Remove from heat, and gently ease sticky apples away from the side of pan with a knife. Refrigerate overnight so that apples firm up and "confit" further.

3. For pastry, preheat oven to 350° about 1 hour before serving tart. Sift flour, salt, and sugar into a bowl. Rub butter into flour mixture with your fingers until it resembles coarse crumbs. Sprinkle in 3 tbsp. ice water and work dough until it just holds together. Form into a ball, wrap in plastic, and refrigerate for 30 minutes. Roll out dough on a floured surface into a 12" circle.

4. Drape pastry over apples and pan. Roll the rolling pin across top of pan to cut off excess pastry and allow pastry to fall over apples against inside edge of pan. Bake in oven (still at 350°) until pastry is flaky and golden, about 20 minutes.

5. Remove from oven, place a flat ovenproof platter on top of tatin pan and invert quickly and carefully. Do not unmold yet. Reduce heat to 300° and return platter and pan to oven for 10 minutes. Remove tatin pan and serve warm.

VARIATION: *Puff Pastry Tarte Tatin*—Follow steps 1 and 2 above. Preheat oven to 350°. Roll out 1 puff pastry sheet on a floured surface and use a sharp knife to cut it into a 12" circle. Bake on a parchment-lined baking sheet for 15 minutes. Pastry will puff, turn golden, and shrink to fit pan. Put on top of apples and bake for 20 minutes. Proceed with step 5 above.

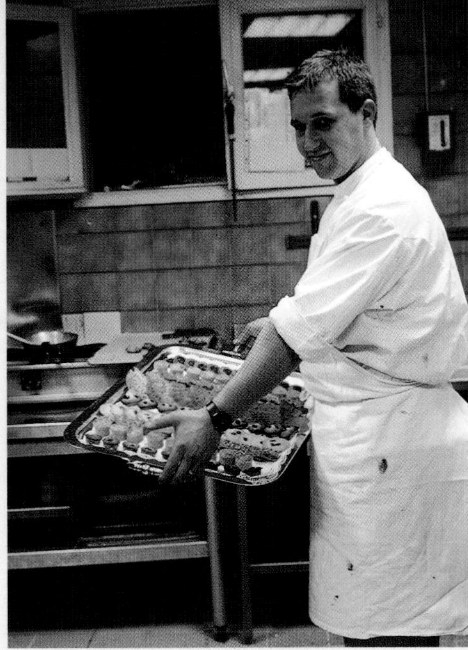

Delicious Accident

Jean Tatin was a baker and pastry chef in the village of Lamotte-Beuvron, in the Sologne, 110 miles north of Paris, and his daughters, Caroline and Stéphanie, opened the Hôtel Tatin there in 1860. In the hotel kitchen one day, Stéphanie, who had learned her father's craft, apparently either accidentally or deliberately upturned an apple tart onto a baking tray and put it in the oven. The results were good, and the tart became a specialty of the hotel. The story goes that news of the new dessert reached the ears of one Monsieur Gaillard, a frequent visitor to the Sologne (where he hunted wild game) and owner of the legendary Maxim's in Paris. He is said to have become a regular customer at the Tatins' table, and he eventually introduced Stéphanie's creation to his own customers—who happened to be the crème de la crème of Parisian society. The rest is dessert history.

Lemon Fest

France's most famous lemon-producing region is the *arrière-pays*, or back-country, around Menton, abutting the Italian border on the Mediterranean coast. So vividly are the lemons identified with the town, in fact, that its annual version of carnival is called the Fête du Citron, or lemon festival. Every year, just before Lent, local enterprises, neighboring towns, and even foreign participants (the German spa town of Baden-Baden, for instance) construct elaborate, massive set pieces out of lemons, oranges, and other citrus fruit, to be put on display in the public garden called Jardins Biovès (below). In a sort of puckery variation on the Rose Parade, floats similarly decked out roll down the city streets on Shrove Tuesday evening, and there are concerts, fireworks shows, art exhibitions, and special dinners, too. Shortly after Ash Wednesday everything stops, and any fruit still in edible condition gets sold off at bargain prices, for use in such local specialties as vin d'orange and vin de citron—wine macerated with spices and oranges or lemons, respectively.

Tarte au Citron

(Lemon Tart)

SERVES 6

AT ONE OF our favorite Lyon bouchons (see page 217), À Ma Vigne, proprietors Patrick and Joséphine Giraud and Francine Ballay (facing page, top right, from left) offer this flaky-crust tart as a specialty. If you have dough left over after rolling out the shell, make a pastry lattice for the top.

FOR PASTRY:
2 cups flour
2 tbsp. sugar
½ tsp. salt
12 tbsp. cold unsalted butter, cut into pieces

FOR FILLING:
1 ¼ cups sugar
2 eggs
10 tbsp. butter, melted and cooled
Juice and minced zest of 2 lemons

1. For pastry, combine flour, sugar, and salt in a large bowl. Cut in butter with a pastry cutter or 2 knives (mixture should resemble coarse cornmeal). Sprinkle with up to 3 tbsp. ice water so that dough holds together, then form into a ball, wrap in plastic, and refrigerate for at least 1 hour.

2. Preheat oven to 375°. Transfer dough to a lightly floured surface, then flatten and roll into a 9" round. Ease dough into an 8" false-bottomed tart pan. Prick the bottom of the pastry all over with a fork. Cover dough with foil and chill for at least 20 minutes, then fill with pie weights or dried beans and bake for 15 minutes. Remove foil and beans and continue baking for 5 minutes more. Remove from oven and set aside to cool.

3. For filling, beat sugar and eggs together in a bowl with an electric mixer until mixture is pale yellow. Continue beating as you gradually add melted butter. Then stir in lemon juice and zest. Spoon filling into tart shell and bake until crust is golden and filling is set and lightly browned, about 25 minutes. Cool completely before serving.

Clafoutis

(Black Cherry Batter Cake)

SERVES 8

THIS OLD-STYLE recipe, given to us by Auvergnat grandmother Jeanne Barbet, calls for unpitted cherries. This is the tradition in the region, not as a labor-saving shortcut, but because the pits are believed to add flavor to the cake. If the idea unsettles you, use pitted cherries instead.

1 tbsp. butter
1 tbsp. vanilla extract
6 eggs
6 tbsp. sugar
1 ¼ cups milk
2 tbsp. kirsch
Pinch salt
¾ cup flour
3 cups black cherries, pitted or unpitted
Confectioners' sugar (optional)

1. Preheat oven to 425°. Generously butter a 9" cast-iron skillet or a baking dish. Combine vanilla extract, eggs, sugar, milk, kirsch, and salt in a blender. Blend for a few seconds to mix ingredients, then add flour and blend until smooth, about 1 minute.

2. Pour batter into buttered skillet, then distribute cherries evenly over top. Bake until a skewer inserted into batter comes out clean and a golden brown crust has formed on top and bottom of clafoutis, about 30 minutes. Dust with confectioners' sugar, if you like.

VARIATION: *Prune Clafoutis*—Marinate 2 cups pitted prunes in 2 cups armagnac overnight or longer. Drain prunes, reserving armagnac marinade, and proceed with step 1 above, substituting 2 tbsp. of armagnac marinade for kirsch, then proceed with step 2 above, substituting prunes for cherries.

Cherries of Controversy

When the Académie Française defined clafoutis as a "sort of fruit flan" some years ago, inhabitants of Limoges—capital of the Limousin region, where the confection was born—protested, forcing the venerable institution to change the definition to the more precise "cake with black cherries". Black cherries are the meatiest, juiciest, and sweetest of varieties, and if you mix plenty of them into what may best be described as a slightly thickened crêpe batter, you'll have the makings of a traditional clafoutis limousin. The recipe is old but not ancient, probably dating from around the 1860s. The unusual name (sometimes spelled clafouti) comes from *clafir*, a dialect word meaning "to fill". Next door to the Limousin, in the Auvergne, the same sort of cake is known as *milliard*, and is made not only with cherries but also with red currants or with prunes soaked in armagnac.

Versatile Chard

Swiss chard (*Beta vulgaris cicla*) is a kind of beet grown for its leaves instead of its root. These leaves have a quilted texture and thick striated ribs typically either bright red or ivory-hued (though there are also varieties with ribs in yellow, pink, and various shades of green). Chard (below, foreground) grows easily and has a mild but pronounced flavor, and perhaps for these reasons is the most appreciated of all greens in Nice and vicinity and in the neighboring Italian region of Liguria. In these areas, it is widely used in soups and stews, as a filling for ravioli and various savory tourtes and torte, and as a coloring and flavoring agent for pasta. In Nice, for some reason, chard has scatological associations: Gnocchi made with potatoes and swiss chard (typically served with a meat sauce or just tossed with olive oil and parmigiano-reggiano) are known as merda de can—dog turds—for their murky green color. And the people of Nice themselves are sometimes jocularly referred to in the region as *caga-bléa*, meaning (to put it politely) that they eat so much chard they positively excrete it.

Tourte de Blettes

(Swiss Chard Torte)

Serves 8

ALL OVER the Mediterranean, greens of various kinds are cooked with pine nuts and raisins; in Nice, this savory combination is turned into dessert. Our version of this specialty is adapted from a recipe given by SAVEUR consulting editor Mireille Johnston in her *Cuisine of the Sun: Classical French Cooking from Nice and Provence* (Fireside, 1990).

FOR PASTRY:

3 cups flour
½ cup sugar
½ lb. butter, softened
2 eggs, beaten

FOR FILLING:

2 lbs. swiss chard, washed, ribs removed
¼ cup golden raisins
2 tbsp. dark rum
⅓ cup pine nuts
½ cup confectioners' sugar
2 eggs, beaten
Grated rind of 1 lemon
2 large golden delicious apples, peeled, cored, and thinly sliced
1 egg yolk, beaten

1. For pastry, sift flour and sugar into a large bowl. Mix in butter and eggs with a fork; mixture will look crumbly. Turn out onto a floured work surface and knead briefly. Shape into a ball, wrap in plastic and refrigerate for 2 hours.

2. For filling, bring a large pot of water to a boil, add chard, and cook for 15 minutes. Drain in a colander, then cool under running cold water. Squeeze out moisture, finely chop, and set aside.

3. Preheat oven to 375°. Cook raisins and rum in a small saucepan over medium-low heat until raisins absorb most of the rum, about 1 minute. Cool, then mix with chard, pine nuts, sugar, eggs, and lemon rind in a large bowl.

4. Lightly butter an 11" x 13" baking dish. Divide dough into 2 uneven balls, ⅓ for the top and ⅔ for the bottom. Roll out both pieces to ⅛"-thick rectangles. Line bottom and sides of pan with the larger piece. Prick all over with a fork and add chard mixture. Arrange apples in a single layer over chard. Cover with smaller piece of dough. Crimp edges, trim excess dough, and prick top with fork. Brush top with egg yolk. Bake until crust is golden, about 30 minutes. Sprinkle with additional confectioners' sugar, if you like, before serving.

Gâteau aux Noix

(Walnut Cake)

SERVES 8

THE CASTAGNÉ FAMILY produces superb artisanal walnut oil at its Huilerie Familiale du Lac de Diane near Martel, in the Lot (see page 100), and makes a cake similar to this one with oil and nuts from their own orchards (like those displayed by Marie-Louise Castagné, left). Walnut liquor is often used to moisten the cake or is served on the side.

½ cup chopped walnuts
3 eggs
1 cup sugar
⅓ cup walnut oil
⅓ cup dry white wine
1 ½ cups flour
2 tsp. baking powder
⅛ tsp. salt

1. Preheat oven to 350°. Place walnuts in a small dry saucepan and cook over medium heat, shaking pan, until nuts are lightly toasted, 5–10 minutes. Set aside.

2. Beat eggs in a medium bowl with an electric mixer. Gradually add sugar and beat until mixture is light and fluffy. Add walnut oil and wine and mix well. Batter will be quite thick.

3. Generously grease a 9" cake pan. Sift together flour, baking powder, and salt into a large bowl. Add egg mixture to flour mixture and mix with a wooden spoon until just combined. Gently fold in nuts, then spoon batter into pan.

4. Bake cake until a toothpick can be inserted and pulled out clean, about 40 minutes. Remove cake from oven, cool for 10 minutes, and then turn out onto a cooling rack. Allow to cool completely, then serve in wedges drizzled with walnut liqueur or accompanied by vanilla ice cream, if you like.

The Nut Party

In southwestern France, walnuts are mostly harvested in October, when whole families head for the orchards to fill burlap sacks with the fruit. The walnuts—franquette, mayette, marbot, and corne are the varieties most often grown—are quite damp when fresh, and must be dried over a gas stove. Most of the shelling is done by hand—and the occasional *soirée dénoisillage*, or nut-cracking party, still takes place. At these get-togethers, veterans whack the nuts with a wooden hammer; skilled practitioners of this art can shatter the shell while leaving the meat intact. This is desirable, since whole walnuts bring a higher price than the cracked ones—called *les invalides*—which are sent to mills to be crushed for oil. Though walnut is now a pricey specialty oil, it was once commonly used by the agrarian poor. Until at least the end of the 18th century, in fact, walnuts were sustenance in the Southwest. Walnut shells were used to make bread in times of famine, and the meat was pressed into a kind of milk.

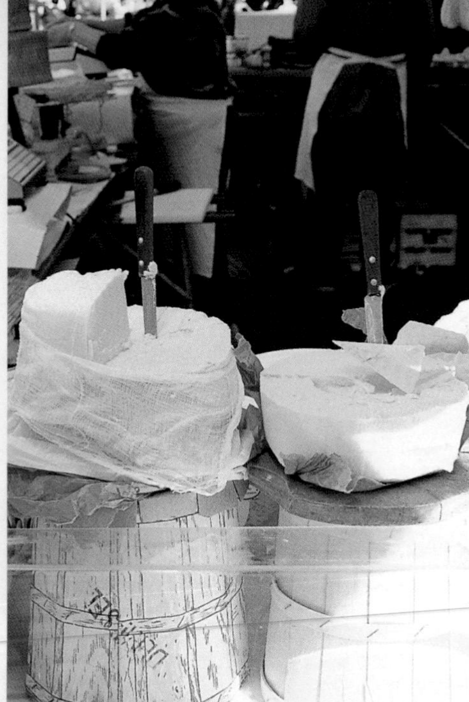

A Butter Culture

Butter, *amann* in the Breton language (the word also means "ointment"), has a symbolic importance in Brittany that must seem all but incomprehensible to the cholesterol-phobic American. In recent memory, older Bretons still placed a slab of butter near somebody suffering from cancer in the belief that it would absorb the disease; even today, mothers often rub a butter pomade on their childrens' bruised elbows. Butter was also used by women to slick their hair back under their starched Breton headdresses. And of course, Bretons *eat* butter. Since the Middle Ages, they've been renowned for their formidable butter consumption, putting it on virtually everything—even fish, which was contrary to the religious and dietary principles of medieval times. The main difference between butter from Brittany and those from other French regions is that Breton butter is almost always salted, with a sea salt content ranging from .5 to 5 percent. The salt allows it to be conserved longer, to have a lower water content and, according to the Bretons, to have far more flavor and character than unsalted butter.

Kouign Amann

(Breton Butter Cake)

SERVES 8

PASTRY CHEFS in Brittany warn that making a perfect kouign amann (pronounced kween ah-MAN) isn't easy, but we've found that this simple recipe yields delicious results.

2 7-gram packets active dry yeast
1 tsp. salt
2 cups flour
12 tbsp. butter (keep 8 tbsp. or 1 stick in refrigerator until ready to use)
1 ¼ cups sugar

1. Dissolve yeast in ⅓ cup lukewarm water in a large bowl. Set aside until yeast begins to activate (it will foam a little), about 10 minutes.

2. Add salt and 1 cup of the flour to yeast mixture, stirring with a wooden spoon. Add ⅓ cup water, and when well blended, add remaining 1 cup flour and another ⅔ cup water. Stir until dough forms into a ball, then transfer to a lightly floured surface and knead with the heels of your palms until smooth and elastic, about 10 minutes. Coat the inside of a large bowl with 2 tbsp. butter, place dough in bowl, and cover with a damp cloth or plastic wrap. Set aside to rise until doubled in bulk, about 1 hour.

3. Preheat oven to 450°. Grease a 9" pie pan with 1 tbsp. butter and dust with flour. Roll out dough on a lightly floured surface into a large rectangle, about 12" x 18", with the shorter side nearest you.

4. Cut chilled stick of butter into 10–12 pieces. Dot middle portion of dough with butter pieces and sprinkle with ½ cup of the sugar. Working quickly, fold short sides towards the center, over the butter and sugar. Edges should slightly overlap. Sprinkle dough with ¼ cup of the sugar and roll over seams to seal. Turn dough again so that the shorter side is nearest you and fold into thirds, as you would a letter. Let dough rest 15 minutes in refrigerator.

5. Roll out dough on a sugar sprinkled surface, dusting with ¼ cup sugar as you go, into a large rectangle. Fold into thirds again and let dough rest another 15 minutes in refrigerator.

6. Roll out dough on a sugar-sprinkled surface into a square slightly larger than the pie pan. Dust with remaining ¼ cup sugar, and ease dough into pan, loosely folding edges towards the center. Melt remaining 1 tbsp. butter, and drizzle over dough. Bake until golden brown, 35–40 minutes. Remove from pan while hot and serve warm.

Gâteau de Riz

(Rice Pudding)

SERVES 8–10

BERNARD PICOLET uses his grandmother's recipe to makes this creamy but cakelike rice pudding at Aux Amis du Beaujolais in Paris. She cooked it for hours near an open fire. Picolet bakes it in the oven, in a caramelized pan, dresses it up with crème anglaise, and calls it a gâteau.

⅓ cup raisins
¼ cup dark rum
6 cups milk
1 cup short-grain white rice (such as Italian arborio)
1 ½ cups plus 1 tbsp. sugar
1 vanilla bean, split lengthwise
4 eggs, separated
Crème anglaise (optional; see sidebar, page 304)

1. Soak raisins in rum in a bowl for 1 hour. Combine milk, rice, ½ cup of the sugar, and vanilla bean in a medium saucepan. Bring to a boil over medium heat, reduce heat to medium-low, cover, and cook, stirring occasionally, until rice absorbs all liquid, about 1 hour. Remove from heat, scrape seeds from vanilla bean into rice, and discard pod. Set rice aside to cool to room temperature.

2. Pour 1 cup of the sugar into a skillet, shaking the skillet so that sugar spreads evenly, and place over medium-high heat. Cook, without stirring, until sugar begins to melt, about 2 minutes, then stir with a wooden spoon until golden and just beginning to foam, about 3 minutes. Remove from heat and carefully pour into a 9" baking pan, then, working quickly before caramel hardens, tilt to coat bottom and sides.

3. Preheat oven to 375°. Stir egg yolks and raisins (discarding rum) into rice. Beat egg whites until foamy. Sprinkle in remaining 1 tbsp. sugar, continue to beat until soft peaks form, then fold into rice mixture. Transfer to caramelized pan, set pan in a shallow pan of water, and bake until a knife inserted into the middle comes out clean, about 1 hour. Cool slightly in pan, then turn out onto a platter. Serve with crème anglaise, if you like.

Friends and Family

"My friend Claude and I [see page 210]," recalls SAVEUR editor Colman Andrews, "went to Aux Amis du Beaujolais, on the corner of the rue de Berri and the rue d'Artois, a few blocks off the Champs-Élysées, all the time. It was Claude's canteen, his hangout. Aux Amis du Beaujolais (With the Friends of Beaujolais) was opened in 1921 by Philibert Bléton, a young man from Fleurie, one of the Beaujolais villages that lend their names to that region's grand cru wines. His brother Georges went to work for him in the late '30s, eventually buying the place from him in 1949. Georges's brother-in-law, Maurice, was in charge when Claude first brought me there—but he is now long since deceased, and the current proprietor is Maurice's son, Bernard. I remember meeting him in 1980, a year before he took over—a nice young man in a stylish suit. 'The next time I come here,' I said to Claude, 'there'll be raw tuna with pineapple beurre blanc on the menu instead of boeuf à la bourguignonne.' I was wrong. The decor has changed (it looks almost Californian in its light-hued stylishness), and there is more fish on the menu than there used to be because that's what people eat these days. But all the old bistro specialties remain, and Picolet cooks them just as well as his predecessors did. His son Christian helps him in the kitchen, and is learning the old ways, too."

Proust on Madeleines

My mother...sent for one of those short, plump little cakes called Petites Madeleines, which seem to have been molded in the grooved shell of a scallop. And soon, mechanically, burdened by the dreary day and the prospect of a sad tomorrow, I raised to my lips a spoonful of tea in which I had soaked a piece of the little cake. But at the very moment that the draught mixed with the cake crumbs touched my palate, I trembled, aware that something extraordinary was happening to me. A delicious pleasure had invaded me, detached, offering no notion of its cause. At once, the vicissitudes of life were rendered unimportant, its disasters innocuous, its brevity illusory, in the same way that love works, filling me with a precious essence: or rather this essense wasn't in me, it *was* me. I had stopped feeling myself mediocre, accidental, mortal. Whence had this powerful joy come to me? I sensed that it was connected with the taste of the tea and the cake, but that it was something infinitely greater than that taste, that it couldn't be of the same nature. Where did it come from? What did it mean? Where could I seize it?"

Madeleines

MAKES 16 LARGE MADELEINES

THE MOST famous of literary confections, the madeleine—which was perhaps named in honor of Madeleine Paumier, a 19th-century French pastry cook—inspired the narrator of Marcel Proust's *Remembrance of Things Past* to embark on his epic exploration of time, memory, and love. This version of the classic recipe was given to us by Michel Richard, whose restaurants include Citronelle in Washington, D.C.

3 eggs
1 cup sugar
1 cup butter (2 sticks), softened
1 cup flour
1 tsp. baking powder
Zest of 1 lemon

1. Preheat oven to 375°. Beat eggs and sugar together with an electric mixer until pale yellow and a little frothy, about 3 minutes. Scrape down sides of the bowl. Continuing to beat, add butter 1 tsp. at a time until all the butter is incorporated, about 5 minutes. (Batter may appear slightly curdled.)

2. Sift together flour and baking powder, then gradually add to the batter, beating on low speed. Add lemon zest and mix until batter is smooth, about 1 minute more.

3. Spoon the batter into a well-buttered and floured madeleine mold. Bake until golden, about 20 minutes. Remove from oven, and allow to cool before unmolding.

Tomates Confites Farcies aux Douze Saveurs

(Sweet Tomatoes Filled with a Dozen Flavors)

SERVES 4

AT HIS THREE-STAR Arpège in Paris (right), Alain Passard serves this unusual dessert exclusively in the summertime—because only small, sweet, perfectly sun-ripened tomatoes will produce a successful interpretation of this dish.

4 small, very ripe and sweet tomatoes, blanched, stemmed, and peeled
12 tbsp. sugar
1 medium golden delicious apple, peeled, cored, and finely diced
1 ripe comice pear, peeled, cored, and finely diced
¼ cup finely diced fresh pineapple
1 tbsp. raisins
Pinch freshly grated orange zest
1 tsp. freshly grated lemon zest
½ tsp. minced fresh ginger
Pinch ground cloves
Pinch aniseed
Pinch ground cinnamon
3 walnuts, chopped
5 almonds, chopped
10 pistachios, chopped
1 sprig fresh mint, finely chopped
2 vanilla beans, split lengthwise
Juice of 1 small orange, strained
Vanilla ice cream (optional)

1. Slice ⅓ of the blossom end off tomatoes and reserve caps. Hull and seed tomatoes, discarding solids. Set tomatoes upside down on a rack to drain.

2. Preheat oven to 400°. Sprinkle 2 tbsp. sugar evenly into a medium ovenproof skillet over medium heat. Cook sugar until it melts and turns golden, about 5 minutes. Add apples, pears, and pineapple, increase heat to high, and cook, stirring, until fruit is coated in caramel juices and just tender, about 2 minutes. Remove pan from heat, then add raisins, orange and lemon zest, ginger, cloves, aniseed, cinnamon, walnuts, almonds, pistachios, mint, and vanilla beans. Mix well, then transfer to a medium bowl and set aside to cool.

3. Remove and reserve vanilla beans from fruit mixture. Stuff each tomato with fruit mixture, then replace tops. Sprinkle remaining 10 tbsp. sugar evenly into same skillet over medium-high heat. Cook sugar until it melts and turns golden, about 7 minutes. Add orange juice and reserved vanilla beans, and cook, stirring, until smooth, about 1 minute. Arrange tomatoes in pan and baste with pan syrup, then transfer to oven and bake, basting often, until tomatoes are soft and filling is hot, 10–12 minutes. To serve, place 1 tomato on each plate, then spoon pan syrup over tomatoes. Serve with vanilla ice cream, if you like.

Give Me Arpège

"At the Parisian three-star restaurant called Arpège," reports writer Thomas McNamee, "the dinner tasting menu costs 1,200 francs per person. That's 200 dollars to you, pilgrim. Service and taxes are included; wine is extra. Surely, no meal, even a ten-course lollapalooza, could be worth maybe 300 bucks a head. At least that's what I thought. Then I sat down for a meal at Arpège, and four hours later, when I floated past the undulating pearwood paneling of the dining room and out into the street, I had begun to understand. I was not drunk. I was not stuffed. Every tiny bite had been...the only word is sublime. This one meal proved to me, beyond the slightest doubt, that food can be a work of art. The food at Arpège appears at first to have been born in a realm of pure abstraction. The owner-chef, Alain Passard, is slight, elegant, contemplative, and unabashedly artistic. His cooking fits precisely the definition of Apollonian: characterized by clarity, harmony, and restraint. Great art is always expensive, always rare, always oblivious to the injustices that make it possible. And his is great art."

Soufflé au Chocolat

(Chocolate Soufflé)

SERVES 3–4

THE FIRST SOUFFLÉS (the name comes from the French verb *souffler*, to blow or whisper) were savory, not sweet like this one. We prefer this more delicate flourless version of the dish to the more traditional flour-stabilized version.

3 tbsp. milk
5 ½ tbsp. sugar, plus additional for dusting soufflé dish
4 oz. semisweet chocolate, coarsely chopped
2 egg yolks
3 egg whites
Confectioners' sugar

1. Preheat oven to 375°. Place milk and 4 tbsp. of the sugar in a small saucepan and stir over medium-low heat until sugar dissolves, about 45 seconds. Stir in chocolate and cook until melted, 1–2 minutes. Transfer to a large mixing bowl, cool for 5 minutes, then beat in egg yolks.

2. Beat egg whites in a clean glass or stainless-steel mixing bowl until foamy, then sprinkle in remaining 1½ tbsp. sugar, beating until stiff peaks form.

3. Butter a small (3 cup) soufflé dish (2½" deep and 6" diameter; soufflé will not rise in a larger dish), then lightly dust with sugar. Gently mix one-third of the egg whites into chocolate mixture, then fold in remaining whites, one-third at a time. Do not overmix. Spoon batter into dish.

4. Make sure oven rack is low enough to allow soufflé room to rise as much as 2" above the dish. Bake until puffed, about 25 minutes. Dust with confectioners' sugar and serve immediately. (Soufflé will begin to deflate after about 2 minutes.)

Surmounting the Uneven Rise

I'd only been at the Cordon Bleu in Paris for a few weeks," reports SAVEUR associate editor Catherine Whalen, "when chef Michel Cliche announced that our next lesson would be on soufflé au chocolat. The thought of tackling this regal dessert brought on an instant surge of what-am-I-doing-in-cooking-school anxiety. Sure enough, my first attempt emerged at a jaunty but unsoufflé-like angle. 'Uneven rise,' Chef flatly diagnosed. My second try was a feeble, sticky pancake. 'Overwhisked whites,' Chef accused, arching a disapproving eyebrow. My next several efforts were all tasty but, in varying degrees, fluffy failures. Then Chef let us in on the secret: Perfectly whisked whites, he said, start with a perfectly clean bowl; even the smallest speck of grease can deflate the volume. The bowl, therefore, should be cleaned with lemon juice, carefully rinsed, and thoroughly dried. I tried it his way, and pulled from the oven what I took to be a masterpiece. I beamed as I showed it to Chef. He just shrugged. 'Pas mal,' he said."

Crème Brûlée

SERVES 4

WHEN HE WAS the pastry chef at Le Cirque in New York City in the early '80s, Dieter Schorner developed his own version of crème brûlée; it became a sensation and introduced New Yorkers to the dessert. This is our adaptation of his recipe. Though there are numerous methods of caramelizing the sugar on top of the crème brûlée, we've found a small kitchen blowtorch to be best for the purpose.

2 cups heavy cream
5 tbsp. sugar
½ vanilla bean, split lengthwise
Small pinch salt
4 egg yolks

1. Preheat oven to 275°. In a small pan, bring cream, 2 tbsp. sugar, vanilla bean, and salt just to a boil over medium heat. Remove from heat and set aside to cool. Scrape seeds from vanilla into cream then discard vanilla pod.

2. In another bowl, whisk egg yolks with 1 tbsp. of the sugar until sugar dissolves. Slowly whisk in cooled cream (if it is not cool, yolks will scramble), then strain through a fine sieve.

3. Divide custard between 4 shallow baking dishes, each about ½ cup in capacity. Place dishes in a baking pan, then place pan in oven. Pour enough cold water into pan to come about halfway up sides of dishes. Bake until custards set, 30–35 minutes.

4. Cover cooled custards with plastic wrap. Chill in refrigerator for at least 4 hours or overnight. Before serving, sprinkle 1½ tsp. sugar on each custard and use a kitchen blowtorch to caramelize tops, holding torch at an angle (flame should barely touch surface) to brown sugar. (You can also brown the sugar in a preheated broiler, taking care to turn the gratin dishes to avoid hot spots.)

A Burning Question

At his Willi's Wine Bar in Paris, Mark Williamson (above) offers a dessert he describes on the menu as "Spécialité du Collège de Cambridge". When his French customers encounter that description, he reports with delight, they unfailingly and innocently inquire, "Excusez-moi, monsieur, but what is this?" Williamson pauses, smiles, and replies, "Why, it's crème brûlée, bien sûr"—and steps swiftly away from their inevitable splutters of indignation. The French, the Catalans, and the English all claim to have created this unique dessert—whose name literally means "burnt cream"—and as an Englishman abroad, Williamson naturally supports the English theory. It was introduced to Trinity College, Cambridge, he says, in the 1850s, by a young scholar whose nanny had made it. It soon became a permanent item on the refectory menu. Unfortunately, university archives supposedly documenting the birth of this dish have never been made available to the public.

Crème Anglaise

To make this delicate custard sauce, put 2 cups milk and 1 split vanilla bean in a heavy-bottomed saucepan and bring just to a simmer over medium heat. Meanwhile, whisk together 6 egg yolks and ¼ cup sugar in a mixing bowl. Reduce heat to low and slowly whisk ½ cup hot milk into egg mixture, then whisk egg mixture into remaining hot milk. Cook, stirring constantly with a wooden spoon, until mixture is thick enough to coat the back of the spoon, about 15 minutes. Remove from heat, strain through a fine sieve, and transfer to a mixing bowl. Stop custard from overcooking by placing bowl immediately into a larger bowl of ice water. Scrape seeds from vanilla bean into custard and discard pod. Cool to room temperature, then refrigerate until cold. Makes 2 cups.

Oeufs à la Neige

(Floating Islands)

SERVES 6

AMONG THE MOST ingenious of classical French desserts, oeufs à la neige (the name literally means eggs in the snow) has become an American dessert tradition, too.

4 cups milk
1 vanilla bean, split lengthwise
6 egg yolks
1 ⅓ cups sugar
4 egg whites

1. Bring 2 cups of milk to a boil in a large heavy saucepan over medium heat. Remove from heat, add vanilla bean, cover, and steep for about 15 minutes.

2. Beat egg yolks in a mixing bowl, slowly sprinkling in ⅓ cup sugar. Continue beating until thick and pale yellow in color.

3. Remove vanilla bean from milk, scrape seeds from bean into milk, then discard pod. Pour milk in a fine stream into egg yolks, beating continuously, then return the mixture to saucepan and cook over low heat, stirring constantly until it forms a custard thick enough to coat the back of a spoon, about 15 minutes; don't rush the process or eggs may scramble. Pour custard through a strainer into a shallow serving bowl. Cool to room temperature, then refrigerate.

4. Beat egg whites until foamy, then gradually add ⅓ cup sugar. Continue to beat until whites are shiny and stiff but not dry.

5. Put remaining 2 cups milk in a large shallow pan and bring to a low simmer. Using a large slotted spoon, form 6 large egg shapes out of whites and poach in the milk for 30 seconds on each side. Do not overcook. Drain "eggs" on a clean towel. Discard poaching liquid.

6. Combine ⅔ cup sugar and ⅓ cup water in a small heavy saucepan. Cook over medium-high heat until sugar caramelizes. To avoid burning caramel, which can happen very quickly, remove pan from heat just before sugar darkens; it will continue to caramelize off heat. Cool caramel for 5 minutes or until it forms into threads when drizzled from the tines of a fork.

7. Using a slotted spoon, carefully arrange "eggs" on top of custard. Working quickly, dip a fork into the slightly cooled caramel and wave it over the dessert to form threads of caramel that crisscross and tangle. Serve immediately.

A
B
C
D

Dacquoise

SERVES 6

THIS CONFECTION was born in the southwestern French town of Dax. Our recipe was adapted with the help of Andrew Shotts, pastry chef at La Côte Basque in Manhattan.

FOR MERINGUES:
2 cups confectioners' sugar
1 ⅓ cups finely ground roasted hazelnuts (see sidebar)
1 ¼ cups finely ground blanched, sliced almonds (see sidebar)
9 egg whites, room temperature
½ cup granulated sugar

FOR GANACHE:
1 cup heavy cream
5 oz. bittersweet chocolate, chopped
3 oz. milk chocolate, chopped

FOR BUTTERCREAM:
2 cups granulated sugar
5 egg whites, room temperature
1 lb. unsalted butter, cut into pieces and softened
3 tbsp. coffee extract

2 cups sliced almonds, toasted
Confectioners' sugar (optional)

1. For meringues, preheat oven to 250°. Line 2 baking sheets with parchment and draw three 8" circles on paper. Sift together confectioners' sugar, hazelnuts, and almonds into a bowl, working any lumps through sieve with your fingers, then set aside. Put egg whites in the clean bowl of a standing mixer and whisk on medium-low speed for 2 minutes. Increase speed to medium and whisk whites to soft peaks, about 2½ minutes. Gradually add granulated sugar while whisking, increase speed to medium-high and whisk until whites form medium-stiff peaks, about 1½ minutes. Transfer whites to a large bowl and carefully fold in ⅓ of nut mixture at a time with a rubber spatula. Divide meringue between parchment circles and gently spread out evenly. Bake in middle of oven, rotating positions hourly until lightly golden and hollow sounding when tapped, for 2–4 hours. Allow to cool.

2. For ganache, heat cream in a medium saucepan and bring to a boil over medium heat. Remove from heat, add bittersweet and milk chocolates, and let sit for 1 minute. Whisk until smooth and set aside until thick enough to spread.

3. For buttercream, combine ⅓ cup water and 1½ cups of the sugar in a small saucepan and cook over medium heat until mixture reaches 250° on a candy thermometer. Put egg whites in the clean bowl of a standing mixer and whisk on medium-low speed for 2 minutes. Increase speed to medium and whisk whites to soft peaks, about 1½ minutes. Gradually add remaining ½ cup sugar while whisking, then increase speed to medium-high and whisk until whites form stiff peaks, about 2 minutes. Slowly pour sugar syrup into whites, whisking until cool, about 10 minutes. Add butter, bit by bit, whisking until shiny and fluffy, about 8 minutes (it may curdle, but will come together). Add coffee extract and set aside.

4. To assemble: Spread ⅓ of buttercream over each of 2 meringues (**A**). Spread ganache over remaining meringue. Layer meringues, placing the one with ganache in the middle (**B**). Spread remaining buttercream on sides of cake (**C**), then cover cake with almonds (**D**) and refrigerate at least 5 hours. Before serving, dust cake with confectioners' sugar.

Nut Tips

Ground roasted hazelnuts add color and rich, nutty flavor to the dacquoise. To prepare hazelnuts, bring 2 cups of water to a boil in a medium saucepan over medium-high heat. Add 2 tbsp. baking soda, and 1½ cups unpeeled hazelnuts. Boil for 3 minutes (water will turn black). Drain, then transfer hazelnuts to a large bowl of cold water and slip skins from nuts with your fingers. Dry hazelnuts on paper towels, then place on a baking sheet and roast in a preheated 350° oven until golden, 15-20 minutes. Remove from oven and set aside to cool completely. When cool, put a small handful of nuts into an electric coffee grinder and pulse into a fine powder. Continue working in small batches, to avoid grinding nuts into nut butter, until all the nuts are ground. Grind 1½ cups blanched sliced almonds the same way. Use nuts in dacquoise or other preparations.

Croquembouche

Serves 16

THE LEGENDARY French chef Marie-Antoine (Antonin) Carême (1784–1833) was noted for creating monumental pièces montées, or edible centerpieces. Among these was the croquembouche—whose name literally means "crunch in the mouth", for reasons that become obvious when you chomp down on one. Carême once proposed that confectionary was a branch of architecture; this extravagant dessert is a good illustration of what he meant.

FOR PÂTE À CHOUX:
12 tbsp. butter
Salt
2 cups flour
9 eggs

FOR FILLING:
1 ½ cups milk
½ cup sugar
4 egg yolks
3 tbsp. cornstarch
½ tbsp. vanilla extract
16 tbsp. unsalted butter, softened

FOR CARAMEL:
4 cups sugar

1. For pâte à choux, preheat oven to 425°. Combine 1½ cups water, butter, and ¼ tsp. salt in a large heavy saucepan and bring to a boil over high heat. Remove pan from heat, add flour all at once, and stir vigorously with a wooden spoon until mixture forms a thick dough and pulls away from sides of pan, 1–2 minutes. Return pan to heat and cook, stirring constantly, for 1–2 minutes. Remove pan from heat, allow dough to cool 5 minutes, then vigorously beat in 8 eggs, one at a time, making sure each egg is completely incorporated. Dough will come together and be thick, shiny, and smooth, and pull away from sides of the pan (**A**). Dip two spoons in water, shake off excess water, and scoop a walnut-size piece of dough with one spoon. Use other spoon to push dough onto a parchment-lined baking sheet. Repeat with the rest of dough, setting pieces 1" apart on baking sheet. Lightly beat remaining egg with a pinch of salt and brush each piece of dough with it. Bake until puffed and light brown, about 10 minutes. Lower heat to 350° and continue to bake until well browned, about 15 minutes. Allow puffs to cool.

2. For filling, bring 1 cup of the milk and the sugar just to a boil in a heavy saucepan over medium heat. Meanwhile, whisk remaining ½ cup milk, egg yolks, and cornstarch together in a large bowl. Slowly pour half the hot milk into

yolk mixture, whisking constantly, then return mixture gradually to milk in pan, stirring constantly with a wooden spoon until it thickens and just returns to a boil. Stir in vanilla and transfer to a bowl; cover with plastic wrap, and refrigerate until cold. In a large bowl, beat butter until pale and fluffy. Add cold filling and beat until smooth, 3–4 minutes. Cover and refrigerate until ready to use. Spoon filling into pastry bag fitted with a plain ¼" tip. Using a chopstick, gently poke a hole in the flat side of each baked and cooled puff. Fill each puff with filling (**B**).

3. For caramel, put 2 cups sugar and ½ cup water in each of two shallow saucepans and stir to mix. Cover and cook over medium heat until sugar turns amber, 15–20 minutes. (Lift covers to check color of caramel after 7 minutes. Sugar will become thick and bubbly, and then begin to turn amber. Swirl saucepans to distribute color. Do not stir.) Remove from heat. Reheat caramel when it becomes too thick. (Making caramel in two saucepans will allow you to re-warm half of the caramel, keeping it fluid, while you work with the other half.)

4. To assemble, dip top of 1 filled puff at a time in hot caramel using tongs or a chocolate-dipping fork. As you dip, place puffs glazed side up on a tray lined with plastic wrap. Form base of croquembouche with 12–14 glazed and cooled puffs, sticking them together with additional dabs of caramel (**C**). Add puffs layer by layer, using fewer at each level as if building a pyramid, to form a hollow cone. Allow caramel to cool slightly, until it is the consistency of honey. With a spoon, drizzle thin strings of caramel around cone (**D**).

Photography Credits

COVER: Front: Rooster in red wine sauce—*Christopher Hirsheimer*
Back: (clockwise from top left) *Antoine Bootz; Hubert Taillard; Christopher Hirsheimer (2); Beatriz da Costa; Christopher Hirsheimer (2); Owen Franken*
2: Lingot beans used in making cassoulet—*J. L. Barde/Scope*
6: Garlic—*Susan Goldberger*

INTRODUCTION

8: Parisian bistro owners eating lunch—*Corbis/Bettman*
10–11: Picking grapes in front of windmill (Bussac); artisanal bakery (rural France)—*Archive Photos;* poster advertising Fromageries Ch. Dayot—*Chisholm Gallery*
12–13: Woman buying pineapple at Montparnasse market (Paris)—*J. P. Owen/Black Star;* covered food market—*Hulton Getty/Liaison Agency;* lithograph of the Marché des Innocents—*Roger Viollet*
14–15: Vineyard workers eating lunch—*Peter Miller/Image Bank;* 18th-century engraving of scene from an auberge—*Roger Viollet;* café in the Latin Quarter (Paris)—*Leonard Freed/Magnum Photos, Inc.*
16–17: Picnic at the Tour de France—*Harry Gruyaert/Magnum Photos, Inc.;* La Bohème café (Paris) —*FPG;* Holiday picnic (Camargue)—*Roger Viollet*
18–19: Julia Child visiting a Parisian kitchen—*Irving Newman/Archive Photos;* omelette restaurant (Mont-St-Michel)—*Hulton Getty/Liaison Agency;* lithograph of dinner party—*Corbis/Bettman*

CHAPTER 1: HORS D'OEUVRES

22–24: Old quarter; Cours Saleya; man on bike; vegetable stand; man playing pétanque (Nice)—*Antoine Bootz*
26–27: Anchovy paste—*Mary Ellen Bartley;* niçois onion tart—*Christopher Hirsheimer*
28–29: Raw vegetable salads along zinc bar, Chez Clovis (Paris); Marcelle Gueneau making vinaigrette (Avallon)—*Christopher Hirsheimer*
30–31: Sébastien Le Ber in vineyard; garlic custard with chanterelles and parsley sauce; Joël Guillet at Le Mas du Langoustier; ingredients for dish—*Christopher Hirsheimer;* Port (Île de Porquerolles)—*Jacques Guillard/Scope*
32–33: Duck terrine—*Beatriz da Costa;* Ariane Daguin and George Faison of D'Artagnan (New York)—*Mark Seelen*
34–35: Chicken liver terrine; Hospices de Beaune—*Christopher Hirsheimer*
36–37: Chicken liver mousse—*Christopher Hirsheimer;* Raymond Fulchiron and Claudie Chaufaut outside the Café des Fédérations (Lyon)—*A. Bailhâche*
38–39: The Pin River (Berry)—*Indre Tourism Office;* pâté in a pastry crust—*Christine Fleurent*
40–41: Parsleyed ham in shop; parsleyed ham in aspic—*Christopher Hirsheimer*
42–43: Stuffed scallops provençal-style; Jacques Maximin (Vence)—*Christopher Hirsheimer*
44–45: Preparation of oysters (3); oysters in champagne sauce—*J. B. Naudin*
46–47: Savory buckwheat crêpes; Patrick Jeffroy (Plounérin)—*Christopher Hirsheimer*
48–49: Burgundian crêpes; Chez Millette (Planchez)—*Christopher Hirsheimer*

CHAPTER 2: SOUPS

50–53: Megan Wetherall eating onion soup; kitchens of Au Pied de Cochon; St-Eustache; Françoise Cornut at Chez Clovis—*Christopher Hirsheimer;* Les Halles (Paris)—*Courtesy Francoise Cornut*
54–55: Tray of French onion soups; in front of Au Pied de Cochon (Paris)—*Christopher Hirsheimer*
56–57: Assorted stocks; preparation of chicken stock (9)—*Christopher Hirsheimer*
58–59: Brown beef stock; bouquet garni in cheesecloth; beef shin—*Christopher Hirsheimer*
60–61: Brown veal stock and demi-glace; preparation of demi-glace (2)—*Christopher Hirsheimer*
62–63: Fish soup; ingredients for fish stock; fish stock—*Christopher Hirsheimer*
64–65: Crayfish soup; Jean Orth and his son, Michel, chefs of L'Écrevisse (Brumath)—*Alison Harris*
66–67: Preparation of lobster bisque; lobster bisque; preparation (2)—*Christopher Hirsheimer*
68–69: Vegetables; cream of squash soup—*Christopher Hirsheimer*
70–71: Village of Frayssinet (2)—*Dominique Vorillon;* fava bean soup—*Christopher Hirsheimer;* Harold Wright with friends (2)—*Dominique Vorillon*
72–73: View from Corsica's southern coast; Corsican soup—*Melanie Acevedo*
74–75: Peasant soup to drink and eat; serving soup at La Tupiña (Bordeaux)—*Martin Schreiber*

CHAPTER 3: CHEESE & EGGS

76–79: Selection of cheeses—*Martin Schreiber;* Courchevel—*Michael Serraillier/Agence Top;* preparing raclette—*Pierre Hussenot/Agence Top;* rooftops—*J. D. Sudres/DIAF;* traditional craftsman weaves baskets (Bessans)—*Pierre Hussenot/Agence Top*
80–81: Fondue Savoyarde—*J. D. Sudres/DIAF;* gruyère wheel—*Corbis/Bettman*
82–83: Preparation of cream puff pastry (3); French cheese puffs—*Christopher Hirsheimer*
84–85: Cheese platter at Arpège (Paris); assorted cheeses—*Martin Schreiber*
86–87: Shallot custard; fresh shallots—*Christopher Hirsheimer*
88–89: Artichoke and mushroom soufflé—*F. Tiano;* Jacqueline Margulis (San Francisco)—*Laurie Smith*
90–91: Lorraine landscape—*Courtesy Lorraine Tourism Office;* quiche lorraine—*Christopher Hirscheimer*
92–93: Buying eggs at market; Lucian K. Truscott IV and family (St-Julien-de-Crempse)—*Owen Franken;* Périgord-style stuffed eggs—*Christopher Hirscheimer*
94–95: Poached eggs in red wine sauce; Stéphanie Guillon at Le Récamier—*J. B. Naudin*
96–97: Eggs in broth—*Christopher Hirsheimer;* parsley—*Ferrucio Carassale;* Chez Millette (Planchez) —*Christopher Hirsheimer*

CHAPTER 4: SALADS

98–101: Vendor selling lettuces at market; woman tends her crops—*Owen Franken;* walnut oil—*Christopher Hirsheimer;* view across newly mowed field (Dordogne)—*Owen Franken;* André Castagné, walnut oil artisan (Martel)—*Pierre Sourzat*
102–103: Chanterelles; chanterelle salad—*Christopher Hirsheimer;* slicing smoked ham—*Owen Franken*
104–105: Rooftops; Catherine-Hélène Barale at Barale; salade niçoise (Nice)—*Antoine Bootz*
106–107: Époisses cheese—*M. E. Bartley;* Mathilde with green salad with Cîteaux cheese croutons —*Christopher Hirsheimer*
108–109: Dry lentils 'du Puy'; lentil salad with roasted carrots and beets—*André Baranowski*
110–111: Salad of haricots verts and green hazelnuts; Jacques Maximin's restaurant (Vence)—*Christopher Hirsheimer;* hazelnut bush—*Hazelnut Board;* Maximin's restaurant (2)—*Christopher Hirsheimer*
112–113: Artichoke and pork belly salad; artichokes—*Martin Schreiber*
114–115: Red mullet; warm red mullet and artichoke salad; artichokes; olive oils—*Christopher Hirsheimer*

CHAPTER 5: FOIE GRAS, FROGS' LEGS, SNAILS & TRUFFLES

116–119: Terrine in bain-marie—*Antoine Bootz;* Lucette Baron with goose (Auch)—*J. D. Sudres/DIAF;* marinating foie gras—*Antoine Bootz;* walnut and foie gras sign (Correze)—*J. D. Sudres/DIAF;* winter foie gras and poultry market (southwestern France)—*J. L. Barde/Scope*
120–121: Foie gras terrine; whole lobe of foie gras; deveining foie gras; soaking foie gras in iced water (Le Cordon Bleu, Paris)—*Antoine Bootz*
122–123: Seared foie gras with green grapes—*Antoine Bootz;* foie gras ducks (Lot)—*M.C. Garcia/SIPA Press*
124–125: Potted foie gras and vegetables; old quarter of Strasbourg—*Alison Harris*
126–127: Frogs' legs—*Martin Schreiber;* frogs' legs in parsley butter—*Christopher Hirsheimer*
128–129: Frogs' leg "Napoleons" with white bean sauce; Jacques Lameloise (Chagny)—*Christopher Hirsheimer*
130–131: Snails; Paule Moine preparing snails for snails in parsley butter (Détain-Bruant) (4) —*Christopher Hirsheimer*
132–133: Live snails; fricassée of snails with parsley and roasted garlic cream—*Christopher Hirsheimer*
134–135: Cèpe fricassée with truffles—*Christopher Hirsheimer;* sack of truffles—*André Baranowski*
136–137: Truffle mass (Richerenches)—*André Baranowski;* Sarladais-style potatoes with truffles —*Christopher Hirsheimer*
138–139: Truffle hunt—*B.Barbey/Magnum;* scrambled eggs with truffles; sliced truffles—*Christopher Hirsheimer*
140–141: Truffled chicken; truffled chicken before it is cooked—*Christopher Hirsheimer*

CHAPTER 6: SEAFOOD

142–145: Fisherman untangling net; various fish; port; bouillabaisse in the pot; Lucien Vitiello bringing out the bouillabaisse (Sanary-sur-Mer)—*J. B. Naudin*
146–147: Bouillabaisse and croutons; Lucien Vitiello presenting second course; Joseph Ubelli; saffron —*J. B. Naudin*

148–149: Breton seafood in broth—*Christopher Hirsheimer;* mackerel—*Martin Schreiber*
150–151: Mussels at fish market; mussels with white wine (Trouville)—*Megan Wetherall*
152–153: Crabs and lobsters at market (Morlaix); lobster in tomato sauce—*Christopher Hirsheimer*
154–155: Le Mas du Langoustier; grilled stuffed sea bream; Georges Richard and Marie Caroline Le Ber, proprietors of Le Mas du Langoustier; deck chairs on hotel grounds (Île de Porquerolles) —*Christopher Hirsheimer*
156–157: Preparation of sole; sole sautéed in butter; preparation (2)—*Christopher Hirsheimer*
158–159: Scorpion fish—*J. B. Naudin;* whole sea bass roasted with herbs; Porto-Vecchio marina (Corsica) —*Melanie Acevedo*
160–161: Skate in clarified butter; Thomas McNamee and chef Vigato in kitchens of Apicius; seafood pavilion at Rungis; Apicius; view out the window of Apicius—*Martin Schreiber*
162–163: Puréed salt cod—*Christopher Hirsheimer;* salt cod—*Martin Schreiber*
164–165: Warm wild salmon filets; Frédy Girardet (Féchy)—*Christopher Hirsheimer*
166–167: Pike perch braised in pinot noir; the Husser family of Le Cerf (Marlenheim)—*Alison Harris*

CHAPTER 7: POULTRY

168–171: Grande Confrérie du Cassoulet de Castelnaudary; the Pont Neuf (Toulouse); cassoles for sale; Castelnaudary; accordionist (Villefranche-de-Lauragais)—*J. L. Barde/Scope*
172–173: Preparation of cassoulet and finished dish (9)—*J. L. Barde/Scope*
174–175: Preparation of duck confit and finished dish (3)—*Christopher Hirsheimer;* canned confit —*J. L. Barde/Scope*
176–177: Carving duck baked in a crust of herbs and salt at Auberge de Noves (Noves) —*Christopher Hirsheimer*
178–179: Roast duck with cider and turnips; François David's artisanal cider; Roger and Claudine Bordelet, cider apples; orchard at Château de Hauteville (Mayenne)—*John Russell*
180–181: Salt farmer (Guérande)—*Courtesy Maison du Sel;* duck breast cooked on the coals —*Martin Schreiber*
182–183: Baby chicken with calvados and cream—*Antoine Bootz;* baby chicken—*Christopher Hirsheimer*
184–185: Preparing rooster in red wine sauce (3); rooster in red wine sauce; poultry market (Louhans) —*Christopher Hirsheimer*
186–187: Breakfast at market; Jean-Pierre Silva at market (Chalon-sur-Saône); coq au vin "cannelloni" —*Christopher Hirsheimer*
188–189: Vineyard in winter (near Marlenheim); farmhouse chicken in vinegar sauce—*Alison Harris*
190–191: Serving chicken with crayfish at Chez Hugon (Lyon); chicken with crayfish—*A. Bailhâche*
192–193: Roast capon with stuffing; roasting capon in hearth at La Tupiña (Bordeaux)—*Martin Schreiber*
194–195: Guinea hen with cabbage; pressure cooker; freshly dug potatoes from Grivot's garden (Vosne-Romanée)—*Christopher Hirsheimer*
196–197: Blossoms of mustard plants; mustard crocks (Dijon)—*Christopher Hirsheimer;* making mustard —*Courtesy SEGMA;* rabbit with mustard sauce—*Christopher Hirsheimer*
198–199: Glasses of wine—*Mark Ferri;* rich rabbit stew—*Christopher Hirsheimer;* Château Lagrazette —*Fred Lyon;* bottles; picking from the crop (Cahors)—*J. D. Sudres/DIAF*

CHAPTER 8: MEATS

200–203: Charolais cattle; Mercurey wine; building facade; happy eaters; road sign (Charolles) —*Christopher Hirsheimer*
204–205: Beef stew Burgundy-style; Millette Coquillon and Giselle Morin (Planchez)—*Christopher Hirsheimer*
206–207: Laguiole knives—*Courtesy Laguiole;* filet of beef with marcillac wine sauce—*Christopher Hirsheimer*
208–209: Beef braised in red wine; Franck and Véronique Cerutti (Nice)—*Antoine Bootz*
210–211: Claude and Pepita Caspar-Jordan in 1964—*C. C. J. Archive;* regular customers at Aux Amis du Beaujolais; slicing meat—*J. B. Naudin;* feeding Claude at a reception in 1988—*C.C.J. Archive;* braised beef with carrots (Paris)—*J. B. Naudin*
212–213: French boiled beef dinner—*Christopher Hirsheimer;* Marina Ganter's grandmother, Hélène, with daughter Caroline and granddaughter Alice—*Courtesy Marina Ganter*
214–215: Nice-style tripe—*Christopher Hirsheimer;* cooking Nice-style tripe; the menu at La Merenda —*Antoine Bootz*
216–217: Arlette Hugon, with husband Henri and son Éric at Chez Hugon (Lyon); veal stew—*A. Bailhache*
218–219: Sautéed calf's liver—*J.B. Naudin;* Jean-Pierre Mouton (Paris)—*Christopher Hirsheimer*
220–221: Veal sweetbreads in the old style—*Martin Schreiber;* Taillevent (Paris)—*Courtesy Taillevent*
222–223: Mountains of the Savoie—*French Government Tourist Office;* Savoyard pork and vegetable stew —*Christopher Hirsheimer*
224–225: Men drinking calvados—*Courtesy Calvados;* pork loin with apples, cider, and calvados—*Christine Fleurent*
226–227: Fresh cabbage—*Alison Harris;* sauerkraut garnished with smoked, cured, and fresh pork—*Christopher Hirsheimer*
228–229: Preparing stuffed pigs' feet (3)—*Christopher Hirsheimer;* Raymond Fulchiron at Café des Fédérations; stuffed pigs' feet—*A. Bailhache*
230–231: Gérard Oberlé; preparation of torte of pigs' snout and finished dish (Montigny-sur-Canne) (4) —*Christopher Hirsheimer*
232–233: Chef Gabriel Asfaux of À Sousceyrac (Paris); lamb stew with white beans—*J. B. Naudin*
234–235: Landscape in the Cerdanya; Catalan-style shoulder of lamb—*Javier Salas*
236–237: View of Piedicroce; tabletop with food and wine; Corsican-style kid—*Melanie Acevedo*
238–239: Rich venison stew—*Christopher Hirsheimer;* shoulder meat and sausage—*David Sawyer*

CHAPTER 9: VEGETABLES

240–243: Harvesting artichokes by hand (Brittany)—*Hubert Taillard;* landscape near coast of Finistère; woman wearing traditional Breton lace caps;—*J. D. Sudres/DIAF;* shady dirt road; Patrick Jeffroy at market in Morlaix—*Christopher Hirsheimer*
244–245: Fresh leeks; warm leeks with vinaigrette—*Christopher Hirsheimer*
246–247: Marinated vegetable and herb salad; lake of Ste-Croix—*Peter d'Aprix*
248–249: Robert Lalleman standing, with his father, André, outside the Auberge de Noves (Noves); white asparagus with olive oil sabayon—*Christopher Hirsheimer*
250–251: Ratatouille—*Mary Ellen Bartley;* vegetable stands at market—*Christopher Hirsheimer*
252–253: Fresh zucchini blossoms; La Merenda (Nice); deep-fried zucchini blossoms—*Antoine Bootz*
254–255: Nice-style stuffed vegetables; window boxes (Nice)—*Antoine Bootz*
256–257: Stacked terrines; Mediterranean vegetable casserole—*Christopher Hirsheimer*
258–259: Grand aïoli—*William Abramowitz;* staff outside Relais Notre-Dame (Quinson) —*Courtesy Notre Dame*
260–261: Borage ravioli; archway; bouquets of borage leaves (Haut-de-Cagnes)—*Christopher Hirsheimer*
262–263: La Formatgeria de Llívia; Catalan cabbage and potatoes—*Javier Salas*
264–265: Fresh cardoons; preparation of cardoons (3); cardoons with anchovy-garlic sauce —*Christopher Hirsheimer*
266–267: Shelling fresh peas—*Owen Franken;* ragoût of peas and morels—*Anita Calero*
268–269: Mandoline; French potato puffs; raw, peeled potatoes—*Christopher Hirsheimer*
270–271: Potatoes baked in milk and cream; dish of cream—*Christopher Hirsheimer;* Dauphiné landscape —*J. P. Nicollet/Tourism*

CHAPTER 10: DESSERTS

272–275: Dessert buffet at La Tupiña; Jean-Pierre Xiradakis at La Tupiña; surrounding countryside; Xiradakis with friends; bridge (Bordeaux)—*Martin Schreiber*
276–277: Grandmother's plum tart—*Martin Schreiber;* Plum eau-de-vie—*Christopher Hirsheimer*
278–279: Apple tart; Lucette Malinouski makes apple tart (Montigny-sur-Canne) (9)—*Christopher Hirsheimer*
280–281: Strawberry tart; drunken strawberries—*Christopher Hirsheimer*
282–283: Upside-down apple tart; Maxim's pastry chef Jean-Yves de Charme—*Christopher Hirsheimer*
284–285: Citrus displays in the Biovès gardens during Fête du Citron (Menton)—*Colman Andrews;* lemons —*Christopher Hirsheimer;* Patrick and Joséphine Giraud and Francine Ballay at À Ma Vigne; lemon tart; young girl enjoys lemon tart at À Ma Vigne (Lyon)—*A. Bailhache*
286–287: Black cherry batter cake—*K. Chen;* fresh cherries—*Christopher Hirsheimer*
288–289: Swiss chard at market—*Christopher Hirsheimer;* swiss chard torte—*Antoine Bootz*
290–291: Marie-Louise Castagné with basket of walnuts (Martel)—*Pierre Sourzat;* walnut cake —*Matthew Benson*
292–293: Buying butter at the market; Breton butter cake—*Christopher Hirsheimer*
294–295: Rice pudding—*Christopher Hirsheimer;* coffee—*J. B. Naudin;* exterior of Aux Amis du Beaujolais —*C. C. J. Archive;* rice pudding; looking into Aux Amis (Paris)—*J. B. Naudin*
296–297: Marcel Proust—*Hulton Getty/Liaison Agency;* madeleines—*Christopher Hirsheimer*
298–299: Sweet tomatoes filled with a dozen flavors—*Christopher Hirsheimer;* Arpège (Paris)—*Martin Schreiber*
300–301: Chocolate—*Christopher Hirsheimer;* chocolate soufflé—*Holly Lynton*
302–303: Crème brûlée—*Erik Rank;* Mark Williamson (Paris)—*Courtesy Mark Williamson*
304–305: Crème anglaise—*Christopher Hirsheimer;* floating islands—*Christine Fleurent*
306–307: Making dacquoise (4); slice of dacquoise; ground nuts—*Mary Ellen Bartley*
308–309: Making croquembouche—*David Sawyer*

INDEX

319: A coq in the poultry market in Louhans—*Christopher Hirsheimer*

Our French Restaurants

FRANCE HAS a restaurant culture, the greatest in the world. France *invented* restaurants. Our first cookbook, *Saveur Cooks Authentic American*, concentrated on home cooks; there are plenty in this book, too, but we couldn't accurately represent French cooking without including professional chefs. In their restaurants, below, some dishes may no longer be available, but you're sure to eat well.

ALSACE

L'Écrevisse
4 avenue de Strasbourg, Brumath
(388.51.11.08; fax 388.51.89.02)
Soupe d'Écrevisses *(Crayfish Soup)*, page 65

Au Crocodile
10 rue de l'Outre, Strasbourg
(388.32.13.02; fax 388.75.72.01)
Baeckeoffe de Foie Gras *(Potted Foie Gras and Vegetables)*, page 125

Aux Armes de France
1 Grand Rue, Ammerschwihr
(389.47.10.12; fax 389.47.38.12)
Volaille Fermière au Vinaigre *(Farmhouse Chicken in Vinegar Sauce)*, page 189

Le Cerf
30 rue du Général de Gaulle, Marlenheim
(388.87.73.73; fax 388.87.68.08)
Sandre au Pinot Noir *(Pike Perch Braised in Pinot Noir)*, page 167

Maison Kammerzell
16 place de la Cathédrale, Strasbourg
(388.32.42.14; fax 388.32.03.92)
Choucroute Garnie à l'Alsacienne *(Sauerkraut Garnished with Smoked, Cured, and Fresh Pork)*, page 226

AUVERGNE

Grand Hôtel Auguy
2 allée de l'Amicale, Laguiole
(565.44.31.11; fax 565.51.50.81)
Filet de Boeuf au Vin de Marcillac *(Filet of Beef with Marcillac Wine Sauce)*, page 206

BORDEAUX

La Tupiña
6 rue Porte de la Monnaie, Bordeaux
(556.91.56.37; fax 556.31.92.11)
Soupe Paysanne à Boire et à Manger *(Peasant Soup to Drink and Eat)*, page 74; Salade d'Artichauts à la Ventrèche *(Artichoke and Pork Belly Salad)*, page 112; Magret de Canard à la Cheminée *(Duck Breast Cooked on the Coals)*, page 181; Chapon Farci Rôti *(Roast Capon with Stuffing)*, page 193; Tarte aux Prunes Façon Grand-Mère *(Grandmother's Plum Tart)*, page 277

BRITTANY

Patrick Jeffroy
11 rue du Bon Voyage, Plounérin
(296.38.61.80; fax 296.38.66.29)
Crêpes de Sarrasin *(Savory Buckwheat Crêpes)*, page 47; Crème de Potiron *(Cream of Squash Soup)*, page 69; Cotriade *(Breton Seafood in Broth)*, page 149; Homard à l'Armoricaine *(Lobster in Tomato Sauce)*, page 153; Kouign Amann *(Breton Butter Cake)*, page 292

BURGUNDY

Hostellerie des Clos
rue Jules Rathier, Chablis
(386.42.10.63; fax 386.42.17.11)
Fricassée d'Escargots au Coulis de Persil *(Fricassée of Snails with Parsley and Roasted Garlic Cream)*, page 133

Hostellerie du Vieux Moulin
Bouilland
(380.21.51.16; fax 380.21.59.90)
Gougères *(French Cheese Puffs)*, page 83; Cuisses de Grenouilles au Beurre Persillade *(Frogs' Legs in Parsley Butter)*, page 126; Pâtes Farcies de Coq au Vin *(Coq au Vin "Cannelloni")*, page 186

L'Espérance
St-Père-sous-Vézelay
(386.33.39.10; fax 386.33.26.15)
Tourte de Groins de Porc *(Torte of Pigs' Snout)*, page 230

La Petite Auberge/Chez Millette
Planchez
(386.78.41.89)
Grapiaux *(Burgundian Crêpes)*, page 48; Oeufs en Bouillon *(Eggs in Broth)*, page 97; Boeuf à la Bourguignonne *(Beef Stew Burgundy-Style)*, page 204

Lameloise
36 place d'Armes, Chagny
(385.87.65.65; fax 385.87.03.57)
Mille-Feuilles de Grenouilles *(Frogs' Leg "Napoleons" with White Bean Sauce)*, page 129

Ma Cuisine
passage St-Hélène, place Carnot, Beaune
(380.22.30.22; fax 380.24.99.79)
Terrine de Foies de Volaille *(Chicken Liver Terrine)*, page 34; Jambon Persillé Maison *(Parsleyed Ham in Aspic)*, page 40

CORSICA

Ferme Campo Di Monte
Murato
(495.37.64.39)
Soupe Corse *(Corsican Soup)*, page 73

DORDOGNE

Le Vieux Logis
Trémolat
(553.22.80.06; fax 553.22.84.89)
Pommes à la Sarladaise aux Truffes *(Sarladais-Style Potatoes with Truffles)*, page 137

LYON

À Ma Vigne
23 rue Jean Larrivé, 3rd arrondissement
(478.60.46.31)
Tarte au Citron *(Lemon Tart)*, page 284

Chez Hugon
12 rue Pizay, 1st arrondissement
(478.28.10.94)

Poulet aux Écrevisses *(Chicken with Crayfish)*, page 190; "Blanquette" de Veau *(Veal Stew)*, page 217

Café des Fédérations
8–10 rue Major Martin,
1st arrondissement
(478.28.26.00; fax 472.07.74.52)

Gâteau de Foies Blonds de Volaille *(Chicken Liver Mousse)*, page 37

Nice

Chez Barale
39 rue Beaumont
(493.89.17.94)

Salade Niçoise, page 105

La Merenda
4 rue de la Terrasse
(no telephone)

Tripes à la Niçoise *(Nice-Style Tripe)* page 214; Beignets de Fleurs de Courgettes *(Deep-Fried Zucchini Blossoms)*, page 252

Normandy

Le Central
5-7 rue des Bains
Moreaux, Trouville
(231.88.80.84; fax 231.88.42.22)

Moules Marinière *(Mussels with White Wine)*, page 150

Paris

À Sousceyrac
35 rue Faidherbe,
11th arrondissement
(143.71.65.30)

Huîtres Glacées en Sabayon *(Oysters in Champagne Sauce)*, page 44; Haricot d'Agneau *(Lamb Stew with White Beans)*, page 233

Apicius
122 avenue de Villiers,
17th arrondissement
(143.80.19.66; fax 144.40.09.57)

Raie Raide au Beurre Clarifié *(Skate in Clarified Butter)*, page 161

Arpège
84 rue de Varenne,
7th arrondissement
(145.51.47.33; fax 144.18.98.39)

Tomatoes Confites Farcies aux Douze Saveurs *(Sweet Tomatoes Filled with a Dozen Flavors)*, page 299

Au Trou Gascon
40 rue Taine,
12th arrondissement
(143.44.34.26; fax 143.07.80.55)

Foie Gras de Canard Poêlé aux Raisins Blancs *(Seared Foie Gras with Green Grapes)*, page 122

Aux Amis du Beaujolais
28 rue d'Artois,
8th arrondissement
(145.63.92.21)

Boeuf à la Mode aux Carottes *(Braised Beef with Carrots)*, page 210; Gâteau de Riz *(Rice Pudding)*, page 295

Chez Clovis
33 rue Berger,
1st arrondissement
(142.33.97.07)

Crudités *(Raw Vegetable Salads)*, page 29; Soupe à l'Oignon Gratinée *(French Onion Soup)*, page 55

Chez Maxim's
3 rue Royale,
8th arrondissement
(142.65.27.94; fax 140.17.02.91)

Tarte Tatin *(Upside-Down Apple Tart)*, page 283

Le Récamier
4 rue Récamier,
7th arrondissement
(145.48.86.58)

Oeufs en Meurette *(Poached Eggs in Red Wine Sauce)*, page 94; Foie de Veau Poêlé *(Sautéed Calf's Liver)*, page 218

Maison Prunier
16 avenue Victor Hugo,
16th arrondissement
(144.17.35.85; fax 144.17.90.10)

Bisque de Homard *(Lobster Bisque)*, page 66; Sole Meunière *(Sole Sautéed in Butter)*, page 156

Taillevent
15 rue Lamennais,
8th arrondissement
(144.95.15.01; fax 142.25.95.18)

Ris de Veau à l'Ancienne *(Veal Sweetbreads in the Old Style)*, page 221

Willi's Wine Bar
13 rue des Petits Champs,
1st arrondissement
(142.61.05.09; fax 147.03.36.93)

Crème Brûlée, page 303

Provence

Auberge de Noves
route de Châteaurenard, Noves
(490.24.28.28; fax 490.90.16.92)

Canard en Croûte d'Herbes et de Sel *(Duck Baked in a Crust of Herbs and Salt)*, page 176; Asperges Blanches au Sabayon à l'Huile d'Olive *(White Asparagus with Olive Oil Sabayon)*, page 249

Le Cagnard
rue Sous-Barri, Haut-de-Cagnes
(493.20.73.21; fax 493.22.06.39)

Raviolis de Bourrache *(Borage Ravioli)*, page 260

Hostellerie de la Fuste
Lieu-dit La Fuste,
route d'Oraison,
Valensole (Manosque)
(492.72.05.95; fax 492.72.92.93)

Tartare de Légumes *(Marinated Vegetable and Herb Salad)*, page 246

Jacques Maximin
689 chemin de la Gaude, Vence
(493.58.90.75; fax 493.58.22.86)

Pétoncles Farcis à la Provençale *(Stuffed Scallops Provençal-Style)*, page 42; Salade de Haricots Verts aux Noisettes Fraîches *(Salad of Haricots Verts and Green Hazelnuts)*, page 111; Salade Tiède de Rougets aux Artichauts *(Warm Red Mullet and Artichoke Salad)*, page 114

Le Mas du Langoustier
Île de Porquerolles
(494.58.30.09; fax 494.58.36.02)

Gâteau d'Ail Confit *(Garlic Custard with Chanterelles and Parsley Sauce)*, page 30; Dorade Farcie Grillée *(Grilled Stuffed Sea Bream)*, page 155

Relais Notre-Dame
Quinson
(492.74.40.01; fax 492.74.02.18)

Grand Aïoli *(Vegetables and Salt Cod with Garlic Sauce)*, page 259

Pyrenees

Gîte Cal Pai
Cal Pai, Eyne
(468.04.06.96)

Épaule d'Agneau à la Catalane *(Catalan-Style Shoulder of Lamb)*, page 234

La Formatgeria de Llívia
Pla de Ro, Gorguja
Llivia, Girona, Spain
(011.34.972.146.279)

Trinxat *(Catalan Cabbage and Potatoes)*, page 262

Index

Table of Equivalents

THE EXACT EQUIVALENTS IN THE FOLLOWING TABLES HAVE BEEN ROUNDED FOR CONVENIENCE.

LIQUID AND DRY MEASURES

U.S.	METRIC
¼ teaspoon	1.25 milliliters
½ teaspoon	2.5 milliliters
1 teaspoon	5 milliliters
1 tablespoon (3 teaspoons)	15 milliliters
1 fluid ounce (2 tablespoons)	30 milliliters
¼ cup	65 milliliters
⅓ cup	80 milliliters
1 cup	235 milliliters
1 pint (2 cups)	480 milliliters
1 quart (4 cups, 32 ounces)	950 milliliters
1 gallon (4 quarts)	3.8 liters
1 ounce (by weight)	28 grams
1 pound	454 grams
2.2 pounds	1 kilogram

LENGTH MEASURES

U.S.	METRIC
⅛ inch	3 millimeters
¼ inch	6 millimeters
½ inch	12 millimeters
1 inch	2.5 centimeters

OVEN TEMPERATURES

FAHRENHEIT	CELSIUS	GAS
250	120	½
275	140	1
300	150	2
325	160	3
350	180	4
375	190	5
400	200	6
425	220	7
450	230	8
475	240	9
500	260	10